Literary Culture in a World Transformed

Literary Culture in a World Transformed

A Future for the Humanities

WILLIAM PAULSON

CORNELL UNIVERSITY PRESS

ITHACA AND LONDON

First published 2001 by Cornell University Press

First printing, Cornell Paperbacks, 2001

Printed in the United States of America

Library of Congress Cataloging-in-Publication Data
Paulson, William, b. 1955
    Literary culture in a world transformed : a future for the humanities /
William Paulson.
        p.   cm.
    Includes bibliographical references (p.   ) and index.
    ISBN 0-8014-3914-0 (cloth : alk. paper) — ISBN 0-8014-8730-7 (pbk.)
        1. Literature—Study and teaching. 2. Humanities—Study and teaching.
    3. Education, Humanistic.   I. Title.
    PN61 .P38 2001
    807'.1—dc21   2001002627

Cloth printing   10 9 8 7 6 5 4 3 2 1

Paperback printing   10 9 8 7 6 5 4 3 2 1

Should life rule over knowledge and science, or should knowledge rule over life? Which of these forces is higher and more decisive? No one will doubt: life is the higher, the ruling force; for any knowledge that destroyed life would simultaneously destroy itself. Knowledge presupposes life; hence it has the same interest in the preservation of life that every creature has in its own continued existence.

Friedrich Nietzsche,
"On the Utility and Liability of History for Life"

From this the poem springs: that we live in a place
That is not our own and, much more, not ourselves
And hard it is in spite of blazoned days.

Wallace Stevens,
"Notes Toward a Supreme Fiction"

Contents

Preface

THIS BOOK owes its sweeping title and bulging subject matter to my attempt to bring together several topics usually placed in separate categories: the world's changing economy and ecology, the role of science and technology in culture and society, the rise of electronic and audiovisual media and their effect on bookish institutions, and the state of the literary disciplines in the academy. It belongs to the curious and not always respectable genre of the "mid-career" book, whose author has come to look askance at his or her field and who tries to muster nagging doubts into a magnum opus.

In my case the doubts had two main points of departure. The first was the all too banal realization that the rapidly changing media environment was calling the boundaries and objects of literary studies into question. Many suspect that we are living in the beginning of the end of the book era. Those who welcome such an event attempt to hasten it by urging that we turn away from print, literature, and the past so as to put our critical acumen in the service of studying audiovisual and electronic media, popular culture, and the present. Not only the definition but the very continuation of literary culture is, in effect, put in play by a scholarly and educational turn away from a literary corpus strongly identified with the printed book.

My second major concern about the state of literary studies arose from a deceptively simple question: among the New Social Movements of the late sixties, why had environmentalism had the least influence in literary studies? Why was there comparatively little "ecocriticism" alongside minority, feminist, and gay/lesbian studies? The answer seemed to be that the latter fields are the direct work of groups of scholars and students seeking to claim and explore their cultural identity. There can be no such constituency or project for a category as nonhuman as "the environment" or "the biosphere." This thought led me to ponder the implications of the tautology that the humanities have been centered in human practices, meanings, and relations: their relation to the nonhuman things of the world seems, by comparison, tenuous, problematic, and perhaps even nonexistent.

None of this would matter if we lived in a world whose nonhuman components were of little importance, or at least could be kept comfortably separate from its human ones. The disciplines could peacefully divide their labor: here we would consider the works and relations of human subjects, there they would investigate and manage the domain of objects. Certainly this arrangement seemed satisfactory to the makers of the modern university in the nineteenth century. Philosophers affirmed that the sciences of mind or culture differed radically from those of nature, while the best artists and writers increasingly believed that beauty and imagination should be cultivated for themselves, as far removed as possible from a hostile or uncomprehending world of science, commerce, and politics.

Such a division still seemed credible as recently as the late nineteen-sixties, when the humanities began to devote considerable energy to denouncing knowledge's complicity with power and high culture's role in maintaining social inequality and exclusion. At the same time, the literary disciplines undertook to provide spaces in which new and hitherto silenced forms of subjectivity could be nurtured and explored. Many literary scholars redefined their task as the critical study of everything whose existence lay in language, text, subjectivity, and sociability—in other words, it seemed, everything that truly mattered.

But with every passing year this division of intellectual labor seems less suited to the world. While cultural constructivism looms large in the humanities and some of the social sciences, geneticists and evolutionary psychologists dazzle the media and the public with stories of hard-wired human predispositions and behaviors. The most intractable aspects of social and racial injustice turn out to be at least as much economic as cultural. The sphere of indigenous and local cultures, and indeed of all non-market institutions and cultural practices, recedes worldwide before the seemingly unstoppable extension and globalization of the capitalist economy. The human remaking of the world alters the physical environment and the biosphere in ways that increasing temperatures and rates of species extinction only begin to measure. It thus seems less and less plausible to suppose that the humanities can comfortably focus on society, culture, and discourse while leaving aside the conditions of the material world on which they depend.

How are the humanities responding—and how should they respond?—to a world transformed by new technologies, the intensification of global capitalism, and the effects of human actions on the environment? The current stance of the literary disciplines does not
seem promising in this regard. Despite many forays into the material
bases of cultural production and transmission, literary and cultural
studies concentrate on the representational, discursive, and intersubjective dimensions of the contemporary world. This focus, inclusive
as it may seem, omits much, beginning with the physical, ecological,
economic, and technological dimensions of the world. Meanwhile, the
humanities pay more and more attention to their own theories and
methodologies, neglecting the cultural texts they presumably exist to
study, especially texts from the past. This neglect is in some respects
a bid for relevance, but in others a recipe for solipsism. By paying less
attention to the past, the out of fashion, and the unpopular, literary
and cultural studies give up some of their strangeness and untimeliness. By continuing to turn their back on the nonhuman, material, and
scientific components of the present, they risk cutting themselves off
from understanding or contributing to the real dynamics of change in
the world.

I have written this book to argue for an alternative future for literary culture, one that refuses a fatalistic or providential view of technology, maintains cultural contact with the past, and whose teaching
mission is not that of training an academic counter-society of cultural
critics, but that of making the strangeness and multiplicity of literary
culture part of an always interdisciplinary or a-disciplinary education
of world citizens —in all the world's dimensions. Rather than letting
go of much of literature in order to hang on to the autonomy and outlook we scholars have come to associate with literary culture, I have
tried to suggest changes to literary culture—understood here in the
sense of the outlooks and practices of the literary disciplines—that
would encourage scholars and students to go on drawing on the works
known as literature, but to do so in new ways.

Making a book that ranges widely requires many decisions about
how much detail and explanation to provide on various topics. If the
book is not to swell like the fabled frog who wanted to be as big as an
ox, some matters must be summarized with eyebrow-raising brevity
so that others can have more space. Almost every reader is sure to disagree with some of my choices in this regard, to feel that crucial docu-
mentation or counter-argument was neglected on some points and/or

that superfluous detail was supplied for others. I can only hope that for most readers, the overall argument and my attempt to link such disparate themes will outweigh inevitable reservations about missing or excessive specifics. I also hope that the many readers who disagree with my conclusions will nonetheless find the path by which I reach them to help focus and stimulate their own thinking about the crucial issues faced by humanistic study.

A "SINGLE AUTHOR" book like this is not really written by one person alone, and it's a pleasure to thank some of the many who have given me so much. I am grateful to the University of Michigan for a Michigan Humanities Award semester, a sabbatical, and other forms of temporal and material support. I also thank Princeton University and the University of California at Santa Barbara for providing academic homes away from home while I was writing. Bernhard Kendler, Teresa Jesionowski, and the staff at Cornell University Press did a fine job of making a book from a manuscript. Many colleagues and friends have offered invaluable encouragement and suggestions, among them Lionel Gossman, Elizabeth MacArthur, Lois Cooper, Mihai Spariosu, Juli Highfill, and Michelle Chilcoat. Marie-Hélène Huet generously read a very flawed draft and even more generously offered support and insight. Dominica Chang has been not only a research assistant *par excellence* but also a very helpful reader and critic. My greatest debt is to Catherine Brown and Santiago Colás, who have helped me think through the issues of this book in more ways than I could describe, who convinced me that it was worth doing and could be done, and whose friendship sustained me on the way. This book is for them.

WILLIAM PAULSON

Ann Arbor, Michigan

Literary Culture in a World Transformed

Introduction: Literary Culture and the Life of the World

DO THE HUMANITIES have a future? Is literature a thing of the past, too much a creature of print to do more than live on as a relic in an age of electronic culture? Can the arts of speech and writing flourish in an era when science and technology have unprecedented power to reshape the conditions of life and human society? What does the culture of words and meanings have to offer the world of matter, creatures, and things?

This book is an attempt to address questions like these by examining literature and literary education in terms of the state of the world at the beginning of the twenty-first century. In this world transformed by technological, economic, and ecological changes, the status, relevance, and role of literary culture seem far less secure than they did a short generation ago. I will argue that the resulting challenges need not and should not be met by encouraging the humanities to pay less attention to literature or the cultures of the past so as to devote themselves primarily to contemporary or popular works and to cultural production in new media. Nor can they be dealt with by a resolute shoring up of the status quo or by attempts to return to the concepts and practices of an earlier time. Instead, those of us who have responsibilities for intellectual life and literary education, especially in schools, colleges, and universities, ought to seize every opportunity to change the ways of literary culture so as to enable literary reading and writing to contribute to the making of livable and desirable futures. We should, in other words, try to bring forth a literary culture that will enhance the life of the larger world.

The unsettled state in which literary culture and literary studies now find themselves has many overlapping causes. Rapid changes in the technologies and media of communication, and the fetishization of these changes by some would-be reformers of education, raise doubts about the kind of place serious reading and writing will or should have in the education of future generations. Meanwhile, anxious to cast off vestiges of an inegalitarian past, many students and teachers denounce literature's privileged role in education as an irrelevant or elitist relic, probably best left behind in favor of more popular, democratically shared forms of cultural production, notably those of the audiovisual and electronic media. In addition, the economic and political pressures on schools, colleges, and universities to become more efficient and accountable weigh heavily on non-empirical, seemingly impractical fields like the humanities. No one can say how extensively or deeply literary culture and literary education will change over the next generation, but these are bad times for anyone who would like to see them continue as they are or to have them restored to what they were a generation or two ago.

At the same time, the world is undergoing even larger transformations and facing bigger uncertainties. New technologies in medicine and genetics, along with the sheer size of industry and agriculture, give human beings unprecedented power to act on the conditions and habitats of life itself, to remake what once seemed a nature beyond human control. Meanwhile, the nonhuman world of bacteria and viruses, oceans and atmosphere, seems ever more resistant to human control, ever readier to bite back. The world of nature and the world of human making, conceptually separated since the Enlightenment, are thus bound together more strongly and in more ways than ever.

Rapid growth of global trade and communications, meanwhile, reshapes markets, societies, and cultures, creating new opportunities and wealth in some places while putting many individuals and communities under enormous pressure to change their ways, and leaving still others in abject poverty. As capitalism intensifies and spreads over the globe, it brings both the upheavals of creative destruction and the specter of worldwide cultural homogenization in the form of American-style entertainment and consumerism. Liberal democracy appears relatively secure in its position as the dominant ideology of government, its tenets often evoked in principle even where they are denied in practice, yet it often seems troubled or dysfunctional, its means of representation and decision overwhelmed by the flow of information, images, currency, and goods across ever more porous borders.

If we think about the world and our life in it, then, we are likely to worry about the staggering and growing inequalities that divide nations from nations and people from people, about economic stability and the future of work, about whether local customs and cultures can adapt and survive in the face of globalization—and about the stubborn persistence, amid so many new problems, of old forms of exclusion, injustice, and oppression. Beyond even these large concerns, on the horizon of the foreseeable future stands the ecological question of whether the intense human remaking of the world will be compatible with the life of a biosphere capable of sustaining us. Economic and technological development is casting humanity, its institutions, and its habitats forward in a great uncontrolled experiment, and no one can confidently or responsibly say how it will turn out. It is doubtful whether anyone—or any government or institution—has much control over the processes that are remaking the life of the world, though they affect everyone. Writer, reader, and critic are all passengers on this wild ride and, to the extent that we are citizens of meaningful democracies, its drivers as well.

But we who are concerned with a book like this one also belong, in all likelihood, to a much smaller community, or rather to one or more of an overlapping set of communities made up of those who care about literature, literary study, and liberal education. In other words, this book addresses primarily those who have an interest in or are professionally committed to what I have chosen to call *literary culture*. By means of this phrase, I will be referring not only to literature itself but to the communities, institutions, activities, and attitudes that cluster around it, without which there could be no such thing as "literature itself."

To speak of literary culture is to refer, in the first place, to the organized and semi-organized groups for whom literature matters, and to the structures and attitudes that define these groups and set their boundaries. One such community is the institution to which I belong professionally: academic literary studies, primarily housed in departments of English, comparative literature, and foreign languages. Traditionally devoted to "language and literature," these disciplines are now often engaged in a wider range of intellectual activities with connections to such fields as anthropology, history, film studies, and women's studies. (This shifting and broadening of interests shows that an institution arising out of literary culture need not always maintain an exclusive relation to literature.) Academic literary culture is but one manifestation of the more general phenomenon of communities and institutions organized around the production, diffusion, criticism, and commentary of books. The company of writers, with its many subgroups—poets, Parisian intellectuals, New York playwrights, and so on—is another strong instance of a community constituted by its interest in literature, specifically by its central role in literary production. Beyond such identifiable categories and communities, moreover, are more diffuse but nonetheless real groups that make up literary culture: students and teachers of reading and literature in the schools, people in the book trade, members of book clubs or reading groups, poetry slam aficionados, subscribers to reviews, and ultimately all those who care about reading and writing.

Of no less importance than the communities and institutions of literary culture are the dispositions, beliefs, and practices that they foster and that define them. A crucial feature of the more restricted, production-oriented literary communities, such as those of writers, intellectuals, and scholars, is their tendency toward autonomy—toward defining and living by their own rules and values. This drive for autonomy can be seen in the scholar's suspicion of a colleague who writes for nonacademic audiences, in the "serious" writer's disdain for the success of the best-selling novelist, and in the literary and artistic assumption that creative individuals should break free from middle-class taste and morality. Autonomy has many virtues: it encourages serious focus on the specific tasks of creative or professional activity, it helps create spaces for invention and experimentation, and under the right conditions it can foster movements of cultural contestation. But it also has its costs. Communities that consider themselves autonomous insist on the boundaries that make them so, such as the lines between highbrow and lowbrow, literature and popular fiction, and the work of maintaining those boundaries takes time and effort away from all other activities. Moreover, literary or artistic autonomy often encourages an emphasis on form at the expense of content (or, slightly more subtly, the assertion that the two are inseparable), since form depends on the techniques and artistry specific to those who create works. A more serious consequence is the tendency of literary communities to become disconnected from the affairs of the city, the marketplace, and the natural world: from aspects of life that are all too easily written off as common, vulgar, or overly material.

The literary disposition to value form is part of an even more general inclination of literary culture: its penchant for assigning special value to language and its works. Whenever we find texts, reading, discourse, or linguistic structure serving as central preoccupations, controlling metaphors, or implicitly dominant models, we are (at least to some extent) in the presence of literary culture. But there are many ways of taking language and text seriously, and the modes of doing so have changed enormously over time. In literary studies, putting language at the center of interest long revolved around *rhetoric*, the appreciation, practice, and apprenticeship of verbal eloquence and organization as these were displayed in refined, ancient, or otherwise admired writings. The rhetorical approach to language and literature survived pedagogically until the late nineteenth century, only to be gradually replaced by an emphasis on knowledge of a national literary canon and its history, or more precisely, the national history that it was generally expected to illustrate, such as French, Spanish, American, and so forth. In the United States, this method of instruction was in turn supplemented (and largely superseded) toward mid-century by the New Criticism, an aesthetically and formally oriented method that emphasized the specificity of literary language and structure while usually retaining the canon of national or comparative literature as its context. In varying degrees, formalist approaches became part of literary education in many other countries as well. More recently, attention to literature and literary discourse as such has been supplanted as a defining characteristic of the literary disciplines, especially in the English-speaking world, by more conceptual and critical ways of emphasizing language, loosely and collectively referred to as *theory*. At the core of theory in this general sense is the notion that not only texts but also culture in general—including political power, social relations, and the collectively constructed psyches of individuals—should be understood as being produced by discourse, and thus as capable of being studied and thought about under such categories as language, rhetoric, and signs. The literary pedagogy of theory emphasizes techniques for stripping away illusions, forms of false consciousness, and other social and ideological effects produced by signs and discourse. Theory proposes less a knowledge of the field of literature than a way of becoming self-conscious about how we use language and language uses us.

Language-centered theory is a fairly recent development in literary culture, its intellectual roots reaching back perhaps a century and its widespread influence scarcely more than a generation. A much longer-term characteristic of literary culture is its orientation toward the cultural rather than the natural world. Since the romantic era, literary culture has defined itself in part in opposition to the outlook and practices of the natural sciences, industry, and commerce—in short, to the modern project of mastering the world of things. C. P. Snow famously described this opposition as that of "the two cultures," literary and scientific: contrasting elites, educated in radically different ways, each with its own outlook and each ignorant of the other's culture.[1] Although many writers and literary scholars are fascinated by science and technology and work at overcoming this divide, the very energy and ingenuity of their efforts point to the gulf that separates the scientific or empirical outlook from the literary or artistic one. Literary culture, in this respect, has long identified with constructivism and freedom against naturalism and necessity, choosing to attend to the made rather than to the found, to the fictive, the inventive, and the imagined rather than to the measured, the encountered, and the unavoidable. It takes far more interest in relations within the community of human subjects than in the world of nonhuman objects or in science's potent knowledge of that world.

Yet literary culture, as I will be using the term, is not restricted to intellectual communities and their outlooks and practices, important and distinctive as these are. It includes not only literary communities and their dispositions but also literary works themselves: cultural artifacts made not of paint or marble but of words. These works now constitute a vast and ever-growing library, its sources extended in both space and time. The phrase "literary culture" also designates the part of culture contained in this library. Relations between this work-centered aspect of literary culture and the more anthropological side discussed above are not simple. The literary archive consists of human cultural productions, not natural objects, and it is largely the work, at least in the modern world, of literary communities. Yet works, once finished, take on something of the status of objects, givens, things out there that can be known, interpreted, used, or ignored. We can, of course, produce knowledge of works and even modify the conditions of their existence by our readings of them, just as scientists make knowledge and modify matter by working with it in laboratories, but

---

[1] C. P. Snow, *The Two Cultures and the Scientific Revolution* (Cambridge: Cambridge University Press, 1959).

we cannot cause the texts we encounter to be other than what they are any more than chemists can make an element like silver or potassium change its atomic number. In reading—and learning how to read—from the vast library of serious writing built up over centuries, we are encountering something that is other, not our own, not ourselves, comparable in this respect to the universe in which we live. It is therefore no surprise to find communities of literary culture that are deeply ambivalent about literature, and works of literature that are seriously disturbing to the values of such communities.

So strong is the tension—yet also the bond—between these two aspects, the works and the communities, that one could describe literary culture, as I will be using the term, as a field organized around two poles, corresponding to the two major senses of the word *culture:* at one extreme, the ways of the literati and associated tribes; at the other, valued works made of letters. The first pole, the anthropological one, corresponds to Snow's (and, subsequently, Richard Rorty's) use of the term "literary culture" in contrast to "scientific culture": the beliefs and practices of those who are trained on books rather than in laboratories. The former, Rorty argues, conduct their intellectual life rhetorically, by proposing new vocabularies and forms of discourse, while the latter endeavor to demonstrate what is true within a stipulated framework of concepts and vocabulary.[2] The second pole of literary culture, the literary part of the archive of human works, has the status of objects: artifactual and not natural objects, to be sure, but in any case things to be known and investigated, traces of human life and inventive activity that now constitute a resource for learning both about the nature of human expression in language and about the life of other times, places, and cultures.

I will argue that we need literary culture in the first sense—the rhetorical, tale-telling, and poetic way of knowing and communicating—because we live in a human world that is social, open, competitive, conflictual, and playful, that is inherently concerned with far more than getting at the truth about the objective condition of things. We need literary culture in the second sense—the vast library of writings out there—because we live in a historically and culturally com-

---

[2] My statement of the distinction follows Richard Rorty, "Nineteenth-Century Idealism and Twentieth-Century Textualism," in *Consequences of Pragmatism* (Minneapolis: University of Minnesota Press, 1982), 139–59. See also Snow, *The Two Cultures*, 1–22.

plex world that we must seek to know with some degree of thorough-
ness and subtlety if we are to act effectively within it. Education in
(and by means of) literary culture is thus caught up in the fundamental Western tension between rhetoric and philosophy, the Sophists and
Plato, orality and writing: between open-ended social negotiation and
stable knowledge about the way things are.

TODAY the works of literary culture are in one crucial sense less stable than they have been for centuries, and this instability lies in precisely what long made them seem so objective and secure. They are
strongly identified with their materialization in books, and thus with
what is often called print culture: the texts, practices, communities,
and institutions associated with books and printed writing. Poems,
tales, and dramas are vastly older than the printing press, of course,
and we still read many works from the pre-print era. However, the
modern category of the literary is very much a creation of a communications universe dominated by print. Even the epics of Homer, the
preeminent Western example of oral poetry put into manuscript writing, survive today primarily as printed books, read silently (and sometimes aloud) off identical pages by individual readers.

As recently as twenty years ago, there would have been little point in
reminding readers that literary culture was closely identified with books
and print. That identity was too obvious to be stated or even thought.
The last decades, however, have brought a growing and perhaps exaggerated awareness that new technologies and media may well be turning print, books, and the forms of expression and cultural organization
associated with them, into something that is dated, out of time, and possibly obsolete. Just as Victor Hugo, evoking the fifteenth century in *The
Hunchback of Notre Dame*, pointed to the printed book and the cathe-
dral and said, "this will kill that," people are pointing today—sometimes with fear, sometimes with desire—to the computer, the electronic
screen, and all their ramifications as the historically appointed slayers
of the book and its culture. People are asking previously unthinkable
questions, such as "how long will we go on reading books?" and "should
schools continue to emphasize print and works written for it?" Of
course, literary culture and print culture are not identical, and many
works and activities of literary culture are migrating to digital media.
Still, it is an open question what will become of existing literary culture—both its works and the ways of its communities—in a media environment dominated by the electronic and the audiovisual. Even

though the products of print culture are probably not about to be thrown out in a great millennial housecleaning, the questions—and the powerful institutional, ideological, and commercial pressure to use "new technologies" in education—put the status of print and thus of literary culture in play to a degree not encountered in a very long time.

This technological challenge to the continuation of literary culture arrives at a time when many old certainties about the value, centrality, and character of literary study have already been swept aside or at least severely contested. The technological turn away from print and toward electronic textuality, hypermedia, and the audiovisual both complements and radicalizes the academic moves away from canonical literature and towards recent, popular, and non-print cultural productions. Professorial controversies and decisions about what to teach are increasingly caught up in—and could yet be overwhelmed by—a changing media environment in which both the educational bases and the functional utility of print literacy are being undermined. Reading and writing have to share space and time in the classroom with ever more new activities, and the practice of reading books is less and less reinforced or supported—whether in school or out of it— by the communications environments in which students actually live their lives. Books and print show no signs of disappearing, but their prestige and status, their role as models of learning and knowledge transmission, and even their centrality to literary culture are not what they used to be.

Not only do computers and electronic media bid to shake up the forms, social practices, and educational bases of writing and reading, they also provide powerful and appealing new metaphors for knowledge and communication, often replacing those of the book. For centuries, people have brought book and world together in the figure of the *liber mundi*, the book of the world. Informally, people speak of "reading" someone's face or actions "like an open book." Descartes, rejecting the overly bookish learning of his scholastic education, wrote in 1637 of his decision to study instead "the great book of the world," thus making the book the touchstone of his notion of study even as he was calling for a turn away from the study of books. And as recently as the flowering of academic literary theory during the seventies and eighties, "reading" came to be a broadly used, positively valued term for engaging in all sorts of acts of sophisticated decoding or understanding; not only did books have to be read, but so too—if they were to be taken seriously and not naively—films, paintings, cities, trials, riots, notorious public figures, and indeed almost any social or cultural phenomenon.

Today, however, the computer and the Internet are more likely than the book to furnish dominant metaphors for study, knowledge, and organization. The reading metaphor often gives way before linking, interfacing, or downloading. The computer has many uses aside from serving as a tool of communication and entertainment, and our sense of its importance as a communications device comes from the totality of its uses, not just those areas in which it is a means of storing, processing, and sending language and images. It thus works as a figure for knowledge and organization from several different points of view: as calculation, as process, as communications network, and as simulation. Above all, perhaps, computers are widely seen as more modern, flexible, and powerful than books as tools for working with information of every kind, and thus—often via a dubious identification of information with knowledge—for learning and knowing in general. Many view the Internet and the Web as a means of being linked not just to flickering texts or images but, somehow, with the entire world, represented by all the people logged on to their terminals, or all the Web pages of individuals and organizations. The computer and its networks thus seem to stand for a well-connected future, leaving the all too familiar book in an uninspiring and isolated past.

Computers and audiovisual media draw interest and support from the modern, capitalist, and especially American cultural privilege accorded to the new, to "the next thing." Though there are, of course, countervailing desires to stick with the familiar and avoid change, the dominant ideology of the modern world is to assume that when something is newer and more up-to-date, it ought to be encouraged in supplanting the old—usually the sooner the better, so that its advantages can be enjoyed and the utopia it seems to promise be realized. Indeed, the predictions and hopes attached to digital communications networks are often virtually millennial: a desire to enter a new world, a new kind of spiritual city or kingdom. The space needles and flying cars of *The Jetsons* having failed to materialize on time, the world of on-line communications and virtuality appears to be the characteristic new space of the twenty-first century. The optimistic projections associated with cyberspace, or simply with the extensive use of digital communications networks, often have a strongly utopian cast that is defined in opposition to a social and cultural order associated with major features of the nineteenth- and twentieth-century world: heavy industry, nation states, centralized structures, and, in communications, the mass-produced, standardized, hierarchical order of book-centered print culture.

Promoters of cyberculture sometimes take books and literary intellectuals as their *bête noire,* and the promise of computers and electronic networks serves as a rallying point for people who feel alienated by, or hostile toward, features of culture that they identify with the predominance of print, literacy, and literature. This strain of thinking goes back at least to Marshall McLuhan, who argued that electronic, audiovisual communications would bring humanity back to many key features of oral cultures, thus putting an end to an era of excessive dependence on typographic, written language and the kinds of authority and institutions associated with it.

Among today's cultural theorists the anti-literary utopianism associated with electronic networks is usually presented less as a return to something like orality than as a culmination of sophisticated postmodern textualism. Hypertext and hypermedia are taken to be exemplary concrete actualizations of poststructuralist theories of language and text, providing decentered symbolic spaces in which language is mobile rather than fixed and where readerly collaboration rather than authorial control is the dominant factor in the making of meaning. With new media, after all, come both new ways of understanding the human subject and a shift in the conditions under which the subjects are formed through interactions with cognitive, communicative, and social environments. The subject of knowledge as conceived under print culture—the reader (and sometimes writer) of single-author books, the apparently self-reliant possessor of a personal library and a corresponding general culture—can perhaps be transformed, under a fully realized electronic culture, into a less fortified, more adaptable and fluid human nodal point in the complex information circuits that make up society, culture, and interpersonal communication.[3] The hopes invested in this kind of mutation can be illustrated by the transvaluation of the *cyborg,* the human being whose body and mind are supplemented by cybernetic prostheses, from science fiction bogeyman to object of theoretical desire.[4]

---

[3] For a brief commentary on the rapidly receding ideal of book-centered general culture, see Louis Menand's essay on Clifton Fadiman, "A). Smart B). Brainy or C). Knowledgeable?" *New York Times Magazine* (2 January 2000), 24–25.

[4] The now-classic statement on the cyborg is that of Donna Haraway, "A Cyborg Manifesto: Science, Technology, and Socialist-Feminism in the Late Twentieth

The rapid development of new ways for human beings to communicate will surely bring far-reaching and still unanticipated cultural and social changes, some of them worthwhile and others less so. What is questionable about much present-day theorizing on these matters is not its sense of change and possibility but its tendency to take new media as all of a piece, usually as either the gateway to a new and better world or as the ruin of civilization as we know it—in any case, as an epoch-making, all-consuming transformation. In *The Electronic Word*, Richard Lanham, perhaps the most prominent and optimistic advocate of a digital future for the humanities, argues that computer hypermedia, through their interactivity and their mixing of the visual, the oral, and the textual, offer nothing less than a rebirth of the rhetorical *paideia* (education/culture) of the ancient and medieval world: an open-ended, playful, competitive, and potentially democratic form of education squelched in modern times by the grimly closed, truth-oriented model favored by reductionist natural science and conveyed by the fixity of print. Lanham, to be sure, does not denounce or discourage the reading of books, but he describes print as an ossifying and elitist medium, deservedly ready to be supplanted by multimedia. For an even more exuberant example of cyber-optimism, one can turn to *Imagologies*, a stylish, eye-popping "anti-book" by the American and Finnish philosophers Mark Taylor and Esa Saarinen. Taylor writes, "I am convinced that recent developments in electronic telecommunications technology have brought us to the brink of an extraordinary social and cultural revolution."[5] He and Saarinen argue forcefully and often convincingly that it is the responsibility of thinkers and teachers to enter the new spaces of electronic, largely image-based communications, but they also argue for the rejection of older, print-based communicative practices, which they view as simply too benighted to be

---

Century," in *Simians, Cyborgs, and Women* (New York: Routledge, 1991), 149–81. On the connections between poststructuralist thought and electronic culture, see Mark Poster, *The Mode of Information* (Chicago: University of Chicago Press, 1990); George Landow, *Hypertext: The Convergence of Contemporary Critical Theory and Technology* (Baltimore: Johns Hopkins University Press, 1992); and N. Katherine Hayles, *How We Became Posthuman* (Chicago: University of Chicago Press, 1999), 25–49.

[5] Mark Taylor and Esa Saarinen, *Imagologies: Media Philosophy* (London: Routledge, 1994), "Communicative Practices," 7. (*Imagologies* is paginated only within sections.)

worthy of continuation: "Literate reason and the literary critic have become relics of the past."[6] Emblazoned on the back cover, this injunction sums up their view of print culture: "If you read books, justify it."

ALL RIGHT. The book you are reading is an attempt to answer that challenge. Taylor and Saarinen are right to point out that the ground of cultural communication is shifting so rapidly that nothing can be taken for granted; nothing, in fact, can simply be as it was before. Books and literature will in all likelihood remain important, but in the context of a communications environment (or *mediasphere*, as the French writer and political thinker Régis Debray likes to call it) in which the form and experience of print is less pervasive than it once was. We cannot and should not try to preserve intact the order of print culture; neither should we rush to assume that because electronic and audiovisual culture is the next thing it is the right thing or the only thing. We have no duty to reinforce the direction of historical change by hastening to turn the new into the dominant, or the dominant into the absolute. We should and will continue to read books, including literary books, even old literary books, but we will need—and want—to do so in different ways, and most likely for different reasons from those that held sway as long as print was the dominant and unquestioned intellectual medium.

It is thus worthwhile to try to understand what is happening to literary culture in the context of what is happening in today's transformed world, and to ask how that culture of books and literature, stricken with obsolescence as it may be, can yet contribute to human society on the planet. For those of us who belong to literary communities, trying to understand what is happening to literary culture in as large a context as possible can be both an urgent task and a remarkable opportunity. Literature and its study, and in a broader sense the part of culture that revolves around the printed word, are losing their obviousness, the self-evidence of their existence, and whatever appearance of autonomy they once had. Their status seems to be shifting from dominant to residual. Literature's overt value as cultural capital for the upper-middle class has been declining for generations, to the point that it is futile either to try to prop up its archaic function as the font of refined, genteel discourse or to claim that one is striking a blow for democratic culture

---

[6] Ibid., "Media Philosophy," 17.

by debunking it.[7] Literature, the humanities, and their communities
cannot expect or hope simply to perpetuate themselves, to make minor
adjustments and go on as before; nor should literature be viewed as such
an effective embodiment of elitist domination that we should unhesi-
tatingly embrace media changes that bid to marginalize it even further.
Our best chance to continue (or to make a dignified end, if necessary)
lies in thinking and acting both as citizens of a troubled world and as
members of literary communities by asking what literary culture can
give to that world—whether (and if so, how) it can transform itself so
as to remain an active part of culture.

This is by no means a call for direct commitment to causes in political economy or ecology or anything else on the part of writers, critics, or scholars. Citizens who are also writers or scholars do well to
commit themselves to political action in which they believe, but that
is not the point of the arguments I wish to offer here. Indeed, the notion that writers, artists, and intellectuals have special authority to
make public pronouncements on political and social questions may
well be a creation of the now departing mediasphere of print culture,
so that intellectual commitment and its forms of expression will be
one of the many things in need of rethinking and reinvention as literary culture adapts itself to a world in which print is a less dominant,
if still important, arena of communication. It may be that literary culture as such can best contribute to the world's life in extremely indirect ways—including that of seemingly turning away from the most
pressing features of the here and now or even the most troubling signs
about the future so as to keep alive a "back country" of cultural reflection and possibilities far from the dominant tendencies of the day.
But the question, "what does literary culture, *now*, have to give to the
larger world?" should at least be raised. To assume that literary culture can go on existing on the strength of its tradition or the inertia of
its institutions, and even be appreciated for trying to do so, strikes me
as the more dubious gamble. At a minimum, asking this kind of question should clarify, in an exploratory and non-reductive way, the current status of literary culture and the possibilities it offers for understanding, and acting in, the world.

[7] On the decline of literature's value as the basis of class-based linguistic and cultural distinction, see John Guillory, *Cultural Capital* (Chicago: University of Chicago
Press, 1993), 55–82.

Moreover, parochial as concern over a decline in book-reading or a turn away from literary study might seem, the changes provoking these trends are part and parcel of the most salient transformations in the world at large. The new modes of communication that are displacing print and books are also changing the human geography of the world by restructuring and vastly increasing the global flow of information. The technologies on which these communications depend are remaking the nature of work, production, and research; they also contribute to rapid growth in the flow of currencies and goods through world markets. New technologies, in other words, help to drive the extension of market thinking and behavior into ever more areas of life. The changing and ever more pervasive economy, in turn, makes literary culture's tradition of setting itself apart from economic, managerial, and policy matters seem an ever more dubious gambit when it comes to thinking about or dealing with society and politics. No less disturbingly, the extension of science and technology into ever more aspects of life is forcing a rethinking (and a reworking) of the boundaries between the natural and the cultural, thereby challenging the authority and autonomy of literary culture and the human sciences in what they once thought confidently was their own house. The recognition that human activity must try to make itself more compatible with the balances and limits of the biosphere further discredits the long-standing notion that the knowledge of culture and history can be kept separate from that of the world of creatures and things. From virtually every perspective, the relationship between literary culture and the life of the world is thus becoming both stronger and more unsettled. Maintaining and enhancing that relationship thus requires a skeptical look at its present course, an understanding of how it got there, and inventive thinking about its options and future headings. The chapters that follow are an attempt to carry out this program.

To UNDERSTAND the possible roles of literary culture in the context of a new and changing world of communications media, it is useful to begin by looking at literary culture itself. The use—and thus the very life or existence—of the literary part of culture depends to a large extent on the workings of literary culture as an institution. In other words, beliefs about literature, conventions of reading, and modes of teaching all shape the ways in which literary texts belong to cultural life and participate (or not) in the processes by which culture, society, and the world are maintained and transformed. Literary culture, no less than print or electronic or audiovisual communications technologies, forms an important part of the media—in the broadest sense—through which the symbolic activity of society is carried out. The capacity of literary words and ideas to touch minds and hearts and to make differences in the world depends not only on such obvious mediations as paper, print, schools, the book trade, and book reviews, but also on the disposition toward literature fostered by the social status of writers and readers, on the image of writing and reading projected by literature's self-representations, on the range of subject matter and style recognized as legitimate by literary communities.

Chapter 1 will thus offer a brief look at literary culture, its place in the modern world, and its dominant outlook. The modern category of literature depends on the rise of a secular public culture and on the dominance of the market for printed matter over other economic bases of literary production, such as patronage. These conditions fostered the development of a modern literary culture emphasizing the distinction between author and reader, the autonomy of literary creators and their communities, and the importance of innovative exploration in the use and indeed the continual transformation of language and discourse. Literary culture became in many ways the opposite number of modern scientific culture, with its assumptions of shared rationality and its goal of clear, even transparent communication. It thus tended to take little interest in the nonhuman and material aspects of the world, in the objects of scientific knowledge. It also came to see itself as distanced from the business of the city, and to define itself as loftier or purer of spirit than political and economic affairs.

Literary study, meanwhile, became an independent academic discipline through successive affirmations of the autonomy of both its objects and methods. Professors of literature, like their counterparts in other academic fields, won the right to define which texts and ideas they would work on and what kind of work would count as legitimate. In recent years, this disciplinary autonomy vis-à-vis both other academic disciplines and nonacademic literary communities has made possible rapid (and often controversial) changes in the literary canon— the works most generally used in literary education and research. It has also allowed for a no less controversial shift of emphasis away from the reading of literature per se and toward the study of literary and cultural theory and of a wide range of cultural texts outside the limits of what was once considered literature. All these changes have taken place in the context of a structurally terrible job market for those who earn the Ph.D. in the humanities, and of an increase in the quantity of scholarly production by literature professors. Literary studies thus form an intellectual community with considerable autonomy but also significant structural problems and conflicts.

Controversy, of course, is not surprising when we consider that much of the current outlook and ethos of literary studies was shaped by events and ideas of the late sixties, probably the most recent historical moment to have had this kind of impact. The second half of the sixties saw the rise of theoretical discourses such as poststructuralism that became prominent in the intellectual landscape of the humanities in the seventies and early eighties, and that remain highly influential in a somewhat diluted form today. The turn to multiculturalism and the politics of identity likewise have their origins in the New Social Movements of the sixties and early seventies (Civil Rights and other activism by or on behalf of racial and ethnic minorities, the Women's and Gay/Lesbian Movements). In chapter 2, then, I look at how the recent state of the literary disciplines responds to the era of 1968, and suggest that the way in which concerns of that time have been institutionalized in the academy, together with changes in economic and social conditions over the past thirty years, have left literary studies out of step with the changing world at the turn of the millennium.

Both the character of late-sixties social protest—perhaps most intensely exemplified in the Paris of May '68—and the theoretical innovations of that era have, for the most part, reinforced literary culture's long-standing preference for radical opposition and critique over pragmatic engagement with the world around it. Academic literary culture's relations to the dominant (and conservative) social and political forces of today can largely be described in terms of three distinct but interconnected stances: the critique of ideology in language and discourse, the demand for rights, justice, and cultural representation by or on behalf of formerly excluded groups, and the practice of local, tactical, and symbolic forms of politics. Valid as they may be, all are at least to some degree institutionalized echoes of the world of thirty years ago, now comfortably integrated into academic literary culture as a semi-autonomous social and communicative system, struggling to counteract the academy's isolation from the larger culture and the problems of today's world.

The New Social Movements and the intellectual ferment of the sixties took place in a context of rising and unthreatening economic expectations; they were largely directed against injustices, repression, and conformism associated with increasingly affluent societies. This helped make them compatible with the idealized (and ultimately romantic) understanding of literary culture as something distinct from and even intrinsically opposed to economic and political power. Today, however, as a result of the acceleration in capitalism's work of creative destruction, people are less and less able to count on a stable material and economic existence upon which they could then base aspirations and critiques in the social and cultural domains. There are thus ever fewer political and social issues that can be effectively addressed by critiques of a literary and cultural kind, with their tendency to neglect the economic and the material. One result of this is a literary academy often unproductively and uncreatively estranged from the problems of the world around it—even while it regularly claims to have special insights into these problems and often erects the making of such claims into a standard of intellectual integrity.

The intensification of the world's economic life has been accompanied by changes in humanity's relation to its earthly environment. The reality of environmental disasters and the possibility of ecological unsustainability provide further evidence that the worlds of ideas and of things, the cultural and the natural, cannot be kept separate. They remind us that taking care of social and cultural life may not be enough. The need to care for the environment also calls into question the long-held progressive idea that human history is, or should be, a one-way march toward the overcoming of necessity, toward the replacement of natural, given conditions of existence by humanly constructed ones. Once again literary culture finds itself out of step with reality. Although many worthwhile attempts at "ecocriticism" have been made in recent years, they have remained relatively marginal in comparison with other kinds of social concerns in the humanities, probably because it is difficult to know how to take ecology and the physical environment seriously in a field heavily committed to viewing linguistic and cultural construction as the most important operation in the making and knowing of the world.

The same problem besets literary culture in coming to terms with a world increasingly made and known through the practice of science and technology. In neuroscience, evolutionary psychology, computer science, genetics, and even the physics of nonlinear dynamical systems, science is investigating many phenomena formerly assumed—at least in modern times—to belong to culture and not to nature. No less important, the sociology, anthropology, and history of science

have amply documented the ways in which science and its explanations of the world belong to culture—a proposition that should not, of
course, be used to deny the power of what the sciences have been able
to discover. There is no such thing as culture without a physical and
biological basis, without places, matter, bodies, and things; conversely,
the concept of nature and everything we know about it are creations
of culture and especially of the part of culture known as science.

Recent work in the cultural study of science offers concepts and
models for a study of culture, including literature, that takes seriously
the role of both the natural and the cultural in making and knowing
the world (Chapter 3). My discussion of this work focuses on the
French philosopher and anthropologist of science Bruno Latour, who
has argued boldly and convincingly for a major realignment in how we
view the relations between nature, society, science, and modernity.
He proposes that nature and society (or nature and culture) should not
be considered foundational givens that become blended together as a
result of the workings of science and technology—for example, when
humanly released pollutants cause a hole in the ozone layer or sociobiologists claim that what anthropologists call nurture is really nature. These are indeed hybrid phenomena, but Latour argues that, as
such, they exemplify the general, primordial condition of natural/so-
cial relations, common to so-called premodern (i.e., science-lacking)
societies and to our own: what is exceptional, and amounts to a very
particular kind of cultural construction, are the representations of pure
nature and pure society produced (at great cost) by the natural and social sciences of the modern West. The West believes itself to be modern by virtue of its scientific separation of a natural world from a social and cultural one. But since the epistemological claims for this
separation, he argues, do not stand up to the scrutiny of an anthropological approach to science, and since in practice technoscience constantly produces ever more extensive nature/society hybrids, *we have
never been modern*, to quote in lowercase the title (and the thesis) of
his most synthetic work. We thus live, he concludes, in a nonmodern
world, one in which we have to take more political and cultural responsibility for the making of technoscientific hybrids, for working
human and nonhuman entities together so as to make a future that is
neither ever more modern nor self-consciously archaic.

Latour's work suggests that the humanities, in the sense of the study
and creative invention of what matters most about human beings,
should be located neither in the purely symbolic and cultural activi-

ties where the academic division of knowledge places them, nor in the naturalistic constructions favored by sociobiologists and champions of Prozac. The humanities are to be found instead in the zone of interaction between human beings, their cultures and societies, their sciences and technologies, and the world around them. The writings of another leading practitioner of the cultural study of science, Donna Haraway, provide examples of the kind of work and writing that can come about when the conceptual and stylistic resources of literary and cultural theory are brought to bear on the sociotechnical hybrids that typify the world's present-day transformations.

The work of a third major figure in science studies, the Belgian philosopher Isabelle Stengers, suggests ways in which humanists should question the ethics of their own modern practices, their way of assuming a position of superiority over those who are said to use language naively or uncritically. The successful work of natural science, she argues, depends on creating situations in which non-humans can become reliable witnesses, in which things can say no to scientists. The social sciences and humanities, unfortunately, often fail to achieve this kind of reliability in their dealings with people and texts.

In short, the new work in science studies strongly suggests that literary culture's best possible future lies not in disciplinary autonomy, not even in cultural or human autonomy, but in crossing over into new territories and inventing new forms and practices of explanation. Literary culture ought to be able to follow the lead of science studies in doing intellectual work that does not start by separating subject from object, culture from nature. On this path it should be possible to transgress the boundaries that have largely kept literary culture away from the economic, the ecological, biological, and physical aspects of the world.

Crossing disciplinary boundaries so as to reach new objects, however, is far from being the only approach to encouraging literary culture to interact with more aspects of the world. It is also worth trying to reimagine and reconceptualize the fundamental goals of literary and cultural study: in particular, in order to find ways of breaking with their current dependency upon critique, denunciation, and stances of superiority.

To create, read, and interpret texts—to learn new forms of speaking and acting from contact with the works of others—is to find and follow one's own path, and also to participate in collective cultural acts of steering or governance. The cultural and political contributions of the humanities need to be strategic as well as tactical, need to concern the maintenance of systems and structures as well as their critique or disruption. The making, reception, and recycling of works, I argue in chapter 4, is a complex, indirect, and often subtle way of sending feedback signals within the ongoing life processes in which history is made. It is also a form of participation in networks of human communication and transmission that mobilize the past and the present, the dead and the living, the far away and the familiar. It is a way of adding to the richness of human life and activity, a way of noticing things that would otherwise not be noticed, and perhaps thereby of provoking kinds of action that would not otherwise be thought of or carried out. The workings and use of literary culture can thus be said to make up part of the cultural feedback systems by which some measure of control can be exercised over processes that make up collective life in the world, part of the transmission networks through which people use language to constitute and participate in communities.

The adaptability and nonreductive working of feedback systems and of discursive communities depends in large part on the variety or diversity of the signals they can process, the voices they can integrate. Texts in foreign tongues and writings from groups long excluded from high culture are important elements of this diversity. So are the poetic and playful inventions of language: the strangeness and beauty that can arise when words are pushed to do and say things beyond the usual norms and habits of discourse. Literature is both referential and rhetorical: it helps its readers to interact with both the variety of the world over time and space and the variety of possibilities for knowing and imagining the world through language. Both modes of reading—directed toward the world and directed toward discourse—are parts of the requisite diversity needed for steering an adaptable course and constructing a viable and pluralistic future.

A crucial element of the diversity offered by literary culture lies in the persistence of literary works from the past. Cultural contact with works from a broad range of past eras matters, because it challenges the routines of the present and contributes to the process of steering a course into the future. If we have never been modern, then we can no longer consider the past as that which has been passed by. We would do well to think twice about the current tendency in education and culture towards *presentism*, towards rejecting much of the literary past as benighted, elitist, or simply out of date and thus reducing the contact students and scholars have with it. In chapter 5 I contend that it is crucial to maintain contact with the many forms of the past if the intellectual project of the humanities is to be one of understanding the world with a view to acting effectively and inventively in it.

People like to say that we are living in the age of computers, because computers, being new, distinguish our moment from earlier ones. But we are no less living in the jet age, the automobile age, the era of industrial mass production; indeed, that of the city, of money, of books, of the wheel, of agriculture, of the hearth. History is no smooth succession of organically coherent eras, each one complete in itself; rather, change and inertia are always mixed together, with different aspects of the human lifeworld enduring and changing at varying rhythms. Computers have joined a host of other fundamental technologies, complicating but not suppressing the many instances of commonality between life today and life in the past, even the distant past.

We will not, in other words, soon be entering a digital age as if emigrating to a new country, and so it is important to stay in contact with the cultural works of the past when so many of our institutions are themselves the persistent creations of earlier times. To neglect works from the past is to impoverish our capacities for representing, understanding, and acting on the historically multilayered world in which we will always live. Works from the past provide spaces of possibility and sources of cognitive noise that add tension, dissonance, and variety to present-day thinking—all qualities that ultimately make thinking stronger, more resourceful and resilient. It is thus both vain and dangerous to pin utopian hopes to a new order of communications expected to jettison both accumulated culture and old habits of communication.

With these considerations and those of previous chapters in mind, I turn in chapter 6 to prospects and prescriptions for the intellectual life of literary studies and for education in the humanities. Literary culture needs to adapt—by drastic change, if necessary—in order to survive and remain pertinent in the post-print order of communications while giving up as little as possible of its genuine intellectual specificity, its difference within the emerging electronic mediasphere. It's not reasonable simply to try to enforce the maintenance of the literary past, nor should we just give up on it or be content with transferring some of its highlights to new formats and media.

In the teaching of literature at all levels, from elementary to graduate school, I argue that it is important to cultivate the relation between language and literature more intensely than has been done in the recent past, and to do so in new ways. If literature and its institutions are to survive as more than an elitist nuisance, then reading and writing need to be made attractive and desirable in a communications and cultural environment where they must compete for attention with other media. Their desirability can only result from being used to do what they do well and that other media do less well. The mediatic specificity of reading, writing, and of literature, their potential niche in the new mediasphere, lies in their being made of language, which is a virtually universal human possession: everyone can respond in kind to works in language and talk back to them. Everyone can use language to speak, to think, and to play. Although print literature has been criticized for disrupting the reciprocity of oral communication by producing a hierarchical separation between author and reader, literary works—even when printed in books—retain a direct connection, in their very stuff, with the words we use to think and talk to ourselves and to talk to one another. Teaching should thus emphasize the interplay between the pleasures of hearing and telling stories and those of reading and writing—that is, between orality and literacy, the spoken and written word. To read and study the literary written word is to add to one's own repertoire of language, to augment one's own capacities of speaking, writing, and thinking.

This does not mean, however, that literary study and research should devote themselves only to local and personal concerns, or to mastering rhetoric or learning to tell and enjoy good stories. A crucial teaching task, and also knowledge-making task, of the literary humanities should be to help people find and enrich languages with which to speak, write, and think about what is most important in their lives and the world. The idea that literature can be a resource for participating in the task of steering the world should not be opposed to, but rather combined with, the idea that literature is one of life's modest but important pleasures, important precisely because of its distance from the weighty seriousness of dealing with the world. For the real power often found in literature comes from being both a serious resource and a ready pleasure, and, better yet, from putting them together. Works of literature are at once abstract and concrete: they systematically exploit the power of language, narrative, and rhetoric to move with speed and agility from sensuous particulars to the heights of abstraction, from real-world reference to the play of signifiers, from the flow of persuasion and enchantment to the discontinuities of irony and resistance. The reader of a thousand-page novel delineating the social complexities of an age is the same person who plays with (and works at making sense of) the words in her own head, the words around her as she leads her daily life. Reading and writing as a matter of serious, world-sustaining, responsibility-oriented education should be of a piece with reading and writing as a matter of individually oriented, liberatory, enlightening, or pleasureful education. People should be encouraged and assisted in thinking about the relations between the local and global networks of which they are a part: on the one hand, their lives, thoughts, modes of interaction, and imaginings; on the other hand, the social, historical, economic, and ecological contexts in which they live, and about which, as citizens, they're called upon to make decisions.

These goals for literary culture, if they are to have any chance of being realized, will require educational changes running the gamut from preschool to the doctorate. In the final section of chapter 6, I focus on possible new directions for undergraduate and graduate education in literature and the humanities. I argue that it is time to rethink quite radically the specialization and autonomy of the literary disciplines and that one place to start would be to stop believing that majoring in either a humanities or an empirical discipline alone, complemented by a few watery "distribution" or "core curriculum" requirements, can constitute a genuine liberal arts education. A further step, one more directly related to the formation of the future literary professoriate, would be to stop training graduate students to write only for a captive academic audience. Such a step might, I suggest, help ease the related internal academic crises of over-publication of unreadable scholarly prose and overproduction of unemployable Ph.D.s; more important, it might set literary culture and the humanities on a path to greater involvement in public culture and the construction of the world's future.

IN THE END, choices about letting go of literary culture or hanging on to it, about what to teach from the works of the past and how to teach it, about whether and how to take the nonhuman world into account in studying human society and culture, are forms of ethical and political choice through which, to however modest a degree, we try to shape our world—both the small world of local and professional communities and the larger world of planet Earth. To assume that literary culture should be superseded by the march of progress is to acquiesce to one kind of future; to defend a primarily critical and oppositional vocation for literary culture is to opt for a slightly different variant. In the pages that follow, I hope to offer as strong an argument as possible for the desirability of a third choice: that we see literary culture neither as a burden to be cast off nor as a privileged or insightful space from which to criticize or reflect upon the world around us, but rather as a resource, as an extension of our collective sense organs, brains, and voiceboxes, near and far, then and now, which we can use as we participate in, and try to sustain, the life of the world.

1 Becoming Modern: The Autonomy of Literary Culture

LITERARY CULTURE, as I noted in the introduction, is a nonstandard term, one that brings together the several related ways in which literature is a part of culture and in which there is a culture associated with literature. If it is possible to speak of literary culture as a distinct entity, however fuzzy at its edges, this is because the works of literature, its institutions, the communities around it, and their ways of thinking and acting form an interdependent ensemble, a recognizable cluster of artifacts, interests, activities, and beliefs. To describe this ensemble thoroughly would require a book far longer than this one; in fact, to define literary culture unambiguously is probably impossible, because that would require the members of its communities—to say nothing of outsiders—to reach a consensus about what exactly it is and where its edges lie. My goal in this chapter is more modest: to offer a brief account of the emergence of modern literary culture as a distinct institution, one whose most characteristic manifestation today is found in the disciplines of literary study in the academy.

Literary culture includes the accumulated works of literature considered as part of the totality of human cultural artifacts. These works are all from the past, though at any given time many of them are so recent that they seem part of the present, especially when they are first being read and commented on, when they are becoming part of the present of many readers. Writings from the past are a part of cultural memory, a form of contact with earlier moments in the world's life. *Literary* writings from the past, however, are not primarily records of what was, but an accumulated set of inventions and imaginings from times and places not our own. They form a verbal annex to the world as it is encountered, lived, and spoken of in the present; a back country not found but made, a set of past attempts to invent and articulate what was once new, what was coming into being.

In one sense, literary culture includes history, philosophy, and indeed every field in which writing is taken seriously. Communities of readers and scholars are eclectic in their tastes and are interested in many things that are not strictly literary. But in a more specific sense the poetic inventions of imaginative literature form the core of literary culture. Novels, poems, plays, and essays are not primarily devoted to describing empirical reality, though they often engage in such description. Nor is their mission that of propounding exact and general truths, though they sometimes dabble in that as well. Works of literature are above all verbal simulations of experience, real and invented. They almost always include elements both abstract and concrete, general and particular. The words of which they're made are public conveyances, their meaning largely shared by all their users, though always shaded and extended by individual versions of understanding and experience. Literary works articulate what is felt or imagined in one singular mind and body into the shared codes of language—the same medium that literature's readers use for talking to others and to themselves. (This active use of the communicative medium—language—by those who read but do not write literary works makes literature very different from the visual arts: most viewers of paintings or sculptures do not paint or sculpt, and many moviegoers do not make images of any kind.)

The enormous quantity and variety of literary works stems from the variety of human cultures and individuals, from the ubiquity of the linguistic medium, and from the robustness of writing (and especially printed writing) as a means of storage and transmission. Literary works from the past remain available as a part of today's culture largely because of the stability of the printed book. I'm referring less to the physical durability of books—which is, in fact, quite uncertain—than to the basic continuity of their format. The multiple and rapidly changing formats of today's media remind us of how exceptional the era of the book—and, going further back, that of the codex or bound volume—has been. Over the past several hundred years the basic format for accessing written language has remained largely the same. To be sure, paper composition, typefaces, and binding techniques have all changed; spelling and typographic conventions have evolved over the centuries; ways of making indexes and tables of contents have gradually been modified. There are certainly historical differences worth studying in the material form of books and in reading practices, but by and large a person living in 2001, opening a recent edition of Rabelais's *Gargantua,* will access the text in ways that the sixteenth-century reader already knew: holding the book in one's hands or on a table or stand; reading lines and pages sequentially; using bookmarks, fingers, marginal scribbles, and page numbers to locate passages or sections; remembering where certain phrases are located on a pair of facing pages without remembering which pages they are; reading the same copy (or identical copies) of the book in different places; discussing the book with others who have read identical copies or similar editions. When compared with the flexibility and imprecision of information passed on orally, with the rarity of manuscripts and their modification by the scribes who copy them, or with the frequent format changes of magnetic and electronic media, the long-term stability of the printed codex seems extraordinary.

The rapid growth of new media is now calling that stability into question, or at least making it less self-evident than it once seemed. But the importance of print to literary culture goes far beyond any computer-age nostalgia for inked paper between binding boards, or even the distinctive continuity of the book format. The nature of writing for print, and especially for a market in printed books, was fundamental to the constitution of modern literary culture. The stable, quasi-independent existence of printed words in books fostered the notion that literary works made up a distinct and separate realm, removed from the messiness and movement of human life. The market for printed goods, meanwhile, put a premium on innovation, and thus enabled authorial originality to supplant convention as a defining characteristic of letters. Literary production for print also sharpened the separation of writers from readers, thereby helping to define literary culture around the communities, practices, and values of those who write for the print market.

Although Gutenberg printed his Bible in the fifteenth century, a literary culture fully organized around the reading of printed works and the production of books for the market did not really come into its own until the late eighteenth and early nineteenth centuries. Until then, print, handwriting, and oral expression shared the defining role in a transitional form of literary culture that Walter J. Ong, S.J., has usefully called "rhetorical culture." Ong devised this term to designate an early modern form of cultural organization that, while largely realized in writing and even print, was still strongly nourished by its roots in orality: in storytelling, oratory, preaching, conversation, and other genres of the spoken word. Far from disappearing with the invention of writing or even printing, the cognitive and social practices of orality—notably its reliance on conventions and epithets shared by speakers and listeners so as to constitute both their cultural memory and their way of relating to one another—lingered on for centuries. Ong describes rhetorical culture as "oral culture shrouded in writing . . . an oral culture whose institutions (in the sociological sense of this term, ways of doing things, patterns of behavior) have been codified, put into manuals, made the object of reflection and of reflective training, and thus both artificially sustained and reinforced by writing— the very instrument which was ultimately to make these institutions obsolete."[1] This was the dominant verbal culture of early modern monarchic Europe, with its courts, salons, and established religious institutions: a world in which writing remained closely linked to the social rules and occasions of speech.

The mutation of rhetorical culture into mature print culture was part and parcel of the democratic and industrial revolutions of roughly two centuries ago. With the decline of fixed and hierarchical institutions such as princely courts and established churches came a shift from patronage to market as the crucial factor in the economic situation of the writer. For the writer engaged in selling work for the print market, the reader is no longer a fellow courtier, academician, or salon acquaintance but one of a mostly unknown mass of consumers whose taste and appetite for novelty can only be guessed at. Writing came to be less and less a matter of "writing down" simulacra of oral forms that served to entertain or persuade an audience of potential peers; instead it directly assumed the task of interesting and holding the attention of solitary readers, who were likely to rent or purchase books only if convinced that they can entertain them or inform them in a new way.

---

[1] Walter J. Ong, "Romantic Difference and the Poetics of Technology," in *Rhetoric, Romance, and Technology* (Ithaca: Cornell University Press, 1971), 261; see also 1–15, 260–70, and Ong, *Interfaces of the Word* (Ithaca: Cornell University Press, 1977), 214–22.

In a study of print culture's coming of age in England, Alvin Kernan interprets Samuel Johnson's career as exemplifying the emergence of the modern print author, a professional producer of copy whose writing seems to reveal a distinctive individual persona:

> There were no writers like Johnson before him, and none like him even afterward, but in the romantic system of literature that gradually developed after him, the authorial personality had to be, and continued in fact to be, like Johnson, in the respect of being strange and interesting enough to impart to writers and writing a psychological dignity and meaning they could no longer derive from a place and function in the social world of palace, great house, and cathedral.[2]

The writer, in other words, came increasingly to be seen as a specific, original, creative figure, not just a particularly skilled practitioner of a rhetorical culture shared by his readers, but someone distinctively inspired or gifted. Eighteenth-century writers like Johnson and Rousseau began putting their personality on display to a degree that previously would not have been accepted or imagined.

This cultivation of writers' individuality was facilitated by their increasing emancipation from the control of church, court, or patron as well as from the socially shared expectations of genres derived from orality and its rhetorical forms. At the same time, it accompanied the growing importance and specificity of the literary market: a distinctive literary personality meant a distinctive product. Thus the transition from "rhetorical culture" to the modern institutions of literature entailed both emancipation and restriction: on the one hand, freedom from many of the forms, prescriptions, and prohibitions that came with a hierarchy of genres derived from oral forms, but on the other hand, the exclusion of many writers and kinds of writing from success in the market for cultural goods or from the new critical and disciplinary category of literature.

The premium placed on writerly originality and the sharp contrast in interests and outlooks between producers and consumers in the literary marketplace have both contributed to the sense that modern lit-

---

[2] Alvin Kernan, *Samuel Johnson and the Impact of Print* (Princeton: Princeton University Press, 1989), 21. Marilyn Butler makes a similar argument, à propos of Coleridge, concerning the "rise of the man of letters" in the romantic generation in *Romantics, Rebels, and Reactionaries* (Oxford: Oxford University Press, 1981), 69–93.

erary and artistic culture stands apart from the values and practices of the larger society to which it belongs. It tends, in other words, to become *autonomous*. The social phenomenon of aesthetic autonomy is the object of extensive analyses by the French sociologist Pierre Bourdieu, who focuses both on the historical development of autonomous communities of cultural producers and on their role in today's markets of artistic and intellectual goods.[3] Bourdieu distinguishes what he calls the *field of restricted production* (e.g., writing for other writers, a "legitimate" activity under the rule of autonomy) from the *field of mass production* (the aesthetically "illegitimate" production to fit the demands of the large-scale public). The distinction between these two fields depends on the divide between, on the one hand, a small group of technically specialized and self-aware producers, and, on the other hand, a larger group of consumers—who, viewed from the first group, are an anonymous collective perceivable only as an alien set of market forces. Bourdieu considers the dominance of a market economy in symbolic goods—as opposed to a predominantly patronage economy— to be a necessary condition for the emergence of the field of restricted production. A largely anonymous market, he argues, frees cultural producers from the direct control of patrons, church, or court, but in so doing it subjects them to the more impersonal, mysterious, and thus disturbing pull of the market itself. A field of production structured by the requirement of its own autonomy thus arises in reaction both to the kind of freedom accorded by the market and to the kind of constraint it simultaneously imposes.

Market forces are particularly strong in the case of printed works, since the reproduced work of each producer must be sold or rented to a large number of consumers, most of whom will not respond to it directly as a patron or court audience would have done. The facelessness and numerical mass of book buyers makes them a more impersonal force than the purchasers of, say, paintings, even in a commercialized art market.[4] As a market of literary goods took shape, writers gained

[3] See Pierre Bourdieu, "The Market of Symbolic Goods," in *The Field of Cultural Production*, ed. Randal Johnson (New York: Columbia University Press, 1993), 112–41, and *The Rules of Art*, trans. Susan Emanuel (Stanford: Stanford University Press, 1996).

[4] Bourdieu does not restrict his arguments to any one artistic or cultural field, but it is the literary field that furnishes, implicitly or explicitly, his most compelling articulation of his thesis. "This movement towards artistic autonomy accelerated abruptly with the Industrial Revolution and the Romantic reaction. The development

enough freedom from direct control that they could see themselves as a community and attempt to strengthen their autonomy. At the same time, however, this motivated them to assert the autonomy of their community as a refuge against the alien pressures of market forces by recognizing only their own judgments as legitimate—even as they often continued to produce works for the mass market. The ideal of autonomy thus encouraged literary culture to distance itself from the larger society, but also made it comparable, in important ways, to other professional institutions, such as the liberal professions and academic disciplines, for which autonomy is also a fundamental principle.[5]

An early embodiment of an intellectual community that claimed at least a measure of autonomy can be found in the seventeenth- and eighteenth-century "Republic of Letters," understood as a cosmopolitan collective of scholars and writers devoted to the advancement of knowledge through the maintenance of community standards for polite sociability and the exchange of discourse.[6] While many of its members produced works for print, the Republic of Letters was also grounded in the oral culture of salon conversation and the handwriting culture of letter-writing. The literary community took on its characteristic modern form in the nineteenth century when the ideal of community autonomy in intellectual judgment, already important in the eighteenth-century Republic of Letters, became more closely tied to the conditions of literary production characteristic of a mature print market.

---

of a veritable cultural industry and, in particular, the relationship between the daily press and literature, encouraging the mass production of works produced by quasi-industrial methods—such as the serialized story (or, in other fields, melodrama and vaudeville)—coincides with the extension of the public, resulting from the expansion of primary education, which turned new classes (including women) into consumers of culture" (*The Field of Cultural Production*, 113). The conjunction of mass literacy and the fully reproducible character of the printed text made print the most advanced or characteristic medium of marketed and marketable culture, and thus made literature a leading early instance of the construction of an autonomous aesthetic field, a construction both facilitated by and opposed to the impersonal and heteronomous cultural market.

[5] On the connections between the formation of modern literary institutions, the professionalization of writing, and the growing importance of professions and disciplines in society, see Clifford Siskin, *The Work of Writing: Literature and Social Change in Britain 1700–1830* (Baltimore: Johns Hopkins University Press, 1998).

[6] See Dena Goodman, *The Republic of Letters* (Ithaca: Cornell University Press, 1994).

Autonomy, for a literary or artistic community, means that the work of the writers or artists who make it up—and thus their right to membership—can only be validated by the judgment of their peers: above all by fellow practitioners of their art, to some extent by fellow creators in comparable aesthetic fields, and at times by other friends or sympathizers whose judgment, for one reason or another, can be equated with those of the cultural creators rather than the consumers. A literary community acquires autonomy in its definition and values by restricting the legitimate judgment and destination of works to its own members. This kind of autonomy—which is common to artistic communities, professions, and academic disciplines—emphasizes judgment according to the professional criteria of peers: writers are judged primarily by writers acting as writers and thus according to writerly criteria, painters by painters as painters following painterly standards, and so forth. In the nineteenth century, the entry criterion for membership in the literary community increasingly became the production of work for the print market, above all in the imaginative or "literary" genres of poetry, theater, and fiction. This standard gradually superseded that of belonging to a literate circle via participation in salons and/or correspondence—although vestiges of the salon-centered criterion survived in the inclusion of some non-publishing friends and sympathizers within the literary and artistic communities. By basing its preferences and judgments on "writerly" standards, valuing what is admired by fellow producers working in the same medium, this kind of community definition favors an emphasis on form, language, and style—i.e., preoccupations specific to those who write—over content or idea, which are less closely identified with the act of literary production. And, unlike the salon-based literary communities of the old regime, in which writers and readers mingled and often exchanged roles, the producer-centered literary community fosters distinctions and even opposition in values and taste between writers and the reading public.

The literary and artistic communities of the nineteenth century found names for the despised, uncreative consumers against whom they liked to define themselves: the bourgeois, the philistine. Bourgeois, in this sense, is not primarily a class term, defined by economic standing or by ownership of means of production. It designates, rather, someone who is neither a writer nor artist (nor one of their close friends and sympathizers) and who is thus felt to lack aesthetic sensibility, almost by definition. The bourgeois, or non-practitioner, seems unable to appreciate works according to the practitioner-centered, and thus increasingly formal, criteria that writers and artists consider to be legitimate. This opposition of artist and bourgeois quickly became a cliché, yet as a defining gesture of artistic, literary, and intellectual communities it has never been fully left behind.

A crucial consequence of the ideal of autonomy (and of attempts to practice it) in literary culture has been a long history of disengagement from such matters as politics, governance, economics, and technology. This disdain for involvement with the undistinguished business of the nonliterary world, no less than a sense of the aesthetic distinctiveness of the literary field, has shaped the critical stance of modern literary culture vis-à-vis society. The notion that the literary intellectual can serve as a disinterested, public-minded critic and reformer can be traced back to the figure of the Enlightenment *philosophe* (and, before that, to the exemplary figure of Pierre Bayle at the end of the seventeenth century). In the eighteenth-century Republic of Letters, however, there was little distance between writers of imaginative works, denouncers of injustice and political abuses, and inventors of theoretical and practical plans for the reform of society—indeed, the major Enlightenment figures combined all of these roles. The *Encyclopédie* of Diderot and D'Alembert, the great enterprise of a substantial literary community in mid-eighteenth-century France, included science, artisanry, and manufacture as well as arts and letters; natural history as well as political history; geography along with philosophy. This inclusiveness was part of the *Encyclopédie*'s critical stance toward the hierarchical and exclusive official culture of its day. In nineteenth-century Europe, however, once the context of literary culture was a partially democratic and heavily commercial society, once the writer's or thinker's despised Other was no longer the noble or the churchman who disdained the material world, but the bourgeois who made it his business, literary and intellectual critique became gradually more distanced from the world of commerce and things, at least in the culturally and economically dominant nations of Western Europe. With a sense of aesthetic specificity and distinction came a distaste for involvement with much of the everyday world. Over the course of the nineteenth century in Europe—and somewhat later in other parts of the world, such as Latin America—literary culture turned away from much of the everyday, the material, and the political. Writers and artists increasingly made whatever political and social critiques they offered in the more rarefied air of principles and utopias.

To be sure, major early nineteenth-century writers such as Balzac, Shelley, and Hugo, while not philosophers or social theorists in the manner of the Encyclopedists and *philosophes* of two and three generations earlier, still retained an active engagement with political life, offering critical analyses of contemporary power structures or visions of utopian resolution of conflict, describing the poet as a guide for society, and sometimes even participating in politics and government themselves. In France in the years just before and after the Revolution of 1830, the followers of the proto-socialist Saint-Simon taught that artists and writers had a social mission parallel to that of scientists and the organizers of industry and finance. The Saint-Simonian doctrine never won mass converts, but the idea of artistic commitment to social reform has remained a crucial (if often contested) part of the literary outlook and of behavior in literary communities. As early as 1835, however, Théophile Gautier allied scorn for the social and political sphere with the cause of literary autonomy under the banner of "art for art's sake," rejecting "social romanticism" and the Saint-Simonian doctrine of the artist's mission. This disdain for practical or world-oriented concerns was to be radicalized later in the nineteenth century in the horror proclaimed by aesthetes and decadents for the natural and the everyday.

The tension between artistic commitment and art for art's sake has continued down to the present. It often plays out not in compromise but in an amalgam of extremes, in which the doctrine (and group dynamics) of intellectual autonomy encourage what social commitment there is to take the form of radical, otherworldly positions and gestures: acts of political commitment, in other words, that also serve to affirm an aesthetic distance from the bourgeois—from conventional behavior and from dominant ideologies.[7] The historical avant-garde movements of the early twentieth-century are a case in point. The avant-gardes tried to break out of the social isolation and neutrality of the autonomous aesthetic sphere via radically disruptive forms or acts

---

[7] Tzvetan Todorov writes, "the model of art seems to have acquired growing importance among us, art itself being conceived in terms of autonomy (the work is beautiful in itself, not because it illustrates a truth or a moral lesson). Along with that, intellectuals, writers, and artists began to apply aesthetic criteria systematically to the field of ethics and politics." Todorov, "Politique des intellectuels," *L'Esprit créateur* 37, no. 2 (Summer 1997): 14.

intended to prepare the way for changes in consciousness and even for political revolution. Yet as Peter Bürger points out in a now classic study, avant-gardes "adopted an essential element of Aestheticism . . . they assent to the aestheticists' rejection of the world and its means-end rationality. What distinguishes them from the [aestheticists] is the attempt to organize a new life praxis from a basis in art,"—namely, from the autonomous aesthetic sphere's rebellion against the every-day bourgeois world.[8] The avant-garde, in other words, is both a re-jection and a radicalization of aesthetic autonomy's self-distancing from the world.

Throughout much of the twentieth century, when writers have con-cerned themselves with matters of politics or policy, it has been in the role, first seen in all its clarity and splendor in the Dreyfus Affair, of the *intellectual:* a person whose standing comes from his/her position as a cultural creator (or scientist or scholar), and who attempts to use this literary, artistic, or scientific authority to intervene in public mat-ters. Such intervention usually takes the form of statements made in the name of general principles of justice or morality rather than at-tempts to enter the arena of practical politics and offer policies. In ad-dition to calling society to account on issues of justice and human rights, intellectuals have characteristically endorsed radical, utopian alternatives to liberal democracy, whether progressive or reactionary. Political commitment and aesthetic autonomy have thus shaped as well as opposed each other, making common cause in creating a sense of radical distance from the conventional, the everyday, and the bour-geois order.

When modern literary culture has turned its attention to society, then, it has generally done so in the name of critique, opposition, and subversion. A gulf divides literary culture, which deals in signs and meanings, from the hard world of politics, money, and things; this chasm helps define literary culture in the modern world—or, more ac-curately, the chasm is central to literary culture's definition of the mod-ern world. The Enlightenment tradition of the man of letters as critic and reformer, the romantic tradition of the poet or artist as opponent (and creative superior) of the crass bourgeois, and the modernist tradi-tion of literature and art as modes of expression that continually bring

---

[8] Bürger, *Theory of the Avant-Garde,* trans. Michael Shaw, foreword by Jochen Schulte Sasse (Minneapolis: University of Minnesota Press, 1984), 49; see also x–xv, 34–54.

the shock of the new—all these heritages encourage literary thinkers to see their engagement with society in critical and radical terms, from a perspective outside (and usually imagined as above) the ordinary messiness of governance, policy, and commerce. The still much-enforced (if often breached) cultural boundaries between the cultivated and the popular, the highbrow and the lowbrow, make it unattractive (and even unseemly) for writers, artists, and intellectuals to live out their political and social commitments in an "everyday" mode of participation in an always imperfect and compromised democratic arena.

LITERARY CULTURE's uncomfortable relations with everyday life and the material world also have their roots in its intellectual genealogy, specifically in its disaffiliation from the modern scientific culture that emerged parallel to it. Literary culture understands its domain to be a cultural rather than a physical world. At its center are human creations in language; in ambitious moments it extends its inquiries from verbal artifacts to a much broader range of humanly created artifacts, behaviors, and institutions. But literary culture is out of its element when faced with the objects of empirical knowledge and action: it struggles like a fish on dry land when it reaches complex and technical human creations that are themselves the objects of empirical knowledge—things like computer chips and national economies—and feels itself in a vacuum (or a rigged, immaterial spectacle) when it comes to things like metals, oceans, and stars, which were made by no one known.

The distinctive position of literary culture was to a considerable extent shaped by the emergence of science as a specific mode of producing, authenticating, and reporting knowledge. Early advocates of empirical research and mathematical reasoning knew that they had to challenge textual authority: Bacon and Descartes took polemical aim at the reliance of both scholastic philosophy and Renaissance humanism on verbal texts.[9] For Descartes, history, erudition, and the verbal arguments of philosophy were far removed from real knowledge. At their worst they were a misleading waste of time and at their best a vaguely broadening experience akin to travel. Bacon denounced the errors and misunderstandings produced by language as the "idols of

---

[9] See Steven Shapin, *The Scientific Revolution* (Chicago: University of Chicago Press, 1996), 65–80.

the marketplace," one of his four "idols" or general tendencies of human minds toward error that needed to be reformed if humankind was to attain genuine knowledge and thus win mastery over nature. The celebrated successes of early modern science, such as Galileo's telescopic observations of sunspots and Jupiter's moons, and Boyle's use of an air pump to produce a vacuum, provided persuasive evidence that ancient authorities could be wrong about natural phenomena and that the use of new techniques and the regulated practice of observation could increase the quantity and accuracy of knowledge. Newton's subsequent formulation of mathematical laws for the motion of bodies and the force of gravity led to the widespread conviction that the "book of Nature" was written, and thus could be described, in a mathematical language that would be more faithful to the actual workings of physical phenomena than accounts in human speech.

Science thus increasingly used language to communicate in ways that dissociated the act of knowing from rhetorical aspects of writing. Boyle and other experimentalists developed an impersonal, circumstantial style of writing to report their results—a writing intended to convey not the authority or conviction of the author, but the experience of witnessing, or more precisely the content of what any rational observer could be expected to observe.[10] This conveying of experience is still an effect of writing, something that we might now call a textual strategy, but it's a particular kind of strategy, distinct from those of the storyteller, the orator, or the erudite scholar; it's a new and strong version of the old rhetorical gambit of denying that one's discourse is rhetorical. In this case, the displacement of rhetoric, though not total, was substantial. The characteristic gesture of founding a scientific discipline, as Thomas Kuhn pointed out, is to create a community of investigators who agree sufficiently on goals, methods, and basic conceptual framework that they no longer need to convince one other of the rightness of their perspective (and no longer care about persuading those outside their group). A science becomes scientific when it acquires what Kuhn famously named *paradigms*, models for research that define acceptable problems and methods and thereby provide an agreed-to context for specialized, often technical work. In the pre-paradigmatic phase of a sci-

---

[10] See Steven Shapin and Simon Schaffer, *Leviathan and the Air-pump: Hobbes, Boyle, and the Experimental Life* (Princeton: Princeton University Press, 1985), 55–69, and Shapin, *The Scientific Revolution*, 106–109.

ence, its practitioners may well hold competing views about the nature of their objects and methods, views for which they argue in books or treatises. Once there is agreement, however, on the definition of problems and the range of methods appropriate for solving them, the status of writing changes, since there is no more need to persuade people of one's view of the fundamentals by means of convincing narratives or persuasive verbal arguments. The exchange of information, usually carried out with the aid of technical or formalized languages, supplants the writing of treatises; the short article replaces the book.[11]

The most influential paradigm in the history of science was established by Newton's mathematical formulation of laws for gravitation and the motion of bodies. This was the "paradigm paradigm," the one that, more than any other, conveyed the idea that stabilized knowledge—clearly defined, universally agreed to—was possible. The mathematician D'Alembert, in his "Preliminary Discourse" to the *Encyclopédie*, spoke for many when he referred to Newton's work as a definitive advance: "Newton . . . appeared at last, and gave to philosophy a form that it apparently will keep." He went on to say that philosophy's Newtonian success and the resulting taste for analytical and mathematical rationality had discredited erudition, created an unfavorable climate for achievement in *belles-lettres*, and chilled the art of conversation.[12]

What D'Alembert saw as a one-sided triumph for scientific philosophy, necessarily if somewhat regrettably pushing poets and scholars into the margins, seems in hindsight to be just one moment in the long history that has led to what C. P. Snow in 1959 called the two cultures, scientific and literary. The notion that linguistic and cultural phenomena, and more generally human meaning and communication, constitute a distinct field of knowledge and creation with its own rules and laws has its roots in the work of Vico early in the eighteenth century, and its great flowering in the thinkers of the counter-Enlightenment and romanticism at the end of that century and the beginning of the nineteenth. Vico drew on an old philosophical idea—that one can truly know only that which one has made—to propose a fundamental distinction between knowledge of the natural

---

[11] Thomas Kuhn, *The Structure of Scientific Revolutions*, 2d ed. (Chicago: University of Chicago Press, 1970), 19–22.

[12] *Encyclopédie (articles choisis)*, ed. Alain Pons (Paris: Flammarion, 1986), 1: 142–43, 156–57.

world and that of the human world of history, law, myth, religion, custom, language, works of art and poetry. Arguing against the Cartesian
view that history, custom, and story could at best be the objects of uncertain erudition and conjecture, inferior to the clear and distinct
knowledge attainable in the study of the natural world, Vico held that
historical knowledge, since it involves the imaginative and empathetic
use of the human mind to understand behavior, motives, and meanings produced by other human minds, was distinct from—and in crucial ways superior to—knowledge of the natural world. Although
Vico's thought did not become widely or thoroughly known in his time
or in the first generations that followed him, his distinction between
knowledge of history and that of nature is a founding text for the division between the natural and human sciences, or *Naturwis-
senschaften* and *Geisteswissenschaften* as they were known in their
influential nineteenth-century German incarnations.

From Vico, and later from Herder, whose influence in early romanticism was more direct, came the idea that language, and what we would
now call culture and communication, are central not only to understanding the world but to living in it: that they constitute the truly
human calling, alongside which the making of things, the getting of
wealth, or the scientific mastery of the world are merely exterior or technical, so many forms of what social thinkers would soon call alienation
and artists would relegate to the despised world of the bourgeois. With
this idea of the centrality of language and culture came that of the specificity and diversity of languages and cultures, the notion that individuals, societies, and epochs possess an expressive particularity that ought
to be understood on its own terms and that cannot be judged according
to general laws of taste or supposedly universal truths. On this view,
that of Herder and of much of the philosophical and theoretical com-
ponent of romanticism, there can be no legitimate aesthetic or cultural
equivalent of Newtonian science. Those who weigh the world and
themselves against one standardized set of quasi-natural laws, or who
measure human cultures and creations along a one-dimensional yard-
stick of value, be it that of economic utility or French classicism, op-
press the human spirit—a spirit that takes refuge, when thus squeezed
by forces of the modern world, in art and poetry, in feeling and irony.[13]

---

[13] See Isaiah Berlin, *Vico and Herder: Two Studies in the History of Ideas* (London:
Hogarth, 1976).

With science driving a wedge between legitimate knowledge and the writerly use of language, with rhetoric largely reduced to ornament and thus becoming more conventional, writing that takes itself seriously as writing would henceforth, beginning roughly in the late eighteenth century, be linked more closely to imagination, fantasy, and emotion than it had been in the early modern era. Fiction and invention would be more important than eloquence or genteel taste to the emerging concept of literature. In his *Letters on the Aesthetic Education of Man* of 1795, Friedrich Schiller describes art and poetry as an exploration of humanity's freedom from both natural law and social convention, a way of reconciling and subsuming the sensual and spiritual aspects of human nature, and a cultural apprenticeship of true political liberty.[14] The autonomous and often individual creative impulse, fostered by secular public culture and the print market, came to be seen in literary culture as a fundamental value, a form of authenticity and truth more important than the merely objective accuracy of science or the pragmatic efficacy of political and economic realism.[15] This idealized sense of mission for the aesthetic and expressive sphere of human activity was often complemented by denunciations of industrial, empirical, scientific, and economic modernity. In the words of the great English critic Raymond Williams, in his *Culture and Society*, literature became, with romanticism, the defender "of certain human values, capacities, energies, which the development of society towards an industrial civilization was felt to be threatening or even destroying."[16] Despite the enormous changes in literature, society, and the world since the romantic

[14] It is to this aspect of literary culture that Bill Readings largely refers in his chapter of that title in *The University in Ruins* (Cambridge: Harvard University Press, 1996), 70–88.

[15] It is important to recognize, however, that modern literary culture often parallels and sometimes imitates scientific culture even while dissenting from it. The scientific and philosophic project of the Enlightenment aimed to eliminate, or at least to stabilize and contain, the accumulated and potentially misleading charms of language, rhetoric and story; the literary or poetic project of romanticism aimed to replace the unity and conventionality of Old Regime poetic diction and rhetoric by an ever-renewed invention and reinvention of literary languages by schools, movements, and individual writers. Rhetoric and conventional diction were denounced and replaced by a succession of innovative styles. In this sense the dynamic of literary innovation, while very different from that of science, in that it proceeds not by making arguments but offering new languages, also imitates the scientific or philosophic gesture of becoming modern by means of purification, by stripping away the confusions and complacencies of the past.

[16] Raymond Williams, *Culture and Society* (London: Chatto and Windus, 1958), 36.

era, a commitment to creative freedom, to cultural specificity and dignity, and to artistic autonomy, though often contested and imperfectly realized, has remained among the most distinctive and positive features of literary culture over the last two centuries.

From these bold and freedom-spawning ideas, however, it is but a short step to the earnest and vaguely righteous notion that the writer, scholar, or humanist can properly ignore what is happening in the world of science and commerce, and thus, for all practical purposes, can ignore the entire domain of understanding and engineering *things*, a pervasive activity that constantly reconfigures the human, cultural, and social world by refitting its points of contact with the material stuff around it. Indeed the act of ignoring the material, technical, and economic world can come to pass for a virtue, a gesture of purity and solidarity—isolation from the inauthentic detour of spirit through things, and support for those who keep faith with the "truly human" project of living in speech, in mind, in unalloyed sociability. The literary side of culture has thus come to identify with a truncated, if reassuringly idealistic, notion of humanity and human activity, cut off from much of the human remaking of the world.

BUT WHERE can we locate "the literary side of culture"? Today's community of writers has little of an autonomous community about it, and even less of an avant-garde. In the world of publishing, the distinction between serious literature and works for the mass market grows ever shakier, and from Gabriel García Márquez to Marguerite Duras to Don DeLillo, writers esteemed by their peers seem to be the first to benefit. Articles on science, politics, and world affairs nestle comfortably among the literary reviews in *The New York Review of Books*. Not only science fiction writers but also "mainstream" novelists incorporate great technical and ecological complexities into their inventions. Many writers, publishers, and reviewers of fiction, drama, poetry, and essays show no particular concern for the autonomy of a literary sphere. The idea that writers should seek the esteem primarily of other writers has been around too long to provide any sort of distinctive legitimation, and indeed the phrase *a writer's writer* is widely recognized as a double-edged sword, suggesting a shameful failure to reach the public as well as the justifiably valued esteem of peers.

If there is a place where the traits of literary culture sketched in the preceding pages have found a home in recent years, it is in college and university departments of literature.[17] This can be seen most obviously in the popular appeal of reactionary denunciations of "tenured radicals" among university literary scholars, long an object of indifference (or, at most, mild ridicule) off campus. Where once one might have fulminated against some subversive vanguard of writers and artists—romantics, aesthetes, decadents, symbolists, surrealists, or beatniks—now the vexingly subversive subculture seems to ferment among professors and graduate students.

This slightly ludicrous situation would not have been possible had academic literary culture not taken on some of the characteristics of an autonomous field of cultural producers. Literary studies have grown in autonomy over the course of the last century, acquiring many of the unworldly and anti-bourgeois characteristics of modern literary and artistic culture. The cultivation of autonomy is not in itself surprising, since it is a standard feature of professions in general and academic disciplines in particular. Academic literary study struggled in the late nineteenth century to differentiate itself from the teaching of eloquence and morality, adopting the scholarly investigation of language, texts, and literary history as the basis for its specificity within the emerging research university. The New Criticism of mid-twentieth-century America marked a further advance in the autonomy of literary studies, one that largely rejected the concerns of philology and literary history as being too far outside the central experience of reading a literary work and responding to its specifically literary language and structure.

The turn to theory, generally identified with structuralism and its aftermath in the late nineteen-sixties and early seventies, began as a challenge to the autonomy of literary studies but has wound up reinforcing the autonomy of the literary disciplines. "The advent of theory . . .," wrote Paul de Man in a late, retrospective essay, "occurs with the introduction of linguistic terminology in the metalanguage about literature."[18] In applying linguistic (and anthropological) terms and concepts to literature, structuralist critics often saw themselves as shaking up the complacencies of literary history and aesthetic appreciation. Yet despite its seemingly intrusive "outsider" stance, structuralism brought an in-

---

[17] For a very different argument that academic literary studies embody the modern or romantic cultural project of literature, see Readings, *The University in Ruins*, 62–88.

[18] Paul de Man, "The Resistance to Theory," *Yale French Studies* 63 (1982): 8.

tensification of literary formalism, ratcheting up the professionalism and technicity of the academic analysis of literature. More important, theory gradually became a set of methods that defined the professional ethos of literary scholars in such a way *as to be no longer dependent on the category of literature itself, or on the contents of literary canons.* The literary disciplines to a large extent transformed themselves into a field of theoretical reflection and cultural critique inspired by the core notion that society and subjectivity, far from being naturally given, are shaped and indeed constituted by language and culture.

This meant that critics and scholars no longer needed to be seen as parasitical on authors and their works: as literary criticism gave way to cultural critique, literary *studies* became more autonomous by serving less as the handmaiden of literature. The literary disciplines could deploy a set of methods and an outlook that are of literary culture without being limited or subservient to literature. In today's literary studies, scholars still inquire into the cultural and social world by means of texts and works of art, i.e., aesthetic and reflective productions, but they also understand this world *as being primarily constructed* via language, discourse, and symbolic creations and behavior, and for many this insight is a more crucial feature of disciplinary identity than any particular set of objects of study. Moreover, literary studies is a highly self-reflexive discipline, at least as concerned with the methods and procedures of its studies as with any actual findings or conclusions about the cultural part of the world.

The intensive theorizing of literary studies in recent years amounts to a modernization of the field, a turning of attention away from a literary canon that once seemed (despite constant changes) a given, and toward an ongoing discussion among members of the contemporary scholarly community. As such, the turn to theory helps make literary studies every bit as much a research discipline as it is a teaching one. It thus corresponds to an increased degree of professorial autonomy in which a scholar's recognition and status is tied ever more closely to peer review of work produced for fellow academics. (In fact, the local and disciplinary autonomy afforded by universities is a cause as well as a consequence of the turn away from inherited canons and toward theory, since this turn depended on the wide latitude scholars have to decide what they will teach and what forms of scholarship they will recognize as legitimate.)

By reducing its dependence on an inherited literary tradition and on the values and interests of the nonacademic literary community, the

disciplines of literary studies have given less attention to their traditional roles as curator or docent in the museum of literature. In his account of the institutions of modern literature and art, Bourdieu notes
that they include, in addition to the two fields of restricted and large-
scale cultural production, a third area that he somewhat awkwardly
calls the "field of instances of reproduction and consecration"—
academies, learned societies, museums, the relevant parts of the educational system.[19] These institutions help enable legitimate works of
art and literature to constitute cultural capital, particularly for the
dominant social class, by authentifying their distinction from illegitimate or "popular" works, by preserving their durability, and by training students to understand and appreciate them.

The most lively energies of literary studies, at least in the United
States, are no longer dedicated to "reproduction and consecration" of
literary works, however much they are still read and studied. Part of
the impetus for this sea change has been responsiveness to contemporary conditions: to the consumer society and the importance of individual desire (emphasizing reading over authorship), to New Social
Movements and newly empowered groups (feminism, multiculturalism, gay/lesbian studies), to decolonization (anti-imperialism, postcolonial studies), to contemporary media and cultural practices (film
studies, popular culture). All of these have produced valuable enlarge-
ments and revisions of the humanities. Given the literary canon's
residual role as middle- and upper-class cultural capital and its near
saturation with white males, it is no surprise that calling it into question should have been a key move in a partial but significant rejection
by literary academics of their role as caretaker and educator on behalf
of inherited literary culture. (Nor is it a surprise that conservative de-
fenders of such a role have objected strenuously.)

What is perhaps less obvious is that in reducing its commitment to
"reproduction and consecration," the discipline of literary study has
intensified its resemblance to the "field of restricted production," the
self-proclaimedly autonomous field where artists and writers produce
primarily for each other, at least for each other's judgment, in an open-
ended dynamic of invention. Literary studies has thus grown to be
structurally more like the modern ideal of an autonomous community of writers or artists, while becoming more independent of today's

---

[19] Bourdieu, *The Field of Cultural Production,* 120–25.

very heterogeneous field of literary production as far as the content of its interests are concerned. Instead of its traditional role of dowdy stepsister or governess to literary production's ingénue, literary studies now plays a part more like that of an estranged twin or former best friend, not unhappy to feel itself purer and more vanguardist than writers. Yet the literary academy's rejection of monumental or edifying stewardship takes place in the context of an institutional status quo, in which the pronouncements of humanities professors, no matter how subversive, don't interfere with serious business, whether in the universities or outside them—which makes the demonizing of the theoretical humanities by right-wing outsiders all the more pointless.

Thus the literary disciplines have become, for better and for worse, a substantially autonomous field of cultural criticism and inquiry. They have done so in part via calling into question their role as guardians and transmitters of a tired, once-hegemonic literary high culture, opening literary study to previously excluded voices, forms, and communities, and that has been a very positive move. But alongside this new inclusiveness has come greater concentration on internal positions, debates and disciplinary abstractions, and here it is harder to be enthusiastic. Contemporary theorizing is doubtless broader and more complex than the much vaguer and narrower conceptualizing of literary studies that preceded it, and that took up a much smaller portion of the curriculum (the occasional proseminar or history of literary criticism). Yet contemporary theory is in some ways narrower and more normative than is the degree of familiarity with a broad spectrum of works from various periods of the past that formerly characterized literary education, a familiarity that has now been de-emphasized so as to make possible the greater attention to theory.

Literary studies have lost something of their untimeliness, their once distinctive otherness with respect to the functionalism and "presentism" of the empirical social sciences; they have largely given up their radical merit of sticking with the long-term, the irrelevant, the unexpected shock of beauty or insight from a fragment of the bygone world. To be sure, one should not idealize the discipline's past, because the ideological constraints and exclusions shaping the canon, the narrowness of formalist criticism, and the inherently divisive nature of a curriculum conceived as a collection of historical periods all kept the potentially laudable engagement with the literary past from being as open or as mind-expanding as it might now seem to have been when viewed nostalgically from the white-collar cubicles of the contemporary theory corporation by people who never knew the life of the old parishes, plantations, and shop-floors. Yet avoidance of misplaced nostalgia should not imply complacency in the real losses entailed by present trends.

When we used to read literature more, and with vaguer assumptions about how we were reading it, it was more of an object of fascination; it was assumed—often, to be sure, on the basis of high-blown and naive ideas—to be something worth knowing and finding out about, a treasure-trove of words. Now that many have lost faith in the richness or beneficence of what literature itself has to teach, believing instead in a critical understanding of how the world is constructed by language and culture, the discipline has become in many ways livelier, more liberating and demanding, and yet in other ways narrower and hastier and more brittle. What has been lost is not so much a "great tradition" of literature—a monumental fiction that well deserved to be brought down—as a sense that the discipline exists to know, however imperfectly, something not itself. Just as in much of modern life humanity's relations with a world not of its making has been replaced by relations with a culturally constructed and altered world in which things found are supplanted by things made, so too in literary study the sense of a large world of works to be encountered and explored has largely given way to urbane, in-house conferencing among experts.[20] The expertise of today's academic critics, like those of court and town elites throughout history, is made up in large part of our subtle knowledge of one another, our familiarity with the respective positions and proclivities of everyone in the circle. Theory enabled us to perfect this disciplinary structure and believe that it was an improvement over the looser, less autonomous, less internally regulated setup that preceded it, and in many respects it was. But theory discourages us from contemplating its own costs, from considering that our gains in sophistication and critical consciousness can also bring an impoverishing loss of wonder and humility, a frosty neglect of whatever is not useable in academic terms.

These qualitative developments have come hand in hand with structural changes in the literary disciplines. In the first place, far more publications are produced today in literary studies than thirty years ago.

---

[20] So little of the world is not fully mediated and controlled by culture that the very category of the natural seems in retrospect to look as though it must have always been a mystification. For some, this discredit extends from the *category* of the natural to the things of nature.

Study of the Modern Language Association bibliography suggests that the scholarly output of the average literary scholar roughly doubled from the late 1960s to the middle 1990s.[21] This is a significant change, especially in view of the largely artisanal character of the work. It seems likely that the literary professoriate is collectively (and, on average, individually) spending much more time writing and publishing than it did a generation ago.

This increase is almost surely related to the difficulties of the academic job market. Once teaching jobs became scarce, colleges that once expected few if any publications for tenure and promotion began to require a substantial amount, often not for any particular educational purpose but simply because the state of the market, with its excess of qualified people seeking positions, enabled them to do so. Moreover, long periods of financial stringency and concerns about unproductive professors have pushed many institutions toward merit pay plans that strengthen the incentives to go on publishing more regularly after tenure and promotion to the rank of full professor. The overall increases in quantity of scholarly production show that universities have made these changes in expectations possible by providing resources for increased publication outlets in the humanities.

The academic job market "collapsed," to use the standard descriptive cliché, around 1970 with the slowdown in the postwar expansion of universities. During the postwar years of rapid growth in undergraduate enrollments, new Ph.D. programs had been created and old ones expanded to keep pace with the rising demand for new professors. Universities and their faculties grew accustomed, even addicted, to having large graduate programs: budgets became dependent on large numbers of low-wage graduate teaching assistants, and professors came to regard devoting a substantial portion of their teaching to graduate students as a basic prerogative of their positions.

---

[21] Membership in the MLA, a rough index of the number of people professionally involved with language and literature in North American higher education, has held fairly steady over this time, rising only from around 30,000 to 32,000 (with a decline to levels of 23,000–25,000 in the middle). Meanwhile, the number of entries for American literature in the annual *MLA International Bibliography* has grown from between 2,000 and 2,500 in 1969 and 1970 to around 5,000 for 1994 and 1995. Entries for French have grown a bit more slowly, for Spanish and Spanish American literature somewhat faster. Entries on literary criticism and theory grew rapidly from under 200 per year in the late 1960s to over 500 in 1972 and 1973, and then more slowly to a recent level between 700 and 800.

The job market has now been bad—with occasional brief periods of modest improvement—for new Ph.D.s for about thirty years, long enough that it seems safe to conclude that the problem is structural and not one of temporary financial stringency. This tight job market has gone hand in hand with an increase in the quantity of publications expected of its survivors. A great many scholars will tell you that there is far too much to read in the areas they're interested in or nominally responsible for, that they can't keep up, and that—fortunately, they may add!—much of it just isn't good enough to bother with. More scholarship is being written and published in the literary disciplines than is really useful or desirable for the intellectual life of those who write and are supposed to read it, or for the collective intellectual sanity of the field. Of even greater concern, the pressure to produce large quantities of scholarship may well be making the product more conventional and predictable, less daring and original, for the simple reason that it is more efficient to work within (or nominally against) established paradigms than to invent new ones.

As more and more professors have published in greater quantities, the literary disciplines have come closer to realizing literally the project of autonomy that, for nonacademic literary producers, has never been more than an ideal: to form a community that writes and publishes entirely for itself. Of course, there is *some* crossover reading of academic books by nonacademics—women's studies and gay/lesbian studies, for example, have done well in this regard by producing work of interest to specific readership communities outside academia. And some professors don't publish at all, while most publish less than the academic stars, and so forth. But the fact remains that a large volume of prose is being published by a comparatively small number of people for a similarly small audience, consisting largely of themselves. Most of it is not drawing many readers: sales of scholarly monographs in the modern languages and literatures, even to university libraries, have fallen to levels that are barely viable in the economics of print publication.[22] As competent, serious, and well-informed as much recent scholarly writing is, this late print-culture experiment in establishing a community of producers who read each other is in trouble.

[22] For a pithy statement of the problems brought on by over-reliance on the publication of scholarly books as a criterion for tenure, see Lindsay Waters, "A Modest Proposal for Preventing the Books of the Members of the MLA from Being a Burden to Their Authors, Publishers, or Audiences," *PMLA* 115, 3 (2000), 315–17.

It's true that many if not all other disciplines face similar problems of scholarly overproduction and thus of difficulty keeping up with it all. (I've heard it said of business and even accounting as academic fields.) It would be foolish to think that many articles on literature are expendable but that everything in the chemistry and mathematics journals is important. Moreover, very few people outside academia (or outside quasi-academic research centers and laboratories) read scholarly or scientific publications in any field: autonomy, in the form of production for peers, is the norm. Nonetheless, there is a crucial difference between the humanities and the empirical disciplines that makes the situation of literary studies both more frustrating from within and vulnerable to attacks from without.

The professional schools, the natural sciences, and the empirical social sciences claim, at least, to do research that can be put to practical use by society. Almost no non-chemists will read chemistry publications, but their social worth—at least potentially, and granting that some of them will turn out to be useless—lies not primarily in the experience of reading them, or in the contribution they make to culture by revealing the structure of the universe or by showing the human mind at work advancing the knowledge of chemistry, but in the value of what can be done with the results they announce: the products or processes or therapies to which they may contribute. A commentary on a theory of international relations can potentially be taken into consideration by policy makers in the State Department or Foreign Office. In other words, the lack of direct symbolic communication between academia and society is offset, in empirical fields, by the presumed technical or social utility of the products or consequences of admittedly esoteric research. This relation both encourages society to be tolerant of paying for research in these fields and reassures their practitioners that what they do can have an effect outside their own professional circle—even if recognition within that circle is central to their professional concerns and ambitions.

The humanities, however, perform mostly a kind of cultural work that is of little social value in the absence of symbolic exchange and circulation. There are virtually no mechanisms or institutions in place to act on or make use of the results of humanistic scholarship, no congressional staff or therapists or engineers or venture capitalists waiting to turn the ideas of literary and cultural studies into legislation or treatments or widgets or software. The social and cultural effects of literary scholarship depend on what it does for its readers' minds, one at a time, page by page.

There is, to be sure, the effect of influencing how literature is taught to undergraduates by influencing the community of undergraduate teachers. Teaching matters a great deal, but the connection between scholarly publication and teaching is frequently tenuous, and too often the positive interaction between the two is overwhelmed by the concrete tradeoffs that must be made: more publishing means less time for teaching, and vice versa. Moreover, the empirical disciplines teach students, too, so that teaching by itself hardly makes up for the awkward situation in which the humanities find themselves when much of their energy goes to producing publications that barely circulate or have value beyond their disciplinary boundaries.

It makes little sense to try to make a difference in society through specialized literary and cultural work in the humanities and yet to leave out the question of communicating and transmitting that work into the political and social sphere, whether via publication or graduate education. Taking for granted the cultural authority of high print culture and the university, presupposing the effectiveness of demonstration and denunciation in print, we practitioners of close reading and critique have largely failed to make the effort of understanding media and transmission that would be needed to break out of our own predicament. Individually and collectively, we do not communicate well with people unlike ourselves. To be sure, the intellectual life of universities should include publication for peers, should provide spaces of communication and exchange that are insulated from the pressures of the market; this is one of their key functions as universities, as institutions that nourish society over the long term by standing apart from its immediate fashions and preoccupations. The university will thus always, and appropriately, be a site of tensions between the demands of the here and now and those of a wider, longer term perspective, between the empirical and the imaginative, between the instrumental and the critical. But one can legitimately hope for a working compromise of these tensions that would be more effective than what we have now, at least in the humanities.

The forms of autonomy and professionalism pursued by literary studies in recent years, I've tried to suggest, have brought the field to a certain number of impasses: in its ability to communicate beyond its borders, in the job prospects of its graduate students, in its power to make the texts and insights of the humanities matter in society. These problems have undermined the very real intellectual successes of the field in opening itself to new texts, new issues, and new perspectives. They underlie both the harshness of the criticisms the profession has taken from conservatives and its relative ineffectiveness in defending itself against them. I have avoided the more overtly political aspects of that criticism, such as the oversimplified and superficial charge of "tenured radicalism," so as to concentrate on the institutional setting. There is, however, something to the notion that the social and political contestation of the late nineteen-sixties was a key historical moment that helped shape literary studies for the succeeding generation. The next chapter will thus take up the strained relationship between the forms of literary studies that emerged from that era and the changing world of more recent years.

2 From *mai '68* to the *fin-de-millénaire*

THE STORY of North American literary studies in recent decades is in large measure that of the startling arrival and exhaustive domestication of a transatlantic import, French theory. It thus seems fitting on several levels to begin a discussion of the literary impact of late-sixties social movements with France's belated and concentrated plunge into the exhilarating turmoil of that time. From the outset, the Paris "events" of May '68 were marked by the participation of aesthetic avant-gardes (notably the situationists); cultural institutions from universities to national theaters to art schools were at the center of the action. In addition, specifically national issues of protest loomed less large in France than in the United States, where the Civil Rights movement and opposition to the war in Vietnam were central. As a result, May '68 in Paris, despite all of its local features, has always seemed a distillation of the worldwide climate of social (and particularly student) protest of the late sixties. What French specificity May '68 *did* possess helped make it a theoretically resonant event: the Parisian students' involvement with (and estrangement from) France's then still strong tradition of working-class militancy underscored the differences between the New Social Movements of the sixties and the class-based movements that had long dominated the theory and practice of social conflict, while the conservative rigidity of French universities and the paternalism of the Gaullist state made authority and hierarchy as such a key target of protest.

In his lucid and moving analysis of May '68, *The Capture of Speech*, the historian and cultural theorist Michel de Certeau described the essential and enduring feature of the events as a loosening of tongues, a renewal of community through the inclusion of the silenced. Writing in the summer and early fall of 1968, de Certeau tried to understand and evoke what it was about May that made it more important than the wild month of barricades, demonstrations, and strikes it obviously was:

> Something happened to us. Something began to stir in us. Emerging from who knows where, suddenly filling the streets and the factories, circulating among us, becoming ours but no longer being the muffled noise of our solitude, voices that had never been heard before began to change us. At least that was what we felt. From this something unheard of was produced: we began to speak. It seemed as if it were for the first time. From everywhere emerged the treasures, either aslumber or tacit, of forever unspoken experience.[1]

This was not the authorized speech of professors, managers, politicians, and the media, nor simply the private comments of individuals cut off from the public sphere. It was, instead, a demand for a generalized right to speak out, for an end to the privileges of those who speak from positions of constituted authority and thereby silence others. The new legitimacy of speaking out was not to depend on cultural or official competence, but was instead to flow from, and in turn define, one's rights as a member of a community. De Certeau quotes a May '68 television interview with a department store elevator operator, who said "I really don't know what to say, I don't have any education," whereupon one of her fellow strikers interrupted: "Don't say that. Knowledge is finished. *Today, education, well, it's all in what we say*" (9).

For de Certeau, the crux of May '68 lay in calling into question a culture that can be possessed, that summons those who have it to speak and warns those who lack it to keep quiet. Such was the indictment of the pre-1968 French university: instrumental knowledge, its form and content determined by the institution and the professo-

---

[1] Michel De Certeau, *The Capture of Speech and Other Political Writings*, ed. Luce Giard, trans. Tom Conley (Minneapolis: University of Minnesota Press, 1998), 11–12. Subsequent references given in parentheses in the text. The French title, *La Prise de parole*, also has connotations of "taking the floor" or "speaking out."

riate, was dispensed to students so as to prepare them to become components of an order over which they would have virtually no control. What the May events challenged, de Certeau wrote, was *"knowledge* identified with a *power* that acts upon *objects"* (47)—a referential and controlling mode of discourse that was essentially the same whether its objects were things, texts, cultures, or human beings. Conversely, the emergent culture of May '68, that of the "voices never before heard," was an attempt to give all subjects the right to speak and to invent, in the collective act of speaking out, new forms of subjectivity and social relations.

These traits are central to the legacy of the late sixties in literary studies, where they have both altered, and been altered by, the institutional setting of the university. The most visible part of that legacy comes from the New Social Movements and their emphasis on cultural politics as distinct from the class and economically based politics that had previously defined the modern left. The focus on cultural and symbolic change resonated strongly in a field that is by definition devoted to language, meaning, and interpretation, rather than to empirical knowledge acquired in view of action. The anti-technocratic, anti-hierarchic impulse of sixties protest fit the romantic and bohemian strain of literary culture. The politics of speaking out, of recognizing the authenticity of individual and minority voices, resonated with modern literary culture's embrace of inventive speech over stable knowledge. Roland Barthes, for example, considered les *événements* of May '68 to be in some sense comparable to the unexpected and destabilizing "events" of avant-garde works and cultural interventions, with their project of changing forms and disrupting settled systems.[2] May '68 and related events of the late sixties thus gave political resonance to the then-emergent theoretical work of structuralism and poststructuralism, which became a crucial force in transforming the aims and practices of literary study, particularly in North America.

Three of the most prominent of the New Social Movements of the sixties—Civil Rights, the women's movement, and Gay/Lesbian activism—led to major changes in literary culture and literary studies: first, by spurring interest in literary production by African-Americans,

---

[2] Roland Barthes, "Writing the Event," in *The Rustle of Language,* trans. Richard Howard (New York: Farrar, Straus and Giroux, 1986), 149–54.

Latinos, Native Americans, women, gays, and lesbians; second, by calling into question the exclusion or marginalization of works by members of these groups from the canons of literary taste and teaching;
third, by making cultural identity a central issue in cultural theory
and interpretation; fourth, and perhaps most important, by understanding literary and scholarly work in these areas as helping to realize a project of social and political change. The creation of African-
American Studies and Women's Studies programs in universities was
one of the earliest and most direct effects of late sixties protests on the
institutions of literary culture. (Gay/Lesbian studies have not attained
the same degree of institutional recognition and status, although in recent years they have become an influential and ever more visible field
of work in and across a number of disciplines.) The movement to hear
from previously silenced voices and to include once excluded identities in all these areas was an important manifestation of the impulse
toward speaking out, toward the refusal of hierarchic authority: groups
and individuals that had previously found themselves and those like
them outside or on the margins of officially sanctioned speech, and
thus subjected to being represented by others as the objects their
knowledge, began insisting on becoming subjects of knowledge, on
taking control of their own representations. The impact of the New
Social Movements in literary culture has thus been directly related to
having members of cultural identity groups actively present as writers, critics, scholars, and teachers.

   This correlation can be seen *a contrario* by the case of environmentalism, usually counted among the New Social Movements from
the standpoint of the activism of the late sixties and seventies, but
only marginally on the map in literature and literary studies: since it
does not articulate the cultural identity or oppositional politics of a
human group, it has had far less influence within academic literary
culture. There are, to be sure, "environmental critics" and "environmental writers," but these are topics one picks up, not cultural identities one works through from a subject position. To speak of the rain
forest or the biosphere is to speak *for*, not to speak *out*. Environmentalists must always speak on behalf of others, constituting them as the
objects of their knowledge, solicitude, and good will—a position less
dubious, and perhaps more necessary, with respect to nonhuman
rather than human others, but still a position outside the community-
and identity-based paradigms of the other New Social Movements.
(This is a problem to which we'll return later in this chapter.)

Of course the literary consequences of the New Social Movements, especially in the academy, go far beyond the simple inclusion of writers and scholars who speak out as individuals representing their groups. The notion that identity is cultural and group-related, that there is no individuality that can be separated from such commonalities as race, ethnicity, gender, and sexual orientation, is an important part of a larger theoretical challenge to atomistic conceptions of the individual's relations to society—the autonomous subject of modern political theory and the utility-maximizing individual of economics and rational choice theory. This mode of understanding individual and society is called into question both by culture-centered, group-oriented accounts of human identity and sociability, and by linguistically or psychoanalytically inspired theories of the unstable and socio-symbolic character of selfhood and subjectivity. Work on minority cultures and identities thus complements and reinforces theoretical critiques of empirical or atomistic assumptions about the relationship of individual and society. Individual identity, according to this critical view, is at once more socially and culturally determined—thus more communal—and less stable, less naturally given, than the dominant paradigms of the empirical social sciences would have it.

The cultural politics of identity are thus strongly connected to the notion that language and culture are central to the making of social reality. (Indeed, many of those concerned with the politics of minorities and particularism hold firmly to linguistic and cultural constructivism so as to distance their work from noxious forms of identity politics bound up with racial or geographic essentialism, with blood and soil.) While bringing new texts into the canon to make it more representative of present-day society, identity-based studies thus participate in the turn from an archivally to a theoretically based definition of literary studies. Within the theoretical framework of linguistic and social constructivism, the New Social Movements have worked to give legitimacy and urgency to scholarship dedicated to the pursuit of social change by academic and intellectual means. Such work assumes that changes in the order of symbol and language already constitute significant steps toward political and social change. This assumption draws strength from the structuralist idea that the crucial determinants of a society or even the unconscious mind are to be found in the fundamental organization of its symbolic articulation of the world— the kinship structures and conceptual oppositions that a culture mobilizes in organizing itself and its environment, and the symbolic order of names, grammatical persons, rules, and prohibitions within which one becomes a speaking and thus a social subject. It also draws on the poststructuralist idea that these linguistic and cultural structures, strong as they may be, are also unstable at the core and thereby subject to disruptive rewriting. Critical and/or destabilizing intervention in the field of language and text are thus expected to lead to differences in the ways cultural groups perceive and are perceived, speak and are allowed to speak—in other words, in the constructed reality of their experience and their place in society.

These ideas seem reassuringly familiar in today's literary and cultural studies, but they did not enter the academic mainstream without much conflict. As deep as were the roots of the idea that modern literary culture should have a progressive political mission, there was no shortage within literary studies of objectified knowledge or of practices as hierarchical, exclusionary, and undemocratic as those of any so-called instrumental discipline. It may have been tempting to think that de Certeau's observation that May '68 called into question "a *knowledge* identified with a *power* that acts upon *objects*" (47) applied mainly to scientific or quasi-scientific fields, to the use of empirical knowledge for power over things in the world. But there are plenty of targets for this kind of questioning in literary studies, where texts and authors are defined as objects over which specialists possess authority by means of their knowledge—a knowledge they transmit to students so as to assure the reproduction of the discipline. From the New Social Movements came the criticism that these objects were chosen and maintained according to exclusionary criteria and that knowledge of them was functioning so as to keep some people in power and leave others out. From the impulse toward speaking out and undoing hierarchies came the insight that magisterial, specialized, "authoritative" talk about texts and authors was as instrumental and alienating a practice of knowledge as anything you could find in the business or engineering schools.

The critique of knowledge's complicity with power lay at the heart of the work of Michel Foucault, and was crucial to both his work's relation to the sixties and to its great influence in the post-sixties humanities. Foucault's first book, *Madness and Civilization* (1961), already showed how organized, institutionalized knowledge could function as a system of power, controlling the objects of knowledge it constructs. But in a 1977 interview, Foucault noted that "it was not until around 1968 that these questions took on their political significance with a sharpness I had not suspected . . . Without the political opening of those years, I would perhaps not have had the courage to take up the thread of these problems and to pursue my inquiry in the direction of punishment, prisons, and disciplines."[3] In other words, as Luc Ferry and Alain Renaut point out in their study of "sixty-eight thought" (*La Pensée 68*, translated as *French Philosophy of the Sixties*), May '68 served to intensify and reveal the importance of certain features of Foucault's work, notably the idea of the equivalence between institutionalized knowledge and power over those it defines and constructs as objects. More historically and archivally oriented than the work of most of the philosophers and literary critics of the structuralist and poststructuralist era, Foucault's writings have been enormously influential in shaping the cultural critique carried out in post-sixties literary studies. Foucault's understanding of *discourse*—an elusive but powerful term designating kinds of language produced according to social rules and in turn constituting what is socially sanctioned as real—has given a strongly pragmatic and institutional turn to the linguistic constructivism of literary studies. The construction of reality, according to this view, depends less on the semantic or representational properties of language than on its rules of utterance, on the kinds of speech both authorized and marginalized. The political project of this kind of work remains very close to that of the anti-hierarchic, "speaking out" impulse of the late sixties, a project of subversion and opposition, of resistance to systems of knowledge that produce power by claiming to represent and speak for others.

Foucault was but one of the most influential theorists who emerged or came to prominence in the late sixties and whose work played a crucial role in transforming the outlook and interests of literary studies. Much of this work (though not that of Foucault) plausibly came to be known as *poststructuralist*, because it came in the wake of attempts to use structural linguistics and anthropology as a paradigm for cultural theory and because it called into question the ordered, systematic, and quasi-scientific tendencies of structuralism. Although such linguistically inspired theory is rarely professed today with the fervor and excitement it often communicated in the seventies and early eighties, it remains a crucial element of the ways in which many

---

[3] Michel Foucault, "Vérité et pouvoir, entretien avec M. Fontana," *L'Arc*, no. 17 (1977): 17; quoted in Luc Ferry and Alain Renaut, *French Philosophy of the Sixties*, trans. Mary Cattani (Amherst: University of Massachusetts Press, 1990), xix.

scholars and critics understand literature, culture, and their own intellectual role. Foucault's enduring hold on literary studies lies in his
understanding of language as discursive: words invested, often illegitimately, with the power to make and regulate forms of individuality
and sociability. The legacy of poststructuralism resides in its theorists'
presentation of language as textual: words woven together into something new, into something that resists discipline and expectations.
Poststructuralist thinkers were skeptical of language's capacity to convey meaning stably or unequivocally, and thus attentive to the multiple possibilities for both mystification or manipulation and for uncertainty or creative disruption to be found in texts and utterances.

Much poststructuralist writing set forth as principles or as criteria
of value the disruption or subversion of claims for the coherence or
truth of systems—and the undermining of strategies by which cultural
hierarchies try to pass themselves off as stable and natural. In *S/Z*
(1970) and *Le Plaisir du texte* (1973), Roland Barthes presented readers' experiences of blissful and transgressive discontinuities in texts
as both more liberating and more authentically literary than the reception and understanding of large-scale patterns and meanings set
forth by authors. He thus celebrated the fragmentation of textual structures and the creative work of reading as ways of bringing forth transgressive "events" and breaking with established codes and conventions of representation.

In a more philosophic mode, deconstruction, as practiced by Jacques
Derrida and Paul de Man, proposed that the rhetorical and textual play
of language undermines its use in the service of unified or intentional
meaning, and thus destabilizes or even subverts hierarchical oppositions central to Western thought, such as presence/absence, man/
woman, cause/effect. Making a claim for the political importance of
his conception of theory, de Man wrote that "more than any other
mode of inquiry, including economics, the linguistics of literariness is
a powerful and indispensable tool in the unmasking of ideological aber-
rations. . . ."[4]

The questioning of established structures of meaning and systemic
claims to knowledge is likewise a major aspect of Jean-François
Lyotard's account of "the postmodern condition," in which he approv-
ingly described the decline of what he called "grand narratives"—sto-

---

[4] Paul de Man, "The Resistance to Theory," *Yale French Studies* 63 (1982): 11.

ries modern culture has told itself about progress toward the conquest of human freedom through democracy and the conquest of human mastery of the universe through science. Instead Lyotard emphasized the importance, for both knowledge and ethics, of local, non-generalizable narratives, and of slippages and irreconcilable differences among competing forms and practices of discourse. Indeed the term *postmodernism* has often been used—with all too little conceptual precision— as an umbrella term for an era and a type of critical thought that includes Barthes, Derrida, Foucault, Lyotard, and many others. Postmodernism, in this sense, can be loosely described by its cultural constructivism; its questioning of the confidence with which the purveyors of empirical knowledge claim to refer to the world; its cultivation of differences, discontinuities, and juxtapositions; and its skepticism about modernity's master narratives of progress and emancipation—a skepticism that does not, however, entail an antimodern or reactionary desire to return to some form of premodern social or cultural order.

Postmodernist and poststructuralist theories played a key role in enabling literary studies to shift the basis of its language- and text-centered practices from the interpretation of literary works to the critique of discursive effects. They have also provided legitimation for understanding literary studies' engagement with history and society as, first, a matter of making *critiques*—of discourses that produce knowledge and power, of representations that objectify subaltern cultural groups, of beliefs about language that enable such discourses and representations to work; and, second, a matter of enabling and authorizing new voices—primarily those formerly excluded or marginalized— to participate in the cultural and educational conversations that take place in and around the humanities. These projects, deeply rooted in the social protests and cultural transformations of the late sixties, have been powerful enough to give the humanities a generation of dynamic and varied activity and to make significant and probably irreversible contributions to the understanding of culture and society. The literary disciplines of today would be vastly poorer without them.

IT IS THEREFORE not without a sense of respect for what has been accomplished since the sixties and seventies that I am arguing, in this book, that the academically codified and perpetuated version of that era's intellectual paradigms, in the face of a rapidly changing world, risks bringing literary studies to an impasse, or at least to a significant loss of audience, credibility, and effectiveness. The world is a very dif-

ferent place than it was in 1968, and that difference depends largely
on the material part of existence, on the ways in which human beings
transform the stuff of the world while refashioning it as their habitat.
A long generation ago, the linguistic and cultural turn from external
reference to internal structure and subversion brought more gains than
losses, both because of its freshness as an approach and because the
world of things seemed more separable from the world of human relations and meanings than it does today. Shaking loose the congealed
certainties of discourse and disrupting exclusionary cultural hierarchies rightly seemed to be of the highest priority for contestatory
thinkers. In the intervening years, however, the scope and pace of scientific and technological innovation has increased, giving us both new
forms of knowledge and new things to know and use. The often dangerous effects of human activity on the environment are far more
known and publicized; the global economy has become both more dynamic and more unstable, demanding and receiving increased attention. Literary studies' assumption that language, meaning, and culture
are what matter most has thus been undercut by developments in the
world's material household: in its economy, ecology, and technology.

In the short term, the French protests and strikes of May '68 had an
economic outcome: they led, via negotiations, to higher wages for
workers, particularly at the low end of the scale, and thus to modest
progress toward greater income equality in France. This result, however, depended on some of the most archaic or residual aspects of May
'68, namely its evocation of a French tradition of workers' uprisings
and the occurrence of a general strike. The most distinctive features
of May as a social movement, by contrast, made it a revolt not against
economic hardship or even class injustice but against the conformism
and rigidity of a technocratic, mass-consumer society still overlaid
with strong residues of a nineteenth-century moral order. This type of
contestation questioned the heavy social, emotional, and spiritual
costs of the *fulfillment* of modern techno-economic projects, as embodied in "organization man," the suburbs, and the explosive consumerism of the postwar economic boom.

By the mid-seventies, however, a new type of problem had emerged
in both the United States and Western Europe: the exceptional economic growth of the postwar years faltered and in many places came
to an end. High unemployment, instability, and insecurity became
major concerns. The renewed success of capitalism in the mid-eighties
and the nineties, while overcoming some of the economic problems

of the seventies, has often worsened social inequalities and contributed to economic insecurity. The exponential growth of the digital "new economy" at the turn of the century is leaving many behind while creating much wealth. The pressures of global competition accompanying the renewed economic dynamism have undermined the ability and/or the will of many governments to protect the economically vulnerable through welfare, retirement, and health benefits. Moreover, the structural unemployment, loss of job security, and weakening of social protection in comparatively wealthy societies such as Western Europe and the United States are by no means the worst problems posed to humanity by its economy—that is, by the present state of its household and material affairs. Enormous numbers of people in the margins or shadows of the prosperous regions suffer the erosion, not to say destruction, of the life known by the generations that came before them, with little prospect of really joining the Western affluence whose simulacra flicker on television screens across the planet. The globalization and intensification of the capitalist economy brings new hardships and problems to the world even as it creates unprecedented prosperity for those who are in a position to take advantage of its opportunities.

As a result of these developments, and even if one takes a more positive view of the rapid economic changes sweeping the globe, it now seems ever less sensible to look at the world through culturally colored glasses, seeing it as above all a matter of human meanings and interpretations. Nor does it seem plausible to assume that the world can be significantly changed in the ways critics and scholars inspired by the sixties sought to change it—by contesting hierarchies and loosening the tongues of unauthorized speech, by tactics of local opposition and resistance to structures of power and official stories. The great human and technological complex of national and world societies and economies, driven by capital, technology, and a monstrous network of interconnected private and public decisions that no one human agency can fully control, has for the past quarter century been growing more complicated and interdependent, changing at ever greater rates of speed, and becoming less and less connected to traditional forms of human needs and social relations. Individuals and communities thus find themselves less able to count on a relatively stable material and economic existence upon which they could then base aspirations and critiques in the social and cultural domains. The reasons to reject the conformity or hollowness of the "affluent society" and to challenge its social injustices have lost little of their force, but it seems ever less plausible or effective to believe that meaningful social change can be effected by working solely or even primarily on culture and relations between subjects; the need for knowledge of and engagement with the things of material and economic life becomes ever more palpable.

The appalling hardships faced by hundreds of millions, at the very least, of the world's people, and by thousands of communities from the harsh zones of urban poverty in the West to the cities, villages, and refugee camps of countries wrecked by colonialism, corrupt neocolonialism, and capricious world markets, go far beyond what most people reading a book like this one, who have the occasion to be involved with literary culture or universities or education, will ever have to confront. The pressures of intensified economic activity, moreover, are hastening the disappearance of indigenous cultures and the loss of much biodiversity, and subjecting the poorest citizens of the planet to its worst environmental degradation. This kind of economic exclusion and cultural/ecological catastrophe is very different from the experience of being marginalized within a prosperous society by dominant cultural or discursive communities, as serious as that discrimination is. Overcoming this material and economic exclusion, to the extent that it is possible, will require not only cultural justice but also successful constructive work in economics, agriculture, urbanism, and education. It makes no more sense to hope that effective political action could come from setting aside the kind of objectifying, instrumental knowledge whose forms and institutions were contested by May '68 than it would to set aside that contestatory critique in the hope that the knowledge-power nexus would spontaneously reform or dissolve itself.

Engagement with economic systems as such is unavoidable, because when people and organizations interact as economic actors, the outcomes are not derivable from, or reducible to, the intentions and culture of the actors. Although economic *behavior* always exists within culture—its often reductive modeling by economists notwithstanding—economic *interactions* and *outcomes* cannot be explained as meanings or discourses or acts of mind; their logic and materiality fall outside the cultural approach of the strictly human sciences. (This is why economics is a separate discipline and not part of politics or sociology or cultural studies—and why it would need to remain a separate discipline even if it came up with behavioral models more sensitive to culture and cultural differences.) Shared, empirical knowledge of the object-like aspects of the social world must complement the cultural, rhetorical give and take of discourses among subjects. Contest the authority of experts, yes, but be prepared to deal with their expertise.

Here is the crucial point: *the material life of the world matters more than it seemed to in the days of countercultural revolution.* The later years of the postwar economic boom now appear, in retrospect, to have been an exceptional time in the history of relations between economic conditions, society, and culture. The late sixties and very early seventies were years in which many aspects of culture changed substantially while economic life and technological infrastructure changed very little. In prosperous Western countries, it was thus easier then than in most times and places to see cultural change not only as something nearly autonomous, but as constituting political change as such—at the very least, as a vital form of political action. The issues central to the New Left and the New Social Movements had little to do with the economic issues of traditional class-based political action of either reformist or revolutionary bent. It seemed credible, at least for brief moments, to imagine a revolution made from imagination. To change society primarily by changing its symbolic order. To analyze problems in society and even political economy as above all cultural problems.

Changes in the economic sphere are by no means the only reasons why culture's relation to the world today cannot be what it was a generation ago. The emergence of major concerns about the natural environment have also taken us away from a time when human activities and institutions could be kept relatively separate from their material contexts. Rachel Carson published her epoch-making *Silent Spring* in 1962, and by the end of the sixties protection of the environment was a matter of widespread concern; environmentalism or "the ecology movement" is generally counted among the New Social Movements characteristic of the era. It reached great public prominence with the original "Earth Day," April 22, 1970. This public mobilization was quickly followed by such governmental actions as the establishment, in the United States, of the federal Environmental Protection Agency in 1970. The political influence of the environmental movement and of "green" parties has since fluctuated, but a series of oil spills and toxic waste disasters—and above all the specter of global warming, which first came to prominence in the hot summer of 1988—have gradually led many people to realize that environmental problems run deep and rarely have simple or easy solutions.

An awareness of the ecological vulnerability of the environment suggests that there must be limits to humanity's freedom to transform the world. If pesticides, industry, automobiles, and indeed any massive use of energy put the environment at risk of being unfit for the many plants and animals facing extinction, and possibly for human beings as well, then these and similar means by which humanity alters its environment may well have to be restricted or outlawed. From its beginnings, political ecology was a cultural movement that challenged not only polluters, industrialists, and technocrats, but one of the basic assumptions of modernity. Its position vis-à-vis literary culture was ambiguous—no surprise given that literary culture has both resisted and embraced modernity. On the one hand, a desire to live more lightly on the earth, or in greater harmony with nature, had strong roots in romanticism and was motivated not only by concern for environmental damage but by cultural and aesthetic rejection of many features of industrial civilization. On the other hand, the embrace of nature and the call to limit or reverse progress toward a humanly constructed world ran counter to the innovative and aestheticist impulses in literary culture.

Environmentalism differed radically from the other New Social Movements in that it was not the struggle of a human group for rights and recognition. Insofar as those in the movement demanded rights, recognition, and better treatment for oceans, rivers, trees, animals, and ultimately the planet itself, they were always representing their mute constituency and not themselves, *speaking for* rather than *speaking out*. Despite the subjective dimension expressed in the desire to go "back to nature," the environmentalist always occupies the position of the "white liberal," taking the floor on behalf of a designated, pitied victim—baby seal, rain forest, spotted owl, ozone layer. Moreover, this delegated representation generally requires some degree of scientific expertise: if we know that there are dangerous levels of pollutants in the air, it is because they have been measured by atmospheric scientists; if we know that tigers are at risk of extinction, it is because zoologists have counted them in their habitats. While many may wish to blame science for making possible the violation of nature through the massive application of technology, the understanding of ecological balance and the detection of ecological imbalance require science and its techniques. The nonhuman actors of the environment are represented not only by environmentalists but by scientists.

Largely because of this nonhuman dimension, the absence of a direct human constituency, and the attendant need for scientific representation, environmentalism—despite some worthwhile (and largely thematic) attempts at "ecocriticism"—has never had an impact in literary and cultural studies comparable to that of other New Social Movements. The rise of feminism, minority studies, and gay/lesbian studies came hand in hand with the arrival (and/or open recognition) of women, African-Americans, Latinos, gays, and lesbians as college faculty; there can be no comparable phenomenon for ecocriticism. Moreover, the need to work with the non-human world, known and interpreted in large part through science, puts environmental thinking and activism out of step with the constructivist outlook of literary culture, especially in the academy. To take into account the equilibria of the biosphere, the finitude of the world and its resources, the long-term heritage of species diversity (which can be dilapidated, but not recreated, within the time scale of human history) is to question the limits of the fundamental modern project of superseding givens with constructions, replacing a found world of necessity with a made world of freedom.

If we cannot (or do not want to—and this is the place of aesthetic and cultural arguments for wilderness and biodiversity) live without preserving the found world in something approximating the state in which it was given to modern humanity as the product of very long-term evolution, then we cannot simply go ahead ordering social and economic and political affairs on the assumption that everything can be remade according to humanly constructed plans. Ecology is the space of unintended and sometimes irreparable effects, of constraints that intrude from outside our societies and cultures. We thus cannot continue to regard politics as exclusively a matter of relations among human subjects. Environmental issues call on those who take them up to think through the relations of culture and society to its non-human, non-constructed outside, and this is something that literary and cultural studies have generally not positioned themselves to do.

Many would argue that this is perfectly all right, and that there is no reason for the humanities to become involved in an issue as dependent on natural science and its objects as is environmentalism. According to this view, humanity's relation to the natural world can be taken care of by the technicians of science, industry, economics, and public policy—along with activists (including literary intellectuals) to

put critical pressure on the bureaucracy and the politicians when ethical and political issues are concerned. But this stance, which accepts
the modern division between the mundane and intellectual spheres,
has a grave drawback. It removes culture from our thinking about the
relation of human beings to the planet, and thus reinforces the risk
that an ecocentric perspective will entail a fundamentalist reification
of nature. Too much political ecology has acted as though an authoritative understanding of nature and its needs had to be imposed on
human politics. It is all too easy for a biological or ecological perspective to shade over into the implicit view that human beings, their
communities, and their cultures have less standing than natural equilibria. The defense of the non-human world as such can easily become
an anti-humanism; opposition to wanton human despoiling of nature
can harden into an affirmation that nature purged of humanity is pris-
tine, unchanging, and even virtuous.

Since all human behavior exists within culture, actions and habits that
sustain or damage the environment can only be fully understood in their
cultural context. There is every reason to try to build cultural and political understanding into thinking about the human/environment relationship from the outset. It is legitimate and necessary to think both
about the cultural implications of steps taken in the name of the environment and about the environmental impact of things done within
culture. Humanity's relations with the environment can only be properly understood if the natural and cultural worlds, the found and the
made, are conceived as commingled, interwoven. Of course, environmentalism did not invent such commingling—it is the stuff of humanity's history of living on the planet. But recent heightened awareness of the environment's fragility and importance has given force and
urgency to the idea that it is not enough to know how to separate nature and culture; one must also be prepared to know and work with
their multiple forms of fusion.

Developments in science and technology are likewise a crucial factor in today's rapid and overlapping changes in society and the world.
New discoveries and techniques are changing the ways of human reproduction and shifting the boundaries between life and death. Ever
more powerful computer chips and new synthetic materials are changing the kinds of goods and services that make up the economy and the
ways in which they are exchanged. Social relations, political discourse,
entertainment, and even ways of seeing and imagining the world are
transformed, seemingly faster than ever before, by new technologies

of communication. When we wonder about the role language and literature will play in an increasingly visual and interactive mediasphere, we are wondering about the future shape of culture in a world remade by technological change. The rise of new media stems from techniques that have drastically lowered the cost of reproducing and transmitting information—successively, print, lithography, photography, telegraphy, cinema, television, computers, the Internet, high-definition TV, and so on into the foreseeable future. Science and technology now challenge literary culture by making print culture obsolescent; they also drastically alter the world in which literary culture resides.

Climate, human life span, and disease seem today less and less the natural givens they once were assumed to be, and more and more the products of interactions between the non-human world and the things people have learned to do with it and to it. The large-scale deployment of technology in industry and agriculture changes the biosphere, the environment of living things; medical and reproductive technologies transform the production and maintenance of human life; expanding scientific research into mind, brain, genetics, and behavior bids to alter our understanding of what it means to be a human being. In ever more areas, it is becoming harder to go on assuming that technical problems can be separated from socio-cultural issues, or even that nature can be distinguished from culture. The tension grows between ever more intense efforts, on the one hand, to emancipate humanity from natural constraints by creating a world of human making and control—an artificial environment for which the virtual realm of the Internet now provides a ready metaphor or approximation—and, on the other hand, an awareness or fear that such emancipation may turn out to be an impossibility or a form of enslavement or both.

This kind of tension has long shadowed modernity and has been particularly striking in reactions to industrialization, to new medical and reproductive technologies, to environmental problems, and now to the digital revolution. It is especially strong today, because science and technology are reconfiguring human action and experience faster and more pervasively than ever. How many aspects of life do not in some way or other become the objects of scientific knowledge? Fewer and fewer. How many aspects of life are not touched by technological change? How many scientific and technological developments are without social or cultural implications?

It has become all but impossible to put boundaries around science and technology, to keep them separate from culture and society. The very basis of Vico's foundational distinction between cultural and scientific knowledge is crumbling: it is becoming ever less possible to use the contrast between the made and found worlds to distinguish the kind of knowledge involved in studying the humanly constructed, cultural and historical sphere from the kind implied in the study of the natural world. Science increasingly acts as the creator (or at least the transformer) and not simply the knower of its objects of study: from elements produced in atom-smashers to synthetic polymers to cloned sheep and mice, scientists tinker with matter and creatures, transforming and remaking them to a degree that would have been unfathomable to Vico or to other thinkers who followed his lead in conferring a distinct status on the human sciences on the grounds that they are engaged in knowing what humanity itself has created.

Awareness of a troubled and risky relation to the natural environment, globalization and the intensified dynamism of capitalism, massive and far-reaching technological changes—all these have taken the world far away from the era of 1968. Today's low unemployment and rising prosperity, unlike that of the sixties, comes in the context of rapid change and anxiety-laden instability. Global warming and species extinction have shown that caring for the environment will require far more than persuading governments to set up environmental protection agencies and pass some anti-pollution laws. Recent technological feats bring not a few men to the moon but a billion to the Internet. Literary studies, meanwhile, has preserved a set of assumptions, topics, and methods that, though by no means unique to the era of Earth Day, Apollo 11, and worldwide student revolt, certainly fit it like a glove.

MICHEL DE CERTEAU wrote that the inevitable *negativity* of the May '68 student movement, its inability to articulate many of its positive aims without recourse to a language of denunciation and reversal, was a sign of "a pedagogy or institutions that are incapable of furnishing other generations with the instruction that would allow them to recognize an experience other than that of their 'cadres' or of their teachers."[5] This kind of generational congealing has, I fear, unwittingly occurred in literary studies since the very era of openness and invention ushered in by the events and ideas of thirty years ago. The turns from literary work to theory, from appreciative criticism to oppositional cri-

---

[5] De Certeau, *The Capture of Speech,* 15.

tique, and from the traditional canon to multiculturalism were, collectively, the last great paradigm shift in literary studies, the last major
refitting of the field's goals, habits, and internal dynamics to the world
around it. Subsequent changes—even the turn to Cultural Studies during the last decade—have been, by comparison, consolidations and adjustments. By institutionalizing a characteristic project of a generation
ago, that of trying to change the world via critical and destabilizing interventions in the field of language and culture, literary and cultural
studies have risked putting themselves deeply out of step with the economically, ecologically, and technologically saturated time and space
of the new millennium.

This assertion may seem surprising or even scandalous to anyone
familiar with the attention that the humanities have given in recent
years to cultural phenomena beyond the text or work of art: to the
body, to new technologies, to the materiality of cultural texts and to
the cultural practices of everyday life. It often seems that the literary
disciplines have boldly claimed the world as their text. But in so doing
they have focused far more on uncovering cultural meaning in material life than on figuring out how cultural texts fit into the world's materiality, or how they might be used as resources for understanding the
complex and multilayered world, always cultural and yet always more
than cultural. Concepts such as text and trope are extended or exported
into areas where materiality and culture intertwine, but this is done
to produce "readings"—i.e., the kind of work that attention to text and
trope always produces. Many fascinating micro-histories and interpretations of hitherto marginalized cultural activity are produced, but
the work done on these cultural texts—with *text* writ very large and
loosely—has little to say on how cultural activity interacts with the
extracultural constraints that help to shape it.

This dynamic has recently been subjected to a magisterial analysis
for the case of the cultural study of technology. In an important and
insightful book, Mark Hansen argues that the critical commentary on
technology that has recently flourished in the literary disciplines has
generally proceeded by treating technology entirely as a cultural and
social construction, and thus as being fully analyzable by the human
sciences without consideration of its material, nonhuman dimension.
Since at least Freud and Heidegger, technology has become a major
preoccupation of theoretical discourse, but at the price of being reduced to a manifestation of thought, psyche, and the discursive construction of subjectivity. "By treating technology exclusively as the

material support for ideology critique and/or identity performance," Hansen writes, "cultural criticism simply amplifies those tendencies of poststructuralist thought most inimical to a robust account of technology." Lost in this mode of critique is what Hansen calls the "exocultural" dimension of technologies, "the largely unmarked alterations they operate on our basic perceptual and subperceptual experiential faculties."[6] Technology modifies both the material conditions in which we live and the ways in which human bodies perceive and experience the world, and it does so in ways that are not reducible to or derivable from the workings of human minds and languages.

Hansen limits his argument to the cultural study of technology, but it is a detailed and sophisticated instance of a complaint that can be directed more broadly at discursive and culturalist approaches to material phenomena. Cultural analysis is extended to material life with the aim of moving beyond textualism or idealism, but the material is then analyzed as if it were a text, as an embodiment or vehicle of meaning. Terry Eagleton, for example, charges postmodernism's approach to the body, in at least some of its versions, with "erasing the biological, and occasionally the economic, altogether. In speaking materially about culture, it began to speak culturally about the material. . . ." For Eagleton, "a *theory* of the body runs the risk of self-contradiction, recovering for the mind just what was meant to deflate it."[7] In a similar vein, Bill Readings noted that in some versions of Cultural Studies, the definition of culture is expanded to include "basically everything that happens, with the proviso that 'everything' is understood as inflected by questions of textuality, is understood as signifying practice."[8] What gets left out when one speaks culturally or textually about the material world, of course, are those aspects of it that are not enrolled in human signifying practices but that provide their nonhuman context, that constrain and interfere with human projects.

The tendency of literary and cultural studies to neglect the specificity of materiality is perhaps most obvious with respect the economy. Consider the reaction in literary culture to the two levels of economic problem mentioned above: insecurity and dislocation in the

---

[6] Mark Hansen, *Embodying Technesis: Technology Beyond Writing* (Ann Arbor: University of Michigan Press, 2000), 9, 2.

[7] Terry Eagleton, *The Illusions of Postmodernism* (Oxford: Blackwell, 1996), 70, 48.

[8] Bill Readings, *The University in Ruins* (Cambridge: Harvard University Press, 1996), 98.

wealthier sector of the world, and poverty and the destruction of communities and habitats in much of the rest. The harsh economic conditions imposed on large segments of the working class in the United States and Western Europe have, by most accounts, contributed to a backlash against immigrants and minorities, accused of taking some of the all-too-scarce jobs. To those who regard culture as central, this racism and xenophobia, by themselves, constitute an essential social and cultural problem, a resurgence of imperfectly buried demons from the past. The rearing of their ugly head, according to this view, calls for a redoubled dedication to critical and contestatory work on the languages and traditions that nurture racism and nationalism. Yet it is also likely that this kind of critique, if pursued by itself and without engaging the forces of economic change, can often look more like elitist moralizing than like a genuine attempt to come to grips with the problems facing society and the world. (On issues of race, both the academic left and the entire right tend to downplay their connections to economic conditions, the former because the specifically cultural critique of racism looms larger, the latter so as to draw attention away from what global capitalism is doing to working people and to demonize modest remedial steps such as affirmative action and social benefits for immigrants.)

Concerning the economically produced predicaments and suffering faced by much of the less industrialized world, literary culture has had less to say. What it can offer are principled denunciations of Western cultural hegemony and efforts to include or promote the literature and culture of formerly colonized peoples. The weakness of these approaches is threefold: they are an unauthorized (and sometimes poorly informed) instance of "speaking *for*" others; they often fail to provide (or make use of) much pertinent empirical knowledge about actual conditions and issues in postcolonial societies; and they usually have little or no communicative or mediatic strategy for reaching an audience or having an effect in the world. It is uncertain what they accomplish. As Aijaz Ahmad wrote scathingly in *In Theory*, "very affluent people may come to believe that they have broken free of imperialism through acts of reading, writing, lecturing, and so forth."[9] Cultural and symbolic contestation has its importance, but in the face of grave economic and ecological problems it does not necessarily help

---

[9] Aijaz Ahmad, *In Theory* (London: Verso, 1992), 11.

people in either the West or in postcolonial societies get a grip on the multilayered world—cultural, economic, and material—in which they struggle and live, and on which they must try to act.

There is no shortage of commentators, like Ahmad and Eagleton, to point this out, yet the problem persists. Readings argued that the allegedly radical focus on culture as the object of analysis and critique only appeared after cultural projects and representations, such as those of modern nationalisms, had ceased to be central concerns of universities, economic institutions, or what remains of states: "In lending primacy to the cultural, critics miss the fact that culture *no longer matters* to the powers that be in advanced capitalism—whether those powers are transnational corporations or depoliticized, unipolar nation-states."[10] In the final chapter of one of his most recent books, Slavoj Žižek calls for a repoliticization of the economy, which too often acts (and is all too generally deferred to) as if it were beyond any political control.[11] The dominant problem to which Žižek is responding is not that the global economy's critics have textualized it or reduced it to an occasion for commentary, but that it is usually treated as wholly naturalized, presumed to be so fully inhuman as to forestall any possibility of contestation or critique. This is the flip side of the postmodern identification of the cultural as the field of critical politics: the depoliticized transcendence of the economic and the material.

But this transcendence, as I have argued, is illusory, a product of no longer pertinent ways of cutting up the world. Challenges raised by the present state of the world household—its economy, ecology, and technology—undermine not only the recent traditions of cultural critique in literary studies that coalesced following the late sixties, but also the longer-term intellectual stance of literary culture toward the world. The canonical form of intellectual intervention by scholars, artists, or writers presupposed that the world could be separated into, on the one hand, a material or bourgeois plane where instrumental reason reigns supremely if perversely, and, on the other hand, a plane of ethical reason and universal values to which the first is held accountable. The material, economic, and communicative complexity of the contemporary world is now undoing these assumptions and giving rise

[10] Readings, *The University in Ruins*, 105.
[11] Slavoj Žižek, *The Ticklish Subject: The Absent Centre of Political Ontology* (London: Verso, 1999), 334–359.

to ever more issues for which the kind of social and cultural critique that can be grounded on the authority of literary culture may simply not be pertinent or adequate. The prospect of global warming caused by the burning of fossil fuel, the flight of high-wage manufacturing jobs from older industrialized countries, and the pressures of global competition on the financing of social democratic programs—all these problems demand, in order to be resolved or even faced honestly, alliances of cultural, political, economic, and ecological inquiry. It is hard to see how the intellectual authority conferred by a sphere of scholarly, literary, or artistic production that holds itself aloof from the messiness of the material, technological, and economic world could form the basis for pertinent intervention in that world.

Nor is it by any means obvious that literary and cultural scholars, as things now stand, are well positioned to heed calls from critics that they pay attention to the global economy, or ecological risk, or the materiality of new technologies. Culturalism and textualism, as out of step with the state of the world as I have argued them to be, are well in step with the state of disciplines, curricula, and career patterns. Given the depoliticization of the economy, the uncertain politics of environmentalism, and the almost invisible politics of technological materiality, what else are literary and cultural studies to do?

To many it may appear that developments such as theory and Cultural Studies have given the literary disciplines a broad enough (and daunting enough) mission. In that case, the kind of obligation I am suggesting—that of engaging the extracultural aspects of the world—is likely to seem excessive and unrealistic. Haven't we already come admirably far from the bad old days of studying only a narrow (and usually elitist) literary canon? There are certainly gains associated with the broadening of attention that theory and Cultural Studies have brought. But there are also losses and risks. One loss, to which I'll return in chapters 4 and 5, is the reduction in focused intellectual engagement with literary works—with the texts that one can expect the literary disciplines to put into cultural circulation, and on which they have long practiced and refined their craft. Of greater concern, at least in the context of this chapter, is the risk that literary scholars, by means of Cultural Studies, will think that they are engaging the larger world while actually doing so only in a very literary or culturalist way. If you study tropes in postmodern poetry, you are likely to see your expertise as very literary and unworldly. If you study tropes of the postmodern body in discourses of medical imaging, you are likely to see yourself as making a much worldlier kind of knowledge, one that takes technology and materiality into account. But what do you do with the biological body, with the medical knowledge that, for scientists, is what matters in how they use medical imaging, as revealing as the cultural implications of their discourse may be? It is my argument that without taking seriously the kinds of knowledge made by empirical disciplines— knowledge situated in zones of the construction of reality where linguistic and cultural rules are not primordial— we will go on leaving out the material world and thus failing to situate our work in the actual contexts where the future of humanity and of culture is being played out. In chapter 6, I address the challenge of fostering this kind of change more effectively than by simply exhorting today's academics to perform new tricks.

If literary culture's mode of engagement with the life of the world now seems unsatisfactory—too attached to an ultimately confining culturalism, insufficiently attentive to the nonhuman complexity with which the human world is shot through—then how might it change for the better? By becoming, I would suggest, either more ambitious or more modest—or both. The way of modesty lies in acknowledging that grand syntheses and worldly interventions will often lie outside the scope of literary culture but that literature and its study have much to contribute to the formation and outlook of interdisciplinary thinkers and to the process of understanding and articulating the issues facing us. Without knowledge of what has been said in the past, without experience of how reading and writing can nurture thought and imagination, without a sense that the fictional and poetic are no less part of our technologies for encountering the real than any supercomputer, efforts to understand and act on the world will be poorer and more reductive than they need to be. What literary culture may best be able to contribute to today's transformed world are not theories but stories, not critical paradigms but works and readings, not accounts of worlds revealed to be words but offerings of words to touch the world.

Yet literary culture can also complement such modesty with redirected ambition. If we scholars and critics and writers want to use culture as a resource for taking on the problems we see around us, want to place our creative, critical, and interpretive work in the large and urgent context of the present, we need to get out of our milieu and encounter the world, at least encounter what people in other fields and walks of life can tell us about it. We need to engage the articulation of material life. The interdisciplinarity now much proclaimed in literary studies is too often a matter of facility or comfort, in which one visits and borrows from only those fields whose outlook and structure are compatible with one's own. This kind of crossover leads to increased circulation within the humanities (and the more interpretive social sciences, such as cultural anthropology) but also to an ever more strongly marked separation of the humanities from the empirical disciplines. The way of ambition, now, lies in seeking not the comfortable but the uncomfortable alliances, in trying to make sense and use of knowledge produced in alien territory. It lies not in succumbing to the fatalism associated with obedience to the real, to nature, or to scarcity, but rather in acknowledging that the cultural order is just one of many layers out of which the world is made, and thus enlarging the scope of constructivism to include the participation of atoms, molecules, cells, organisms, and machines.

3 Becoming Nonmodern: Learning from Science Studies

How can literary and cultural study cope with a world made out of much more than texts and culture—out of *things* that have their own patterns and necessity, often incommensurate with what human desire and interpretation make of them? That is the challenge to the intellectual and political ambition of the literary disciplines in today's materially dynamic world. To face it, literary studies should first question their own disciplinary strictures and habits. Because formalism and language-centered theory have contributed so much to the autonomy and identity of literary studies, scholars have steered unnecessarily far from topics and approaches that depend on using language to refer to things that cannot be taken to be cultural texts. But "rediscovering" (or, more accurately, relegitimating) language's referential function will do little by itself. Literary and cultural studies need to look for models of successful intellectual work that span the great divides of the cultural and the natural, the made and the given. Here is where the emerging field of "literature and science" is trying to do its work. Here, too, is where "science studies," or the social and cultural study of science, offers concepts and models to which the literary disciplines can look as they try to include things that are not primarily cultural into an enlarged field of cultural study.

Cross-traffic between the sciences and the humanities is by no means new. The empirical (and largely quantitative) social sciences—economics, most of political science, much of psychology, and some of sociology—have long treated cultural and social phenomena as matters not for humanistic understanding but for detached observation, experiment, and statistical analysis. This approach even extends (on a small scale) into the literary humanities, with computer-assisted analyses of word frequencies and distributions used to determine authorship or to provide empirical bases for stylistic typologies. Conversely, and more recently, the study of nonlinear dynamical systems, often known as chaos theory, has led some natural scientists to look anew at time-bound, contingent, even historical phenomena that once seemed to fall outside science's reach, thereby trading the hard sciences' traditional goal of deterministic, quantitative prediction for a more qualitative and probabilistic approach.

Despite such crossovers as these, however, the sciences and the humanities largely remain distinct intellectual enterprises, more likely to encounter each other in conflict than in convergence. Chaos theory, for example, has been used and interpreted very differently in the sciences and in the humanities. For most practicing scientists, it is above all a new tool of mathematical modeling, a way of extending the rationality and lawfulness of science to domains formerly thought to be irreducibly random and incalculable. Guided by a yearning for openness and surprise, many in the humanities read the same chaotic dynamics as evidence of intrinsic unpredictability even in systems describable in simple, deterministic terms. They see this as evidence that a new scientific development is turning science into something less confident of its predictions and truths. These contradictory interpretations are possible because, as Stephen Kellert wrote in his compact and lucid book on the subject, the understanding gained from chaos theory simultaneously "provides an account of the limited [quantitative] predictability of chaotic systems" and "allows for new [qualitative] predictions at a different level of detail."[1] Nonlinear dynamics has indeed given the sciences and the humanities something to talk about, but for the most part they have done so with fundamentally different styles, interests, and objectives.

Yet nowhere, perhaps, do the contrasting outlooks and principles of the natural and human sciences come into sharper conflict than in the extension of the hard sciences into the study of the brains, minds, and behavior of human beings. Science is redrawing humanity's boundaries by helping to reconfigure the frontiers of body and life through

---

[1] Stephen Kellert, *In the Wake of Chaos* (Chicago: University of Chicago Press, 1993), 100.

transplants, in vitro fertilization and other aids to reproduction, gene therapy, and computerized prostheses, but also by challenging the boundaries of nature and culture in defining the human. Many areas of scientific inquiry—neurophysiology, cognitive science, sociobiology and evolutionary psychology, the biology of gender difference or sexual orientation—are making inroads into areas of mind, personality, and behavior that have long been thought the province of the human or social sciences.

One ostensible goal of a natural scientific approach to human beings and their behavior is to make the line of demarcation between nature and culture more precise by specifying with increased detail and accuracy just what is given to humans as the outcome of their biological evolution. Within what boundaries can humans go about remaking themselves through cultural change? Studying humans by way of natural science ostensibly participates in the modern, Enlightenment project of stripping away the errors and confusions of traditional belief. Whether or not it can be carried out completely and unambiguously, this kind of research has crucial implications for culture, politics, and ethics. For example, if sexual orientation were found to be determined in some measurable degree by biological structures such as differences between the brains of heterosexuals and homosexuals, it would become intellectually less coherent either to condemn being gay or lesbian as a sin or to interpret it as an entirely social and cultural phenomenon. A segment of the boundary between nature and nurture would have shifted: the givens of biology would have gained territory at the expense of the constructions and choices of human groups and individuals.

When science sets out to identify and define natural bases for human behavior, it steps on what was thought to be the province of the humanities and social sciences and raises serious questions about not only the division but the use of knowledge. The familiar scientific project of advancing human freedom by knowing the realm of necessity, which can thus be overcome insofar as possible, takes a strange turn in these cases, because the newly specified necessity comes at the direct expense of human freedom. Cultural constraints are presumably subject to cultural change, however difficult that may be to accomplish. Natural constraints seem much more intractable; worse yet, the possibility that particular cultural conditions or constructions would be erroneously hardened into "natural laws" raises the specter of cultural rules or beliefs fraudulently masquerading as precultural destiny under the guise of mistaken or biased science.

Even if knowledge of the biological determinants of human behavior were accepted as accurate and unbiased, it would be almost by definition anathema to the social-scientific version of modernity, in which human beings become enlightened and thus potentially free by showing that what was long assumed to be natural or traditional is a matter of social construction and thus subject to political and cultural change and control. It would similarly clash with the humanistic and aesthetic variant of modernity, for which enlarging spaces of innovation and disruption is a paramount good. When these social and cultural versions of modernity find themselves working on the same territory as the scientific version, for which progress is achieved by expanding knowledge of a non-social or non-cultural nature, controversy seems inevitable.

It is hardly surprising, then, that recent decades have been marked by an upsurge in intellectual conflict between the natural and the human sciences. The conflict has generally been messy and frustrating, in part simply because most scholars do not perform well far outside their own disciplines. But much of the trouble stems from confusion over the basic stakes and premises of the conflict: are humanists just criticizing bad science or is their quarrel with science itself? Are scientists just denouncing humanists' errors or are they questioning the premises of the humanities? Rhetorically and politically, the first of these two options—denouncing error—is often the more respectable and effective move, but it is far from the whole story. As I suggested above, even the prospect of completely valid naturalistic explanations of human behavior (to assume for the moment that such a thing is possible) is deeply disturbing to the progressive and liberatory project of the human sciences. Not just the errors but the very existence of a natural science of the human are thus of concern to people committed to reshaping the human world by modifying the languages and other codes that situate us in it. Conversely, the activities of scholars committed to destabilizing and/or poetically inventing knowledge and symbolic structures can be both troubling and perplexing to scientists, most of whom see their task as that of bringing new territory into the domain of stabilized knowledge.

Thus, in the recent and notorious "Sokal Affair," we have, on the one hand, editors of a humanities journal so pleased to hear a scientist say that new developments in physics would bring the triumph of postmodernism over scientific objectivity that they published a phony text full of scientific howlers and sloppy literary theory, and, on the other hand, a physicist (and later his philosopher co-author) so outraged over some conceptual and metaphorical borrowings from science in literary and cultural theory that they felt it wise to publish a book denouncing the theorists as impostors.[2]

The "science wars" have been an academic sideshow both highlighting and obscuring some serious and fundamental issues. The humanities have probably looked sillier in the public eye, but that is not in itself too surprising or disturbing. Of more concern is literary culture's relative absence from public sphere debates over the natural scientific approach to mind and behavior. Scientists (and science writers) have, for their part, been able to tell stories about the natural bases of mind and behavior that, contentious or even dubious as they often may be, are intriguing and powerful. Such is the prestige of natural science in society at large, and the ideological dominance of naturalistic explanations, that they draw far more attention and praise than cultural constructivist critiques offered by the academic humanities, which circulate primarily in-house. Even in a major organ of (non-academic) literary culture such as *The New York Review of Books*, the principal critics of sociobiology and evolutionary psychology are themselves biologists, Stephen Jay Gould and Richard Lewontin. And one thing they do not do is try to rule these sciences out of bounds by saying that they are cultural or linguistic constructs; nor do they deny that there could be interest and valid science in the project of evolutionary psychology, if done on conceptually and empirically sound bases. The cultural con-

---

[2] Alan Sokal's initially unannounced parody was "Transgressing the Boundaries: Toward a Transgressive Hermeneutics of Quantum Gravity," *Social Text*, nos. 46–47 (Spring/Summer 1996): 217–52. He subsequently revealed the hoax in "A Physicist Experiments with Cultural Studies," *Lingua Franca* 6, no. 4 (May/June 1996): 62–64. The co-editors of *Social Text*, Bruce Robbins and Andrew Ross, replied in "Mystery Science Theater," *Lingua Franca* 6, no. 5 (July/August 1996): 54–57; this issue also contains a brief forum on the controversy (54–64) with statements from Sokal, Evelyn Fox Keller, George Levine, Franco Moretti, and others. The above items, together with a large and useful selection of additional comments on the affair, are brought together in *The Sokal Hoax: The Sham That Shook the Academy*, edited by the editors of *Lingua Franca* (Lincoln: University of Nebraska Press, 2000). Sokal's denunciatory book, written with Jean Bricmont, is *Fashionable Nonsense: Postmodern Intellectuals' Abuse of Science* (New York: Picador USA, 1998).

structivism of academic literary culture is barely in the game, exercising little influence in the public sphere while consolidating its position in its disciplinary home.

Yet the issues raised by the constructivist critique are fundamental. When brain scientists point to contrasting magnetic resonance images of male and female brains engaged in the same cognitive task as evidence of natural differences, someone needs to point out that these brain states are the outcome of nurture as well as nature. When evolutionary psychologists describe children as assets in whom parents invest, or assert, as does Steven Pinker, that "the struggle to reproduce is a kind of economy,"[3] someone needs to point out that the powerful cultural (and ethnocentric) category of capitalist economics is a major ingredient of the naturalistic explanation. In other words, practitioners of these fields often confer natural or universal status on what may well be culturally specific forms of behavior or discipline-specific models of explanation, such as those of the "selfish," utility-maximizing subject of the modern capitalist economy and its accompanying theory. Such models assume that biological organisms (including but not limited to human beings) attempt to maximize utility in the manner of economic agents (as theorized by economists). It is almost inevitable that the resulting depiction of human behavior will be a hybrid of the hominids of the savannahs and the investors, consumers, and managers of late capitalism.

The type of problem exemplified here by evolutionary psychology has provided significant motivation for a sociological critique of scientific knowledge, a move toward explaining such knowledge as socially constructed rather than dictated by nature. According to this view, ideological importations such as the economic categories cited above, or still nastier ones such as the underpinnings of "scientific" racism or sexism, must be denounced and exposed for what they are; scientists must not be allowed to get away with making them seem natural. Historically, the first impulse in the sociology and/or cultural critique of scientific knowledge was to focus on overt ideological content of this type, above all as it manifests itself in scientific *error*—generally, error as determined retrospectively by subsequent developments in the science itself. This presupposes that when science is correct it has discovered what really is by way of having properly un-

---

[3] Steven Pinker, *How the Mind Works* (New York: Norton, 1997), 394.

derstood nature. But when science is incorrect, social or cultural bias has intruded on the pursuit of knowledge and has interrupted or perverted its dialogue with nature. Truth and error were explained asymmetrically—the former by nature, the latter by society. This type of argument has appeared in many variants, from traditional histories of scientific progress that acknowledge missteps caused by nonscientific considerations to pointed critiques of the role sexism and racism play in controversial or discredited scientific theories.

The sociology of scientific knowledge took a decisive step toward both audacity and methodological rigor in the nineteen-seventies with the principle of *symmetry:* namely, that scientific truth needed to be explained socially in the same manner as scientific error. For the sociologists of scientific knowledge who came to be known as the Edinburgh School, what mattered were the ways in which social factors determined the form of science's questions and the outcome of its controversies. Similarly, more thoroughgoing feminist critics of science focused not simply on the role of gender bias in producing error but on the masculinist character of habits and concepts underlying whole scientific disciplines and modes of operation. The critical perspectives of these scholars paralleled other forms of constructivism flourishing in the human sciences during recent decades. The strength of the Edinburgh School lay in showing, far more effectively than could critiques focused on scientific errors and dead ends, how social and cultural factors shaped the practice and advance of science. Its corresponding weakness was a limited ability to account for either the pragmatic successes of science, its ability to produce techniques that can be used to act with consistency on the natural world, or for how nonhuman, nonsocial factors also enter into scientific processes alongside social and cultural ones. No less important, sociological approaches beg the question of what is the "society" or "culture" that is supposed to explain scientific knowledge.

These problems have led many recent scholars of science and culture to question the dualistic intellectual framework in which scientific realism and sociological relativism seem to be the only alternatives. It is from this branch of science studies, I believe, that literary and cultural studies have the most to learn about coming to terms with a world in which science and technology, themselves cultural formations, are knowing and reshaping a world that extends far beyond the cultural. Science studies have developed a distinctive conceptual tool kit, different from the ones that are standard issue in the human sciences, as a result of having to work on a part of culture—science—that interacts strongly with the noncultural world. After serving as the tools of science studies, the seemingly familiar notions of *society, construction,* and even *subject* and *object* look very different and can be used in new ways. Science studies is thus a form of cultural study whose methods do not cease to work at the boundary of culture; or, better yet, it is a form of cultural study that does not require (or even accept) dividing the world between the natural and the cultural.

Among the key figures working along these lines are the French philosopher and anthropologist Bruno Latour, the American women's studies and science studies professor Donna Haraway, and the Belgian philosopher Isabelle Stengers. What they offer the literary disciplines is a model for cultural study that does not bracket or set aside the noncultural parts of the world.

Bruno Latour

I TURN FIRST (and at greatest length) to Bruno Latour, one of the most inventive, controversial, and far-reaching practitioners of science studies in recent years. Author (and coauthor) of historical and anthropological studies of the social practice of science and its role in society, such as *Laboratory Life* and *The Pasteurization of France,* Latour has generalized and drawn implications from his work in science studies in three major programmatic books, *Science in Action, We Have Never Been Modern,* and *Pandora's Hope.* In the first he tries to show, in the words of his subtitle, "how to follow scientists and engineers through society": how to trace the social and material processes through which measurements are made, data accumulated, correlations calculated, results reported, hypotheses and theories argued, controversies settled, machines produced, groups of technology users constituted. In doing this, Latour avoids making ontological or even methodological distinctions between human actors, machines, measuring devices, and the forces and objects acting on the machines and devices: all are *actants*—a semiotic term that generalizes the notion of actor to include nonhumans—in networks of processes in which scientific results are produced and technological objects made and put to use. (It must be noted that Latour began using *network* in this context well before the term became closely associated with the Internet and thus took on a meaning he has subsequently described as "transport without deviation, an instantaneous, unmediated access to every piece of information." By contrast, a network, for Latour, was "a series of *transformations*—translations, transductions—which could not be captured by any of the traditional terms of social theory."][4] In Latourian actor-network theory, the making of science and technology is assumed right from the start to be both social and cultural, natural and technical, all the way through.

Latour takes a series of unconventional steps to reconceive the problem of accounting for social and natural causes of scientific knowledge. He first notes that as long as scientific controversies continue, scientists "believe representations to be sorted out among themselves and the actants they represent,"—in other words, they are constructivists—but once controversies have been settled, the same scientists "believe that representations are sorted out by what really is outside, by the only independent referee there is, Nature"—they become realists.[5] Thus historians and sociologists of science cannot use representations of nature to explain how and why scientific controversies are settled, since these representations are the outcome of the settlement. But he goes on to point out that society is no more suitable than nature as a cause of the outcome of scientific and technical processes, because the state of society is in no small measure one of the products of their outcome.[6] One cannot say, to take one of Latour's technological examples, that a social demand for easy to use, inexpensive cameras was the cause of George Eastman's development of the roll film camera, since the social category of snapshot photographers did not come into being until it was on the market. Eastman's rearrangement of the photographic process produced both a technological object (the roll film camera) and a social group (snapshooters). Neither the object nor the group could be taken as the cause of what he did.[7] The making of sociotechnical networks, i.e., the work of science and engineering in action, gives rise to a new state of society, new objects, and new representations of nature.

[4] Bruno Latour, "On Recalling ANT," in *Actor Network Theory and After*, ed. John Law and John Hassard (Oxford: Blackwell, 1999), 15.

[5] Bruno Latour, *Science in Action* (Cambridge: Harvard University Press, 1987), 98.

[6] This is a crucial point in the major published debates between Latour and leading representatives of the sociology of scientific knowledge. See the Bibliographic Essay, p. 196.

[7] Latour, *Science in Action*, 115, 122, 124, 131, 137.

From this set of insights, Latour (and his colleague Michel Callon) derived a "generalized principle of symmetry": instead of explaining *both true and false* scientific representations of nature on the basis of true representations of society, practitioners of science studies should explain the representations of *both nature and society* on the basis of the networks and processes (involving both human and nonhuman actants) in which nature and society are sorted out. "Nature and Society do not offer solid hooks to which we might attach our interpretations . . . but are what is to be explained," Latour writes in *We Have Never Been Modern*. "The appearance of explanation that Nature and Society provide comes only in a late phase, when stabilized quasi-objects have become, after cleavage, objects of external reality on the one hand, subjects of Society on the other."[8]

We Have Never Been Modern begins with the observation that the contemporary world is saturated with hybrid natural/social entities and phenomena not unlike the networks one finds when following scientists and engineers through society. In which department of the newspaper should one put stories on issues such as global climate change, AIDS, Mad Cow disease, or lawsuits over frozen embryos? Politics, economics and business, society, culture, science and medicine? The long and complex socio-technical networks attached to these stories defy clean separation into natural and social components. Such hybrid phenomena are not new, but they have become far more pervasive in recent years as a result of the rise of environmental problems and ecological awareness, the development of new medical and reproductive technologies, and the expansion of natural scientific approaches to human nature and behavior.

For Latour, this proliferation of hybrids is making it ever harder to hold onto one of the fundamental conceptual resources of modernity: the separation of nature and society. Beginning in the Enlightenment with the Scientific Revolution and its interpreters, modernity has defined itself and its up-to-dateness through the act of condemning traditions, folk wisdom, authorities, myths, religions, and social arrangements to an obsolete past, because they illegitimately blended the knowledge of nature together with elements of society and culture. The objects and methods of this critical stance have proven to be in-

---

[8] Bruno Latour, *We Have Never Been Modern*, trans. Catherine Porter (Cambridge: Harvard University Press, 1993), 95. Subsequent references given in parentheses in the text.

finitely multiple—it can be used, as noted above, by cultural critics against the received ideas and practices of natural science, and in turn by scientists against their postmodern cultural critics—but its fundamental operation remains the same: the separation of what is nature from what is society or culture is said to make possible a distinction between truly clarified knowledge and illegitimately blended belief, and thus between present insight and past error.

With this decisive yet endlessly reiterated gesture, modernity claims to distinguish itself from a now premodern past. By the same token, modern Western society, as the proud title-holder to science, modernity, and critical reason, relegates all other societies to a premodern or archaic status—sometimes romanticized or otherwise recuperated as desirable or authentic, but always incommensurable with the standards and dynamism of the modern Western ascendancy. Not only does the West use its science and technology to conquer, colonize, inventory, and represent the rest of the world, it also assumes intellectual superiority on the basis of its privileged access to a nature that transcends the social and cultural conditions of its knowing.[9]

Yet this act of self-definition and self-distinction via the separation of nature and society is only one half of what Latour calls the "modern constitution"—the implicit fundamental law according to which both science and politics are carried out in the modern world. Alongside the official separation of the natural and the social comes their ever more extensive hybridization, their weaving together in ever longer and more complex networks—for example, those that now link farmers, activists, nations, consumers reading labels in supermarkets, genetics laboratories, agribusiness companies, and international trade organizations together around the question of genetically modified foods. Through the work of science and technology, the modern world enlarges, extends, and develops sociotechnical hybrids on an unprecedented scale, binding nature and society ever more inextricably together in practice while distinguishing between them ever more thoroughly as objects of knowledge.[10]

---

[9] Latour argues that even among those who concede that the modern West has no valid claims to *cultural* superiority as such over other societies, many, such as the great structural anthropologist Claude Lévi-Strauss, maintain that science gives the West a kind of supra-cultural access to nature as it really is (*We Have Never Been Modern*, 97–98, 104–106).

[10] Many would argue that modern hybrids are in fact radically different from premodern ones, precisely because they are grounded in scientific truth, i.e., in real

This making of hybrids and extending of networks, Latour argues, shows that modernity has never really been what it said it was: a decisive break with a premodern past, with the mixing of nature and society. The separation of nature and society is not a starting point or foundation, but simply one kind of sorting out and extension of human/nonhuman collectives. It takes a lot of scientific work, a lot of network building, to produce representations of pure nature; it takes a lot of objects and institutions, and a lot of social science, to produce representations of pure society.

Latour thus argues that in an important sense we have never been modern. There can be no radical break with the world of natural/ social hybrids. To say this is not, however, to denounce modernity as a mere illusion. Modernity enabled certain kinds of changes to the networks of humans and nonhumans—in particular, their considerable enlargement and complication. The differences between the modern West and other societies are, as Latour puts it using a double-edged French expression, *de taille:* they are *sizable* but they are only *of size,* not of essence or radical rupture. "The difference between an ancient or 'primitive' collective and a modern or 'advanced' one," Latour writes in *Pandora's Hope,* "is *not* that the former manifests a rich mixture of social and technical culture while the latter exhibits a technology devoid of ties with the social order. The difference, rather, is that the latter translates, crosses over, enrolls, and mobilizes more elements which are more intimately connected. . . ."[11] This is an alter-

---

knowledge of the natural. But even if one holds that well-made scientific statements describe an independent reality and are thus true completely outside the contexts of their making, such purified truth is a rather thin and abstract thing as far as actual practices are concerned. The destiny of scientific discoveries that make a difference is to be used in social and technical networks that weave human and nonhuman entities inextricably together in complex institutions. Even if the laws of aerodynamics are held to be independent of human concepts and actions, how are these laws most influential—as disembodied truths about the nonhuman world or as ingredients of aeronautical engineering and commercial aviation? In other words, Latour's thesis about the non-separation of nature and culture in the so-called modern world is clearly valid insofar as we are concerned with scientific knowledge not as it is accumulated in idealized collections of statements bearing the imprimatur of epistemologists but as it is actually put into circulation, via the processes known as research and development, in the human lifeworld.

[11] Bruno Latour, *Pandora's Hope* (Cambridge: Harvard University Press, 1999), 195.

native way of looking at the kinds of differences that are conventionally described in such terms as premodern versus modern, unscientific
versus scientific, custom versus critical reason. In this nonmodern perspective, construction and truth, or fabrication and fact, are not antithetical but parallel.

Latour concludes *We Have Never Been Modern* with a plea for what
he calls the "nonmodern Constitution," a new dispensation ending
the modern "separation of powers" between "the two branches of government, that of things—called science and technology—and that of
human beings" (138). This nonmodern dispensation displaces humanism—understood here as the study of what it is to be human or
what the ways of being human are—away from the social and cultural
pole (where it now resides in the academic division of knowledge)
without sending it all the way over to the naturalistic and scientific
pole (where sociobiologists and some geneticists would relocate it). Latour's road map for a nonmodern future refuses what both naturalistic reductionists and postmodern antifoundationalists are trying to do,
which is to locate the essence of the human at one end of the modern
polarity, in either a transcendent naturalism or an immanent social
constructivism. Like the antifoundationalists, he defines humanity
not by a given nature but by the freedom of humans to reshape themselves and the world. He locates this freedom, however, in the act of
constructing both nature and society, i.e., in the entire process of making and remaking the human/nonhuman collectives.

Latour's nonmodern perspective makes it possible to take into account the great importance of nonhuman delegation and mediation in
today's highly technologized collectives, where one can no more take
seriously the notion that subjectivity is only socially and linguistically
constructed than one can accept that human nature is just what biological evolution has made it. If human freedom can only be realized
in the continuing processes of transforming human/nonhuman collectives, of remaking both things and society out of society and things,
then it becomes necessary to recognize that much of human politics
and culture is in fact being carried out by science and technology
through the modification of the nonhuman side of the collective. Social relations keep being changed as human lives and practices are re-
organized around the new objects science and technology make.

Such reorganization is obvious, but recognizing the world as nonmodern entails an altered understanding of the historical change that
accompanies it. No longer will socio-technical choices be seen as a

matter of simply modernizing, i.e., of denouncing mixtures of nature and society and announcing breaks with the past by separating them, while at the same time lengthening and complicating networks on the assumption that such is the nature of progress. "The illusion of modernity was to believe that the more we grow, the more distant subjectivity and objectivity would become, thus creating a future radically different from our past."[12] One of the benefits of acknowledging the world's nonmodernity, by contrast, should be that "we can combine associations freely without ever confronting the choice between archaism and modernization" (141). The work of science and of critical reason cease to be identified with a direction for history; the past ceases to be conceived as something that must be overcome.

Is Latour's nonmodernism just an idiosyncratic way of avoiding postmodernism, the condition of being *no longer modern?* In its embrace of multiple, composite times, nonmodernity resembles postmodernity, but without the sense of anachronism and disconnection that comes from believing both in the modern temporality of continuous renewal and in its failure or impossibility.

Jean-François Lyotard famously defined postmodernity as a loss of belief in the grand narratives of modernity, those of humanity's progressive political emancipation through the democratization of knowledge and of humanity's intellectual progress and mastery over nature through the free pursuit of scientific and speculative inquiry. Such narratives are, to cast them in terms closer to Latour's, accounts of how modernity separates society from nature to provide for the unfettered development of each. Postmodernity, then, would be akin to Latour's notion of the discovery that we are no longer and/or have never been modern. It would involve the realization that what Latour calls the top half of the modern constitution, the half that separates nature and society so as to provide emancipated access to both, is no longer viable by itself.

In an article (and subsequently a book chapter) written some years after he first presented his definition of postmodernism as the failure of the two great modern stories, Lyotard describes the actual condition of the planet as one of runaway techno-economic development that no longer has any connection either to the modern narratives or to any identifiable human needs. The ultimate end of this process might well be the replacement of living humans by informational ma-

---

[12] Latour, *Pandora's Hope*, 214.

chines and/or the abandonment of the earth (whether by the biological or by the techno-informatic descendants of humans) in favor of in-
terstellar colonization.[13] This inhuman nightmare is Lyotard's grim
and monstrous version of Latour's contemporary world of proliferating networks and hybrids—with this difference, that Lyotard sees the
ever lengthening networks as radically inhuman, whereas Latour sees
them as everywhere a hybridization of the human and the nonhuman.[14] For Lyotard, the failure of modern emancipation leaves genuine humanity only one desperate refuge, that of artistic, poetic, and
philosophic resistance to the inexorable and inhuman expansion of information, technology, and exchange. In other words, the global triumph of long, massive, inhuman, and purely instrumental networks
being inevitable, Lyotard sees the only possible antidote to be the making of deliberately small, fragile, networks in the most purely and conventionally humanist genres: art, poetry, philosophy. (And, as an observer of the postmodern scene might add, in the small, localized
networks of symbolic disruption and renegotiation that constitute
much of the contemporary academic humanities.)

For Latour, postmodernism is an inadequate response to a proliferation of hybrids that can no longer be ignored: it is a disappointed, critical reaction to the realization that modernity can no longer be said to
have been what it had been claimed to be. Postmodernism, he argues,
supposes that we are *no longer* modern: that the modern revolution
really took place but has now failed, leaving nature, society, and discourse no longer in a state of creative tension or even—as in some of
the greatest of modern philosophies—dialectical contradiction, but
rather in a condition of radical incommensurability in which fragmentation, collage, and ironic reflexivity become the order of the
day—along with free-floating denunciation and critique, a carryover
from modern intellectual habits now cut loose from any sense of overall project or direction. Latour's nonmodernism would jettison postmodernism's pervasive irony and negativity while retaining its con-

---

[13] Lyotard, "Time Today," in *The Inhuman,* trans. Geoffrey Bennington and Rachel
Bowlby (Stanford: Stanford University Press, 1991), 58–77.
[14] Mark Hansen judiciously argues that Lyotard rightly foregrounds the "exocultural" character of technology's autonomous growth, its irreducibility to human projects, but also that he overemphasizes the inhuman or cosmic force of technology to
the point of irresponsibly disempowering human actors and excluding a much needed
"*anthropology* of the technical age." *Embodying Technesis* (Ann Arbor: University of
Michigan Press, 2000), 36, 65–74.

structivism, its refusal of naturalization, and its sense of multiple tem-
poralities (134). It thus has some affinities with the work of thinkers
such as Fredric Jameson for whom postmodernism's emphasis on incommensurability and fragmentation is but one moment of a process
of mapping the contemporary world in its complexity.[15]

I've described Latour's reconfiguration of nature, science, politics, and
society at some length, because I believe it offers a strong and original
conceptualization of the present-day life of the world and the major cultural categories in which we think about it (nature, science, technology,
modernity, Western and non-Western societies, and so forth). His nonmodern rearticulation of these categories shifts the grounds of the human
sciences, suggests an enlargement of democratic politics into areas that
have been bracketed as technique, and questions the assumptions behind the epochal concepts of the modern and the postmodern. His work
in "following scientists and engineers through society" suggests possibilities for research into "Literature in Action" that would follow the
workings of writers, texts, and critics in analogous ways. His call to look
at the hybridizing, bottom half of the "modern constitution" can be
translated into the aesthetic field as a program for understanding how,
during the era of "art for art's sake" and of the art/life antithesis, aesthetic works rarely attained self-referential purity but were instead hybrids referring both to themselves and to ever more parts of the world.

All of these conceptual and methodological moves have major implications for literary culture, at least insofar as it tries to take seriously its
relations with the larger world. When literary culture was establishing
itself as a distinct formation, that world seemed relatively divisible into
such categories as nature and society, technique and culture, instrumental and autonomous, bourgeois and artist. This is no longer the case,
and literary culture needs to adapt by finding new ways of addressing
this changed and changing situation if literary culture is to present its
achievements, resources, and practices in ways that matter to the world.

Donna Haraway

THE WORK of another major practitioner of the cultural study of science, Donna Haraway, offers a strong sense of the concrete contribu-

---

[15] See Fredric Jameson, *Postmodernism, or the Cultural Logic of Late Capitalism*
(Durham: Duke University Press, 1991).

tions science studies and the humanities can make to each other. Although Haraway is not a literary scholar, her work is strongly informed by the kind of recent theoretical work in the humanities that has flourished in humanities departments. She is in solidarity with most of the aims and many of the core assumptions of oppositional and activist scholarship in the humanities, yet she is no less committed to taking serious account of natural science and the non-human world it investigates.

A Ph.D. biologist and now a professor of science studies, feminist theory, and women's studies, Haraway is probably best known in the humanities for a 1985 article, "Manifesto for Cyborgs: Science, Technology, and Socialist Feminism in the 1980s," subsequently reprised in her 1991 book *Simians, Cyborgs, and Women* under a slightly different title.[16] The manifesto is an overt attempt to "build an ironic political myth" around the science fiction figure of the cyborg, or cybernetic organism, a hybrid of human and machine. It becomes, for her, a figure of boundary-crossing and multiple identities, a mode of refusing both dualistic oppositions and the fantasy of overcoming such oppositions by means of a return to some primal wholeness or unity. While constructing the cyborg as a mythic figure, an exemplum of conceptual and pragmatic possibilities, she also insists on its connection to the contemporary condition of human bodies and societies and the disciplines devoted to their study: "communications sciences and biology are constructions of natural-technical objects of knowledge in which the difference between machine and organism is thoroughly blurred; mind, body, and tool are on very intimate terms" (165). Haraway's cyborg is an allegory of the world of hybrids, a figure bringing visibility to what Latour would call the bottom, or hybridizing, half of the modern constitution.

The mythic and speculative character of the "Cyborg Manifesto" makes it somewhat uncharacteristic among Haraway's writings, though it is by no means exceptional; it exemplifies the performative, constructive dimension of her work, with correspondingly less emphasis the conceptual and the critical. She offers a conceptual synthesis of her position on relations between scientific knowledge and cul-

[16] Donna Haraway, "A Cyborg Manifesto: Science, Technology, and Socialist-Feminism in the Late Twentieth Century," in *Simians, Cyborgs, and Women* (New York: Routledge, 1991), 149–81. Subsequent references to this volume given in parentheses in the text.

tural critique in a 1988 essay, entitled "Situated Knowledges: The Science Question in Feminism and the Privilege of Partial Perspective," collected in the same volume. The "science question" is the problem of trying to accept both the constructivist (and, in particular, feminist) critique of science's knowledge claims *and* the possibility of real, useable knowledge of a nature not reducible to the stakes of social or discursive games. In her words, the problem

> is how to have *simultaneously* an account of radical historical contingency for all knowledge claims and knowing subjects, a critical practice for recognizing our own 'semiotic technologies' for making meanings, *and* a no-nonsense commitment to faithful accounts of a real world, one that can be partially shared and friendly to earth-wide projects of finite freedom, adequate material abundance, modest meaning in suffering, and limited happiness. (187)

Haraway's solution consists in displacing traditional assumptions about both the subject and object of scientific knowledge. Evoking recent scientific work on vision, she points out that the sense of sight, traditionally the dominant sensory figure of the knowing subject's distance and mastery, is itself something partial, situated, and embodied: a particular case of primate binocular vision shaped by specific cultural practices and often supplemented by a range of concrete technologies. "The knowing self is partial in all its guises, never finished, whole, simply there and original . . . a scientific knower seeks the subject position not of identity, but of objectivity; that is, partial connection" (193). As for the object of knowledge, she conceives of it "as an actor or agent, not a screen or a ground or a resource . . . the world encountered in knowledge projects is an active entity" (198). Scientific knowing, according to this view, is not an encounter between autonomous subjects and passive objects, but rather a situated transaction among embodied actants, both human and nonhuman.

Despite considerable differences in emphasis and style, and some outright disagreements, Haraway's view of science and culture questions is in the main compatible with Latour's, as she has signaled in recent works. She has criticized the military and agonistic metaphors, such as "mobilization" and "trials of strength," that dominate *Science in Action,* and in a larger sense has faulted Latour for evacuating matters of gender and race from both the technical and social sides of his analyses.[17] Yet she has stated her general agreement with his argument that "we have never been modern" and with his mediation of the nature/society polarity: "where Latour and I fundamentally agree is that in that gravity well, into which Nature and Society as transcendentals disappeared, are to be found actors/actants of many and wonderful kinds."[18] Her work thus usefully shows how the Latourian perspective I sketched above, in which some might see tendencies toward an apolitical pragmatism or empiricism, can be compatible with more pointedly critical and political work. The concrete details and readings with which Haraway, in her less programmatic essays, composes her own kind of nonmodern picture are charged with controversy, animated by a sense that social stakes and strife are just as real as technoscientific objects and networks.

Haraway thus shows us what a practice of cultural studies, informed by but not limited to literary culture, can look like in the hybrid spaces of nonmodernity. She is also a user of literary theory outside its customary borders, since she is not a literary scholar herself and she does not write primarily for a literary studies audience. She is, perhaps of necessity, extremely adept at explaining her literary and cultural theory references clearly; less predictably, she writes with theoretical concepts in a creative, ludic, literary way. Moreover, she draws extensively on the knowledge and cultural practices of literary texts and literary communities, reading science fiction as part of the same cultural networks as scientific discourse, finding inspiration for transgressive readings of technoscience in the activities of science fiction fans (such as the women who rewrite Captain Kirk and Mr. Spock as gay lovers in *Star Trek* fanzines). Her own reading of a John Varley science fiction story, "Press Enter," offers neither literary appreciation nor critical denunciation; instead, she both appropriates the novella's heroine as a "guide figure" through the spaces of virtual reality and treats her vio-

---

[17] For Haraway's critique of *Science in Action*, see *Modest_Witness@Second_Millennium.FemaleMan©_Meets_OncoMouse™* (New York: Routledge, 1997), 33–35, 279 n. 19, 279–80 n. 1, and *How Like a Leaf: An Interview with Thyrza Nichols Goodeve* (New York: Routledge, 2000), 156. For her views of Latour's neglect of gender, see "The Promises of Monsters: A Regenerative Politics for Inappropriate/d Others," in *Cultural Studies*, ed. Lawrence Grossberg, Cary Nelson, and Paula Treichler (New York: Routledge, 1992), 304 and 335 n. 33.

[18] Haraway, "The Promises of Monsters," 329–30 n. 6. On Haraway's agreement with Latour's argument about modernity, see also 331–33 n. 14; and *Modest Witness*, 191, 283 n. 21, and 306 n. 36; and *How Like a Leaf*, 23.

lent, pornographic death as a provocation to "active rewriting as reading": "I cannot read this story without rewriting it."[19] Haraway is completely unconcerned with the autonomy, vanguardism, or even existence of literary studies, concentrating rather on what can be borrowed from literature and literary culture—and what must be jettisoned or rewritten—for work that addresses the complex technical and social issues besetting the world. Literary scholars, in turn, can find in her work a model for writing about things outside the conventional boundaries of culture without resorting to a naive naturalism or abandoning their critical and constructive faculties.

Isabelle Stengers

IF SCIENCE STUDIES can thus help literary studies learn to emerge from a posture of defensive isolation from much of the world's life, they also provide an occasion for questioning the deeply modern presuppositions of literary culture itself. The recent work of the Belgian philosopher Isabelle Stengers interrogates the connections between modernity, science, democracy, and cultural practices in ways that lay down new challenges to literary and cultural studies.

Stengers first came to public notice as the philosophical collaborator of the controversial Nobel laureate Ilya Prigogine, a specialist in non-equilibrium thermodynamics best known for arguing that recent developments in his field pose fundamental challenges to long-held assumptions about the determinacy and time-reversibility of physical systems. Stengers, trained as a chemist and philosopher, coauthored two books with Prigogine, *La Nouvelle Alliance: métamorphose de la science* (1979) and *Entre le temps et l'éternité* (1988). The former, translated in 1984 as *Order out of Chaos*, attracted considerable attention for its contention that the study of time-irreversible systems, whose instability made precise quantitative prediction impossible, would make natural science more compatible with the historical sciences and the humanities, which had long dealt with open systems and unpredictable change.

More recently, Stengers has turned her attention to the human sciences and their connections to therapeutic practices, taking on such

---

[19] Haraway, "The Promises of Monsters," 325–27.

topics as ethnopsychiatry, hypnosis, and drug use. She has also written a series of philosophical essays and books on the often difficult coexistence of modern science with other forms of knowledge and with the practice of democracy. In a seven-volume series under the general title of *Cosmopolitiques,* Stengers proposes an "ecology of practices" for dealing with "the discordant landscape of knowledges that come from the modern sciences."[20] Cosmopolitics is concerned with how we relate in collectives to persons and things beyond our polity, beyond the familiar city: outsiders, first of all, people of other cities, people so distant from us that we barely encounter them as fellow subjects, and even nonhuman creatures and entities—ultimately, the cosmos itself. To those of us in literary studies and the humanities, cosmopolitics poses the challenge of how to know, and to conduct politics with, those persons, creatures, and things outside of the sign systems and discursive communities we find so fundamental and perhaps inescapable.

Yet cosmopolitics, for being cosmic, is no less a form of politics. For Stengers, it is not enough to decide to include nonhumans in collectives, or to acknowledge that societies live in a physical and biological world, as useful as these steps may be. The crucial point is to learn how new types of encounter (and conviviality) with nonhumans, which emerge in the practice of the sciences over the course of their history, can give rise to new modes of relation with humans, i.e., to new political practices. Science is made and transformed by learning new ways of allowing itself to be influenced by its "objects." Paleontology's relation to its Other is not the same as that of Newtonian physics. But the human sciences, politics, and cultural and therapeutic practices are also "laboratories" of new forms of relations. The space of cosmopolitics is one in which inventions in relations to things can influence inventions in relations to others, and vice versa.

In her provocatively titled final volume, *Pour en finir avec la tolérance,* Stengers lays down the challenge of "overcoming tolerance": doing away with the configuration in which I or we have *knowledge* while you or they have only *beliefs*—beliefs that I, or we, will then tolerate out of a condescending liberality. This is the stance, according to Latour, of the modern toward the pre-modern, science toward non-science, the West toward the rest. Considering themselves

[20] Isabelle Stengers, *La Guerre des sciences. Cosmopolitiques I* (Paris: La Découverte, 1997), 7.

to have crossed the great divide into real knowledge, moderns reduce what predecessors and others knew to the status of belief. In Stengers's view, far too many of the human sciences practice this type of modernity, predicated on reducing those they study to holders of belief, worthy of interest and tolerance but not of the respect accorded to one's peers in the making of knowledge. She thus proposes a strong link between scientific reliability and democratic politics.

One can only call scientific knowledge reliable, Stengers notes, if its objects have been addressed in such a way that they have had the possibility of testifying independently of the scientists' will or desire, and thus of proving hypotheses to be wrong, revealing questions to need reformulation, and so forth. For many epistemologists, this means that any situation not comparable to that of a well-structured laboratory cannot produce reliable scientific knowledge. You have to be able to do experiments in which hypotheses can be falsified, as Karl Popper said. But for Stengers, such a criterion should be at once loosened (so that its terrain is not limited to experiments nor its means to falsification) and extended (potentially to all situations in which knowledge is produced, or is claimed to be). What matters is that the knowledge and assumptions of the knower be put at risk: that whatever the knower is interacting with have the power to make a difference in the process.

In the domain of the human sciences, she argues, this risk-taking implies encountering what one might be tempted to call one's *object* as a fellow human *subject:* as a peer or colleague, in at least some important sense. This means that one should not try to produce knowledge by extracting opinions from people presumed to have naive beliefs. The person who polls housewives may run the minor risk that his hypothesis about how many of them would say "yes" to a question will turn out to be wrong, but the "Stengersian" risk, the one that could make the whole enterprise valid, can only come if the housewife has the capability to tell the researcher that his questions are off base. This may be because she belongs to a collective of women who are working on understanding their lives and with whom the sociologist has decided to collaborate.

In other words, Stengers insists that people should be treated, in inquiries conducted by the human sciences, as they ought to be in both science and democratic politics: as collaborators in thought and speech who have the power to make a difference and to put what others think they know at risk. What the scientific stance can bring to the hu-

manities and the public square is not transparent communication, rational safeguards, or the transcendence of dialogue and politics. To the
contrary, translating the model of scientific reliability into democratic
politics entails giving people (and their textual delegates) a say and
treating them with respect—not making them into pretexts or into objects of condescension. (I borrow the concept of *delegate* and *delegation* from chapter 6 of Latour's *Pandora's Hope:* a delegate is an actant,
often a thing rather than a person, to which human action has been
shifted.) We in the humanities should not consider ourselves off the
hook on the grounds that we deal with texts, not people, and that
Stengers's challenge is addressed only to our colleagues in sociology
and anthropology! In a recent paper commenting on the Sokal affair,
in a sentence that cuts close to home for literary scholars and critics,
Stengers writes: "what would be implied and required by the ethical
challenge that, in dealing with people, and even with dead or absent
authors, we should be able to present ourselves to them, to explain directly how we intend to deal with them, and the reasons why they
should accept that we do so?"[21]

What are the implications of this question, and of Stengers's criterion of risk, for literary and cultural studies? It's worth noting that they
correspond to much of what has been accomplished in the humanities
during the last thirty years: the enlargement and opening of the canon
acknowledges the importance of hearing from previously silenced
people and peoples as subjects of discourse rather than forever constructing them as its objects. The empire has to write back if knowledge of it is not to be merely imperial. And yet it immediately seems
that this principle has often entailed tolerance rather than the respect
that would generate real risk, knowledge, or democracy. Because the
non-canonical (or newly canonical) literatures have been studied in a
non-canonical moment, when those studying them believe more in
the power of their own interpretive communities to negotiate meaning than in the power of a text to impinge forcefully on that negotiation, these texts have often been either celebrated for their exoticism
(i.e., tolerated) or used to confirm cultural theories, meaning that those
who study them have risked little and therefore learned little in the

---

[21] Isabelle Stengers, "La Guerre des sciences: et la paix?" in *Impostures scien-
tifiques: les malentendus de l'affaire Sokal,* ed. Baudoin Jurdant (Paris: Editions La
Découverte, 1998), 289. Translation by Isabelle Stengers (from a typescript version in
English).

encounter. Moreover, the principle of recognizing the textual other as a fellow subject and colleague has been somewhat selectively applied: it is only infrequently extended to works from the past and rarely to authors (as in "What is an . . ." or "The Death of the . . ."). Absent texts, especially from the past, are often taken as that from which the living must be liberated, and as such it seems all right to treat them with a roughness bordering on discourtesy, the better that we may attend democratically and collegially to living voices whose right to be heard had been compromised by practices involving those absent texts and their authority. All this is understandable, and came hand in hand with some very beneficial developments; the question remains, however, not whether we should now seek justice for some category such as "insulted or marginalized dead writers," but whether we foster or stunt our own intellectual health by studying texts in ways that do not enable them to testify meaningfully, or in other words that do not put us at any intellectual risk.

A key question is how to let texts testify without giving up one of the basic cultural functions of writing, reading, and criticism, which is to enable processes of analysis, disagreement, and recycling that have very different rules from those that govern human behavior in face-to-face interactions. We can and do treat Jane Austen's texts very differently than we would treat Jane Austen if we could meet her in a drawing-room, and there is no point in losing that special kind of interaction that texts provide. It is, nonetheless, crucial to think about how to give not Jane Austen but her texts the opportunity to talk back to us, to question and complicate whatever it is we want to do with them. To do so is very difficult, not least because it probably requires us to make assumptions about, even speak on behalf of, an absent writer. In so doing we run the risk of being accused of manipulation, inauthenticity, or liberal hypocrisy, charges that most scholars and critics would much rather avoid. Yet the result of this risk avoidance can be an aggressively defensive intellectual life, in which one judges and criticizes others so as not to take positive positions oneself that could be subjected to criticism. Stengers challenges literary studies to acknowledge that these fine methodological precautions, in spite of their usefulness, can also become obstacles to reliable and democratically obtained knowledge of the Other.

When one claims knowledge on the basis of superior or more lucid understanding of the workings of language, which is said to have misled others, one is casting those others—writers, perhaps, and surely earlier or less educated readers—in the role of dupes; one is accusing them of believing in something that one is now too knowledgeable to believe in. And one is saying, implicitly or explicitly, that what really matters and needs to be changed is *language,* the way people believe in it or are influenced by it: changes in thoughts and maybe even things will presumably follow as a consequence of changes in the symbolic domain (or, in more extreme versions, are not viewed as all that important anyway). This kind of practice—a consequence of what has often been called the "linguistic turn" in the human sciences—has probably done some good in fields such as history and sociology where the structuring and mediating effects of language had long been neglected or underestimated. But it is a move that takes few risks, and thus offers few genuine intellectual rewards, in a discipline such as literary studies, which has long revolved around works in language and the teasing out of their liminal meanings and implications.

THE WORK OF Latour, Haraway, Stengers, and their colleagues matters to literary culture for reasons both positive and negative: as an opportunity and as a warning. On the positive side, their common refusal to treat either nature or society as transcendental, Latour's commitment to symmetry, Haraway's use of science fiction, and Stengers's challenge to extend the conditions of scientific reliability to the humanities all put scientific and non-scientific culture on a surprisingly equal footing. Their work encourages students of culture to reject the depressing (if sometimes delectable) idea that technoscience describes and rules so much of the real world that the dubious privilege of the humanities is to get to play gratuitously with residues and margins. But they also point to a path away from the self-satisfying idea that the things of nature and technology are so trivial with respect to what really matters— relations among subjects, cultural identities, creative and disruptive practices—that they can be safely ignored (or at least bracketed) by humanists who are triumphant in the certainties of their own enclave. Latour, Haraway, and Stengers also show that one can avoid traditional dualisms and philosophical essentialisms while retaining conceptual richness and producing unconventional interpretations of cultural phenomena; dissolving oppositions and giving up traditional levers of critique, by their example, need not result in descriptive empiricism.

On the cautionary side, however, Latour's account of how society as well as nature is constructed, Haraway's point that social constructionism can mimic and legitimate the most imperialistic power games of science, and Stengers's critique of the unreliability of postures of critical superiority underline the weakness of claims that the domains of discourse or society alone provide sufficient access to the central locus of human freedom and sense-making. Because technoscience and its hybrids pervade contemporary society, because nature is not passive but active, it is untenable to equate humanism (or, if one prefers to displace that starchy concept by a shift in terms, *posthumanism*) with only those parts of the world customarily isolated as society, discourse, and culture.

The contemporary humanities often assign themselves an ethical or political mission that might be described as that of propagating the contestatory forms and energies of modernist and postmodernist literature and theory. The questioning and dismantling of the ideal (or nightmare) of a unified, controlling human subject, the critique and deconstruction of discourses that convey right knowledge and thus serve power, the affirmation of free and open cultural creation in the face of social and economic conformity—all these are felt to be critical, contestatory virtues illustrated by the works of successive literary, artistic, and theoretical vanguards, virtues that, if spread through democratically accessed education, could help to overcome the conformism, inertia, individualism, and oppressiveness of the contemporary political and economic order.

There is much that is admirable in this project, as I suggested in a different context in chapter 2. Its great weakness, however, is that the aesthetic and theoretical traditions it draws on emphasize the autonomy of art and the primacy of discourse. Subjectivity and social relations are not simply matters of language and culture: they cannot be reinvented or transformed exclusively by means of aesthetic or discursive models and practices, any more than they can be reinvented or transformed *without* such models and practices. Subjectivity is an effect not just of language and relations between subjects, but also of body, brain, senses, and relations to the material world. Sociability is mediated and indeed constructed through objects and technologies no less than through discursive and cultural rules and dynamics of power. The nature/culture hybridity of the emerging nonmodern world requires getting away from a language- and culture-centered critical stance, from the idea that discourse is either a consoling refuge to which to withdraw or a fulcrum on which to place the levers of critique.

The recent insights of science studies thus argue for a practice of cultural study not limited to what is conventionally called culture, especially not to its emergent epiphenomena, as though this were a way of keeping up with the forward march of time, a way of staying modern, or postmodern, or post-postmodern. It would be better to acknowledge, modestly, that culture, language, and the literary tendency within culture and language neither found nor transcend human life: they are simply one set of components within a complex and multiply articulated world. Those of us who choose to specialize in literary culture may want to offer not so much pronouncements from its perspective as gifts from its substance, explorations of how its stuff and its tools can enter into networks and hybrids larger than itself.

"THE UNIVERSE is made of stories, not of atoms," wrote poet Muriel Rukeyser. This is modern literary culture's proud, desperate, and beguiling claim, its grab for the center in a world whose foundational and generative story is that it is made of atoms. Premoderns were said to see stories and things—to use a nonmodern generalization of atoms—as immutably bound together, changes in either one putting the other's stability at risk. Moderns claimed that atoms and stories could be (and indeed had to be) separated so that true knowledge of the former could supplant and circumscribe the pseudo-knowledge offered by the latter. At the same time, the moderns wrote truly fabulous stories about atoms and their kindred, making them into a marvelously real wealth of things, all the while looking the other way from these activities. Literary and artistic moderns accepted and even reinforced the separation, proclaimed the superiority and centrality of stories, and generally cut themselves off from the immense construction and traffic of real-world atomic fiction, setting themselves apart as a community of tellers, tales, and listeners like the characters of Boccaccio's *Decameron* isolating themselves from plague-ridden Florence. Their postmodern cousins remained at their side while admitting that they had lost faith and interest in the stories, mischievously pointing out that the atomic plague, like Poe's Red Death, had stolen in among them.

If literary culture is to have a future enriching the life of the world, this state of affairs will not do. The tellers of tales—their purity lost, as the postmoderns predicted—will have to go back down into the city, realize that it has never ceased to string languages and things together, and offer their words, their narratives, their commentaries. With skill and luck, they may help to build a renewed city, stories *and* atoms through and through, once again inoculated by words against the atomistic plague of proliferating things, still stirred by science out of the closed circle of unquestioned tales.

4 Equipment for Living: Strategy, Feedback, Networks of Discourse

ANY THINKING about how to make differences in the ways people live and relate to one another and to the world must take into account the full sphere of human action: the continual adjustment, reordering, and remaking of the natural/cultural world. The care and transformation of humanity's world must deal with constraints as well as degrees of freedom, with the existence of weighty, resistant networks of economic institutions and material processes alongside the lighter, more malleable symbolic networks of artistic, literary, and theoretical invention and subversion. To many people who note the rapid pace of technological and media change in today's world, its implications for literary culture are obvious and devastating: the era of print-based understanding and representation of the world is ending, and literary culture is fast becoming a useless if not downright harmful relic of a largely irrelevant past.

Some readers may feel that my own arguments imply this as well: that if we accept that today's world is no longer that of the industrial and romantic revolutions or even that of poststructuralism and student barricades, then we must try to supplant literary culture as soon as possible with something much broader, perhaps drawn from the concepts of science studies and the emerging cultural texts of hypertext and multimedia. The remainder of this book, however, will take a different approach. I will argue that we need to enlarge the framework and ambitions of literary and cultural study, but that we should attempt to do so without reducing intellectual and educational contact with verbal texts, particularly those of literature and of the past.

Instead of throwing out the works of literary culture so as to preserve that culture's intellectual habits and arrangements, I am suggesting that we change those habits and arrangements as needed so as to go on learning from those works under admittedly much changed circumstances. Literary culture would do better to stop claiming that it possesses a superior critical perspective because of its insight that the linguistic and the cultural are what matter most in human reality, and instead offer its special interest in, and knowledge of, the portion of culture residing in language as a contribution to a larger project of enacting human freedom and working on the world in all its dimensions and directions. Such a project cannot be that of either literary or scientific culture alone, nor can it be that of only governance or only opposition. It will include, at appropriate times and places, the care and maintenance of specific human institutions—and, at other times, their disruption or dissolution. It will involve both creating global connections and protecting local particularities from being lost to global connectedness, as each is appropriate. It will at times mean separating nature and society, at times stitching them together, both in the interest of making better collectives and new kinds of history.

My project here could be described as an updated attempt to flesh out the simple but provocative title that the literary critic Kenneth Burke gave to one of his essays back in the 1930s: "Literature as Equipment for Living." Literature and other cultural works should ultimately be understood as resources that can help people, both individually and collectively, to live their lives and to shape and sustain the world. This does not imply that the making, reading, or study of literature (or of other cultural forms) should be narrowly utilitarian, or should be subjected to tests of relevance or virtue. Literature and art contribute to the sustenance and transformation of individuals, communities, and the world's life in multiple and often highly indirect ways, notably by offering invented domains as far removed as possible from everyday concerns with practicality, realism, and efficiency. Even the purest and most unworldly of aesthetic creations can at times give people insight into their perceptions and thoughts and into the inventions of their fellow human beings—and thus help them to understand, perhaps through subtle or sublime detours—their lives and the world in which they live.

Perhaps I should add an alternative formation, "... help *to edu-cate* people *so that they may* understand ...," in order to emphasize that the contribution of cultural works to the goals of living in and acting on the world need not be direct, and therefore does not imply that cultural works, in order to participate in this process, would have to be *about* the world and the problems of living in it. The making of works is done for all sorts of motives and reasons. Even the reasons offered explicitly by their makers, which are never the whole story, range from austere professions of the imperative to create pure objects of beauty (poet Archibald MacLeish's "A poem should not mean/But be") to declarations of social helpfulness (performance artist Karen Finley's "I try to fix things with my art").[1] In other words, to make a work is *sometimes* an attempt to act on the world, to understand the world, to give others the opportunity to do so ... but not necessarily, and that's as it should be. The freedom of fiction and art, which must include the freedom to be gratuitous no less than the right to be outrageous, is a foundation of their distinctiveness and value. But the act of commenting on works, of using them in education or in the making of knowledge, almost always implies some project of understanding, and thus potentially of preparation for life, of enhancing faculties for action.

And if this is or ought to be a major goal of literary culture and literary study, then some effort of thought, discussion, and organization should be put into how best to accomplish it. This is all the more true since the world is in such a troubled, unsettled condition, changing in ways that often seem out of control—even as many human beings are subjected to more and more insidious and instrumental regulation. This is why we participants in literary culture should care about its engagement with the social, material, economic, and ecological processes of human life in the world. If we want to see literary study continue for worthwhile reasons, and if we also care about the world and would like our acts of teaching, reading, and writing to help preserve and enhance its life, even if only in the most modest or indirect ways, then we ought to try to answer the question: what, and how, can literary culture give to the world?

---

[1] Quoted in *The New York Times*, 22 September 1997, p. B1. A similar remark comes from the novelist Barbara Kingsolver: "Everything I do, from writing to raising my kids, is about preparing for the future" (quoted in *The New York Times Magazine*, 11 October 1998, p. 55).

The dominant answer in recent years, at least in the most influential circles of literary studies, has been that literary culture's most crucial gifts are a critical spirit, models and methods for resisting ideologies and conventional representations, tactics for shaking up the languages and symbols by which people and things are kept in their social and cultural places. Literary studies have thus emphasized techniques for suspending and discrediting the truth value and effectiveness of discourse, tactics for resisting closure, and a reflexive questioning of strategies for producing consensus or certainty, including within its own field. This critical and oppositional stance amounts to a hardening into theory and method of one of the central functions of modern literary culture, prominent in various guises since the romantic era: that of exploring disorder, breaking habit and convention, setting the freedom of art and sensuous particulars against the dreary necessity of the technocratic and bourgeois world.

This impulse to question and shake up an existing cultural order perceived as rigid and oppressive can be described as one of two fundamental and antithetical orientations or motives of intellectual and imaginative work, the other being the drive to make order and master disorder. It has often seemed reasonable to see these contrasting stances as corresponding to fundamental divergences in ideology or temperament. Those who see society and culture as unjustly or excessively ordered tend to desire and work for breathing space, maneuvering room; they try to open the structures, to tear the fabric of convention's umbrella to let surprise and chaos rain in. Those who see the social and cultural order as leaky and storm-threatened are always trying to fix the roof, to make their sheltering structures larger and more solid.

The particularity of the present historical moment, as I suggested in chapter 2, lies in the conjunction of these two impulses, the impossibility of separating them, and the need for both in understanding and acting on the contemporary situation. For more than a century, literary culture has stressed the one while empirical or scientific culture has emphasized the other, but both modes often impose themselves on the same minds—whether literary or scientific. I will argue here that recent literary culture's distrust of the global and the synthetic—its emphasis on local knowledge, tactics, opposition, and resistance—can usefully be complemented by an engagement with strategic, systemic, large-scale, and long-term perspectives. This argument begins with the observation that today's academic literary culture has a disturbing tendency to distrust and neglect what lies outside it, be it economic life, the physical and biological environment, or scientific knowledge—or simply literary works sufficiently alien to the cultural here and now as to bring discomfort.

The issues of scale (small versus large) and position (nomadic versus sedentary) have something of a contemporary *locus classicus* in discussions of the respective merits of two terms of military art, *tactics* and *strategy*, as intellectual values. (It may well be that what most needs to be questioned is the recourse, on both sides of the debate, to concepts of war, but here I suspend that issue and look at the debate on its own terms.) Writing about what he called "oppositional practices" in cultural and everyday life, Michel de Certeau, whose sympathetic and insightful analyses of May '68 I referred to in chapter 2, chose tactics over strategy because of the latter's complicity with established power. Only those who possess some proprietary mastery over a domain of space and time, he wrote, can engage in strategy as a form of knowledge or practice. Tactics, by contrast, are improvisational and uncentered; they are the ruses of the weak, who create and defend pockets of dignity, freedom, and conviviality for themselves and in their immediate surroundings without attempting to master others or to confront large-scale powers. As de Certeau points out, tactics are a rhetorical art akin to that of the Sophists, whereas strategy corresponds to philosophy and more generally to systemically organized knowledge.[2] Oppositionality, according to de Certeau, resides in tactics that create or preserve localized deviations, spaces and moments of freedom and pleasurable rebelliousness, within and around the territory controlled by hegemonic powers.

De Certeau's analyses are held in justly high regard in literary and cultural studies, and his preference for tactics over strategy has been shared, implicitly or explicitly, by many thinkers in the humanities. It is a postmodern preference corresponding to a loss of trust in society's big institutions and a loss of belief in the potential for revolutionary change, whether in the short run or for all time. Tactical thinkers hope to avoid complicity with authority while working out ways of living and forms of symbolic subversion or critique that palliate, or compensate for, their own lack of power. The choice of tacti-

---

[2] Michel de Certeau, *The Practice of Everyday Life*, trans. Steven Rendall (Berkeley: University of California Press, 1984), 29–42.

cal over strategic thinking thus fits into the longer-term pattern
according to which literary intellectuals conceive their political activity in the idiom of critique or resistance, rather than that of policy-
making or governance, although the emphasis on tactics or oppositionality also amounts to a shift from abstract or general criticism to
concrete intervention in local situations. In still more general terms,
opting for tactics over strategy is another instance of modern literary
culture's stand with rhetoric against philosophy in their ancient and
ongoing opposition. The intellectual preference for tactics also corresponds to the social and cultural legacy of the sixties, which lay in
changes in individual consciousness and ways of living, the microp-
olitics of local and/or identity-based activism, and the politics of empowerment and minority rights characteristic of the New Social Movements.

Thus concerned with questions of localized freedom and identity
and with opposition to structures of symbolic authority, literary and
cultural studies have had no trouble focusing on the evils of state
power, totalization, and authority, but they have few traditions to prepare for engaging with dysfunctions of markets, unstable ecologies, or
effects of rapid technological change—in other words, for dealing with
the issues in which nonhuman materiality and logistics impinge on
human politics and culture. The general targets of liberatory cultural
politics are forms of humanly made order, experienced or understood
as excessive, exclusionary, or abusive. Yet today's world, rapidly re-
shaped as it is by technology and economic activity, contains not only
regularities both useful and oppressive, but also new kinds of chaos,
unexpected forms of uncertainty and chance, the global and unpredictable results of so many humanly created patterns and adaptations
acting on those parts of the world that lie at the rough edges of human
control. The burning of fossil fuel seems to lead to changes in the
weather; a Department of Defense computer network gives rise to a
worldwide medium offering new spaces for interpersonal communication, commerce, pornography, and the crossing of national boundaries. When attempts to remake and control the world have produced
not only order (and its ever troubling excesses) but new forms of unpredictable and unmasterable disorder, then new kinds of explanation
and new narratives of understanding and coherence become no less
important than liberatory undoings of the stories of old or the dictates
of yesterday. Indeed those liberating dissolutions may seem strangely
dated, insolent, and out of phase with the frightening new unpre-

dictabilities of humanly and rationally produced disorders—all the more so if they are produced and promoted by tenured professors, whose residually secure status shelters them from some of the major uncertainties and pressures experienced by many citizens of their societies.

The drawbacks to the critical, tactical, and oppositional modes that have recently held sway in academic literary culture seem more evident now than they were thirty or even fifteen years ago. In the choice between tactics and strategy, the side of tactics accepts that the global contexts of its maneuvers will continue to be defined by its opponent's strategy. Tactics thus appear, at any rate, to leave the big systems relatively untouched, as if they were intractable or unimportant (or both). But the material, ecological, economic, and communicative complexity of the contemporary world, and in particular the hybrid character (cultural/natural/material) of so many of its problems, puts an ever greater premium on strategic thinking, and does so despite widespread recognition that strategic planning and action, as carried out by such entities as states, defense establishments, and large corporations, is often responsible for many of the messes we confront.

It is therefore not surprising to see other thinkers who, like de Certeau, were deeply influenced by the social movements of a generation ago, offer sharp criticism of the intellectual preference for tactics over strategy, for the fragmentary over the synthetic. Régis Debray, one-time companion of Che Guevara in Bolivia in the sixties, wrote in 1991 that "the exaltation of margins, interstices and dissidence has led us to the point of suspecting a moral fault, if not a program of dictatorship, in large-scale views or in the slightest attempt to put things in perspective."[3] Debray, arguing for his own project of a *mediology*, or general approach to the role of media and transmission in all phases of society and culture, adds that the allegedly moral preference for local, fragmentary, and anti-systemic knowledge amounts to a lack of intellectual generosity that fits all too easily into traditional academic overspecialization.

The French philosopher and essayist Michel Serres, who taught for a time at the unorthodox Université de Paris-Vincennes (opened in response to the events of May '68), provides an example of a thinker who has condemned the militaristic aspect of strategic thinking while em-

[3] Régis Debray, *Cours de médiologie générale* (Paris: Gallimard, 1991), 16.

bracing its global and anticipatory qualities. Near the end of a 1976 essay, Serres sets down the injunction, "Break forever with any strategy." His preoccupation here is with the military, death-dealing character of strategy, always present whenever anyone or anything dominates a space and the pathways and energies associated with it. "The non-thanatocratic solution is thus to fragment space, undo the concentration of energies."[4] Yet writing over a decade later in *The Natural Contract,* first published in French in 1990, he announces, "We must anticipate and decide."[5] Here his chief concern is how human interaction with the natural environment has both given humanity responsibility for the fate of the earth and made the earth an actor in a history that can no longer be called simply human history. Serres continues to avoid "strategy" because it is a term of war, but his call to "anticipate and decide" and to extend political governance to the steering of the world implies a long-term, large-scale project, certainly closer to strategy than to tactics.

Unlike Serres, the Anglo-Canadian semiologist and systems theorist Anthony Wilden, who once described the sixties as "the explosion of the context of life itself,"[6] does not hesitate to endorse strategy as an enabling intellectual and political principle. He describes it not as the prerogative of established authority but as an empowering mode of thinking that concentrates on contexts and codes rather than on messages or events—in other words, that turns its attention from phenomena to the conditions of their possibility, from events to the systems in which they occur. As a practical rule for democratic society, he proposes "Everyone a strategist." In other words, if there is to be genuinely democratic governance, people have to have tools to understand the contexts and patterns in which the events and circumstances that are the object of politics and governance come about. They should not try to do politics simply by resisting or making do, no matter how subversively or resourcefully. He contrasts his "Democratic Rule" of strategy for all with what he calls the "Colonial Rule": "Teach tactics, and above all kamikaze tactics; make strategy and the very idea of strategy a secret never to be revealed." Making tactics the

[4] Michel Serres, *Hermès IV. La Distribution* (Paris: Minuit, 1977), 290.

[5] Michel Serres, *The Natural Contract,* trans. Elizabeth MacArthur and William Paulson (Ann Arbor: University of Michigan Press, 1995), 5.

[6] Anthony Wilden, *The Rules Are No Game* (London: Routledge and Kegan Paul, 1987), 308.

main tool of the oppressed, Wilden reminds us, can be a strategy of oppressors to make sure that the dominant order is not overturned: without strategy, the weak will always try to fight—and will generally lose—the same little battles rather than shift the context of their action to one in which they might win where it counts. Strategy is a practice of knowledge that focuses on wholes and contexts and a form of action that aims to shift and change contexts and rules. For Wilden this is closely akin to literacy, understood as knowledge that is empowering because it provides the means to effective communication and action.[7]

Wilden does not comment directly on the relation between strategy and the exercise of power, but George Orwell in effect did so in some characteristically blunt remarks on Rudyard Kipling and his reception by writers and intellectuals. Orwell used the example of Kipling to argue against the embrace of tactics, critique, and opposition as the general political modes of literary culture. Kipling, wrote Orwell,

> identified himself with the ruling power and not with the opposition. In a gifted writer this seems strange to us and even disgusting, but it did have the advantage of giving Kipling a certain grip on reality. The ruling power is always faced with the question, "In such and such circumstances, what would you *do?*", whereas the opposition is not obliged to take responsibility or make any real decisions. Where it is a permanent and pensioned opposition, as in England, the quality of its thought deteriorates accordingly.[8]

The "grip on reality" that comes from identifying with "responsibility" and "real decisions" is the strategic, large-scale, comprehensive thinking that comes with (but perhaps need not be limited to) the exercise of power. The opposition, if it is comfortable with remaining forever in opposition rather than taking power, can be satisfied with resisting and thus with tactics. Orwell acknowledged the conventional modern antithesis between literary culture and political power ("in a gifted writer this seems strange to us and even disgusting"), but he pointed out that this oppositional stance comes at a serious cost in ability to engage with certain features of the real. The oppositional lit-

[7] Ibid., 49, 58; cf. 279.
[8] *The Penguin Essays of George Orwell*, 2d ed. (London: Penguin, 1994), 215.

erary culture of the academy, having no program whatsoever for taking or exercising power, and indeed much institutional privilege to lose in the unlikely event of a real revolution, has little need to worry about those parts of reality on which it loses its grip.

Why should it be important, one could argue against Wilden and Orwell, that everyone in a democracy—and writers, scholars, and literature students in particular—be versed in strategic thinking or capable of assuming something of the cognitive task of governance? In a highly specialized society, an oppositional intellectual culture that does not clutter its collective mind with the problems of running the system may be a source of both stimulation and integrity. Wouldn't it be an improper demand on literary culture to try to replace the occasional rigidity of the "politically correct" with an ultimately much more confining demand for the "scientifically and ecologically and economically strategic"?

There is, indeed, no reason to expect every cultural utterance to be accurate or to fit into a strategic or governing outlook; such a constraint would itself be an example of short-term, reductionist thinking. It is, however, one of the central theses of this book that the kind of specialization and separation represented by a purely oppositional literary culture, unengaged with the long term and with the non-human complexity that is bound up with the human world, is ill-adapted to today's conditions. Not only are the insights produced by such a culture almost non-communicable to the outside world, but the quality of its own thought suffers, as Orwell suggested, from being disconnected from important parts of worldly realities. As I have argued, the historical conditions that encouraged (and, indeed, may have justified) literary culture's autonomy and oppositionality over the past two centuries have by now largely dissolved, revealing a more elaborately interconnected world in which literary culture runs the risk of isolation or irrelevance. Thinking in ways compatible with strategy and governance thus matters even in literary culture, although it should never become an exclusive or obligatory consideration, and should never be allowed to drive out imagination and playfulness from the making and recycling of cultural works. My concern in this chapter is less, however, with the free and inventive character of literary production than with the educational and intellectual uses of literature, or with the activity of the literary disciplines. I am focusing, in other words, on literary culture's stance when it turns its attention to society or is considered as a resource for living in the world. It is in this vein that at the beginning of a new century I question the historical suitability of literary culture's almost exclusive preference for critique, local knowledge, and tactical or oppositional politics over large-scale, strategic thinking and involvement in governance.

A CENTRAL TASK of human beings—a task at once cultural, political, and technological—is to shape the human and nonhuman collectives, as Latour would say, in which they live. We can exercise control—by both producing and regulating change—over the grounds and circumstances of our existence, which are at once local and global, natural and cultural, technical and social. Can we find a framework for thinking about how literary culture contributes to this process?

One promising approach, as I suggested in the last chapter, is to draw from science studies, which offer fruitful models and concepts for literary and cultural studies that are concerned with engaging the larger world. In the balance of this chapter, however, I want to proceed in a different way and offer some alternate figures for thinking about how literary culture can participate in large-scale, world-oriented, and synthetic approaches to understanding and living in the world. Because of the inextricably mixed character of these collectives, and the near-impossibility of describing them in known languages without recourse to such polarities as human and nonhuman, I will propose two provisional conceptual models for literary interaction with them, both hybrid: the first, *feedback*, is closer to objects and machines; the second, *networks of discourse*, is closer to humans and language.

To introduce the first of these tentative models for thinking about how people use culture to interact with the state of their world, I begin with a simple if perhaps unexpected metaphor, that of *steering*. Many readers may know it best from driving a car. Its traditional actor is the helmsman, steersman, or pilot of a boat; in Greek, *kubernetes*, in Latin *gubernator*, from which come the words *governor, govern*, etc., and also *cybernetics* and its many recent *cyber-* derivatives. To steer is to engage in a process of control, and is done through what is now known as feedback. The pilot must feel or observe whatever deviation there is between the present heading and the desired course, and feed this information back into the process by transforming it into corrective action, a slight turn of the rudder. This kind of process is actually very common and is not limited to cases where clearly there is something to control—a ship or a society—and someone in charge of controlling it—a pilot or governor. It doesn't imply control in a political sense, or control that is rigid or manipulative. For example, to raise a coffee cup to your lips, you don't simply impart a certain force to your arm with your muscles and then hope that this will be about enough to get the cup all the way to your mouth but not so much that it will crash into your teeth: instead your mind and senses continuously measure the distance your hand has yet to travel to reach its goal and adjust the muscular action of your arm accordingly so that the coffee reaches your mouth with no excess momentum. Or, to take a different kind of example, when you teach, you adjust your behavior, or input to the learning process, on the basis of the output of your previous teaching, the effect you see it having with students. In the simplest possible terms, you pursue what has brought positive outcomes and de-emphasize what hasn't worked. This doesn't mean that you're "controlling" or "governing" the class in an authoritarian manner, or even that you're exercising control over the people in it. What you're trying to control is the educational quality of your interaction with students; your goal—the state you're trying to reach and/or maintain—needn't be one of order and surely should not be one of domination. Steering, or participating in processes involving control, is a basic property of individuals—and entities of all kinds—that interact in real time with their environments.

One crucial aspect of living, in other words, is that of steering our course through the space of possibilities we encounter. Another, at least if we are active citizens of a democratic society—and perhaps even if we are not, for politics is not the whole story here—is that of doing our part, modest though it may be, in steering the world by trying to exercise some human control over the processes that shape the environments—cultural, social, economic, ecological—in which we will live. Of course, no one steers the whole world or even very much of it. But individuals and small groups can sometimes succeed in modifying some things in their part of the world, and individuals can participate in large groups whose collective response to the way things are sometimes makes them different.

I'm not just talking here about exceptional efforts, crusades to clean up the neighborhood or save the world, though such things have their place. Attempts to work on some part of the world go on all the time, and are a big part of what we normally expect from political and cultural activity and even daily life. Voters who put the opposition party in power, writers of essays for the op-ed page, teachers who try to change the way they relate to their students or urge new methods on their colleagues, proposers of ideas about the role of literature or culture, strikers who protest the government's plan to reduce their pensions, central bank governors who set interest rates—all are engaging in acts of steering: sending corrective signals to some process based on their perceptions of how that process is not going the way they believe it could or should. Knowing and understanding the world is a crucial step in all such attempts; the scholar who spends years figuring out and explaining some small thing may be contributing to more effective decision-making and action in the future. Of course, there are huge variations in the quality and pertinence of knowledge about the world used as input to action: voters may be shrewd about their interests and yet be misled when it comes to policy, central bankers may be fantastically well-informed about the bond market but structurally blind to the effects of its fluctuations on the well-being of working people and pensioners. The action of steering can never wait for definitive and certain knowledge; it always involves acting *now*, in real time, on the basis of the best understanding provisionally available. There are no guarantees, in other words, that human attempts to shape the world will turn out well, but there is no escaping that such attempts are a major part of life, and there is every reason to try to make them more effective, to enhance (and share as widely as possible) the modes of understanding and representation on which they depend.

Steering a steady course is an example of *negative feedback*, in that there is a change of sign or direction in the signal before it is fed back into the system: the helmsman transforms the perception "heading to port" into the action "head to starboard," just as in the working of a home thermostat, the signal "temperature too low" will be transformed into the corrective action "turn on the furnace." In general, negative feedback reduces deviation from the heading or set point, and thus works to hold processes steady or within bounds; *positive feedback*, which amplifies deviation, drives them to new states and to extremes. An everyday example of positive feedback can be found in what is commonly referred to as feedback in sound systems: when a microphone is placed too near a speaker, the output of amplification becomes its input, and the sound level is quickly driven to the maximum of which the system is physically capable. Positive feedback is also the dynamic involved in economic growth, the spread of rumors or epidemics, and population increases.

There is such a strong tendency to identify all feedback loops with control and stability that it's important to emphasize that not all feedback, by any means, is negative or stabilizing. To change heading, a pilot continues to steer. Positive feedback reinforces trends, amplifies tendencies. To think of cultural production and commentary as part of a feedback loop by which people act on, maintain, and transform their relations with each other and with the world is not to assume or advocate that they will be tightly controlled and thus unchanging. It is not to prescribe norms for the making or reading of works, but to describe them as part of a process, or rather of many interconnected processes.

If poets or artists or critics see the social world as too tightly controlled, steered on too straight a course, they can try to destabilize it, loosen it up, with disruptive works or commentaries, but this too is part of a feedback loop, a process of interacting with the world so as to modify it and be modified by it. J. Hillis Miller, for example, writes that "the university ought to have as its primary goal working to establish conditions propitious to the creation of the ungovernable," and thus would probably be appalled at my arguments in favor of governance and control models.[9] Yet his own statement, from my perspective, is an attempt to redirect the activity of making knowledge away from its present state and toward one he considers more desirable.

Conceiving of the work of culture as a form of feedback, I submit, takes away none of its potential diversity and strangeness, but provides a framework for thinking about how it does or does not make differences in the world, for how it acts in real time—as opposed to conceiving of it as headed toward definitive knowledge at some ever-deferred future time. It is true that in the 1950s writers, critics, and artists often decried *cybernetics*, as Norbert Wiener named the science of "control and communication in the animal and the human being," as a repellently technocratic ideology, yet neither Wiener nor his critics should be given the last word. The anthropologist Gregory Bateson, for one, suggested that cybernetics could help provide an understanding of human communications and relationships that would help to untangle some of the communicative pathologies played out in twentieth-century history. A pioneer in using feedback-like concepts in analyzing patterns of behavior, Bateson was most concerned with understanding the communicative dynamics through which processes are transformed: "saying that the important things are the moments at which attitude is determined, the moments at which the

---

[9] J. Hillis Miller, *Black Holes* (Stanford: Stanford University Press, 1999), 181.

bias of the thermostat is changed—this stance is derived directly from cybernetics."[10]

Writers, artists, and indeed all cultural producers select words, forms, ideas, images from all that has gone before, both in their genre or medium and what they know of other arts and the world at large. They amplify, damp down, recombine, reprocess, and reformulate these samplings of the existing world and its cultures in order to send something new back out to the world as a signal, sometimes countering and sometimes amplifying the things and tendencies they have perceived. In this way they regulate, reinforce, or otherwise act on what was already out there before their intervention. The feedback provided by art, philosophy, and other cultural productions can be either positive or negative, and is most often both at once, as in a work that is critical of some received idea or aspect of social life—thus providing negative feedback along one loop—while echoing and amplifying an incipient movement of cultural protest or alternative affirmation—thus providing positive feedback along another.

The making and studying of cultural works are among the means by which people respond to the state of the world and attempt to act on it. In this sense, cultural and critical productions or interventions are forms of feedback at work in the processes that make up human life in all its aspects. Works are made in response to realities that are themselves moments within processes; their creators base them on perceptions and knowledge of present and past states of some of the myriad subsystems of the world's life. These inputs or conditions of creation undergo various kinds of transformations in the production of a new work or statement, which is then sent out in the world to have whatever effect it will have on its processes—sometimes on the same processes whose states were crucial to the work's production, sometimes on completely different ones. Even the most pure, gratuitous work of art responds on some level to the state of the world, of culture, of art; it acts on the world if only in the sense of adding itself to it, as if the artist were saying implicitly, "I prefer the world with this work in it to the world without it" or "I am changing the world in the direction of adding this work to it." And thanks to the many circuits of reception and commentary of works of art, this most rad-

---

[10] Gregory Bateson, "From Versailles to Cybernetics," *Steps to an Ecology of Mind* (New York: Ballantine, 1972), 476.

ically unworldly of creations may become part of someone else's process of figuring out something important about art, society, or history. Of course, a great many cultural works participate much more directly in processes of knowing the world or acting in it: Balzac's novels, for instance, offer elaborate explanations of social phenomena, critiques of the existing political and economic order, and arguments for restoring the authority of throne and altar. No serious reader of Balzac takes all of this at face value, of course, but that skepticism by no means cancels the knowledge-making capacity of his fiction; it simply requires that the works be taken as inputs to the reader's efforts at knowing the world rather than as finished expressions of superior knowledge.

Knowing cultural works—of art, literature, and philosophy—is a part of the collective process of knowing the world, both the natural and the human. The path of knowledge and action that goes through such works is for the most part a roundabout one, a route that turns away from knowing or acting in the most direct or immediate way possible. The making, reception, and use of cultural works is thus a complex, indirect, and often subtle way of sending a feedback signal to the ongoing processes in which history is made. It is a way of adding to the richness of human life and activity, of noticing things that would otherwise not be noticed, and perhaps thereby of provoking kinds of action that would not otherwise be envisioned or instigated. Faced with the permanent task of educating ourselves (and helping others to become educated) so as to know and act in the world, we include the already existing works of culture in the tool kits of language and experience with which to form our minds.

A major task of the humanities, of literary culture, should thus be to contribute to the collective, real-time project of knowing, maintaining, and enhancing those parts of the world that are subject to human intervention and control—to the task of steering or piloting processes that depend at least partially on us for their direction. Cultural works and their study provide multiple, varied, and indirect paths of feedback; they add diversity and subtlety to the process of knowing and acting on the world. Their contribution is crucial, because the effective working of feedback control systems depends on the quantity and quality of the feedback signals they can process.

The notion that the complexity of feedback must be commensurate with that of the system being controlled was formulated by the British cybernetician W. Ross Ashby, and subsequently by Anthony Wilden, as the *principle of requisite diversity* (this is Wilden's term; Ashby's is *variety*). It states that a system of given diversity can be effectively and appropriately controlled, regulated, increased, or re-created only via feedback signals of a corresponding degree of diversity. To give a simplistic but, I hope, clear example: if you have a complicated house, with lots of differently shaped and constructed rooms exposed in varying degrees to the elements—some walls insulated, others not, some spaces swept by winds, others well sheltered from the elements, and so forth—then you will only be able to regulate its temperature thoroughly if you have a correspondingly complicated heating and thermostatic system, with multiple sensors and means of directing quantities of heat to specific locations. In the same way, if you are trying to intervene so as to amplify, redirect, or stabilize a social process, you need capacity for knowledge and communication that is comparable in complexity to the process itself; if this is not the case, you will control reductively, steering badly or doing damage while steering, turning the process you are trying to guide into something rigid or simplistic. To go against the principle of requisite diversity is to commit a version of what William James, in *A Pluralistic Universe*, called "vicious intellectualism": the mistake of assuming that a representation or concept is adequate to the real when it is not, and thus acting reductively on the real in accordance with the concept.[11]

Literature contributes significantly to the requisite diversity of cultural systems both via its voicing of the past—the topic of chapter 5—and by virtue of its fictive and poetic qualities. Fictions are alternate versions of reality, possibilities explored in speech where knowledge of the real, narrative schemas, imaginative invention, and the arbitrariness of chance intersect. To use fiction as input to knowing and acting on the world is to conceive of life as a space of possible variations and perturbations, of hypothetical trajectories. It is thus a means of increasing one's repertoire of imaginings of the world and thus the flexibility of one's responses to it. Chess players (and now computers programmed to play chess) consider many possible moves—their own and those of their opponents—for every one they actually make. Doing so is a necessary part of processing the complex information about the present state of the game so as to decide on their next move in it, their next attempt to exert control over its subsequent development. In a similar manner, fiction heightens the sense of complexity and possibility in our knowledge of social situations past and present, thus sharpening our ability to respond to the world in varied, distinctive, and specific ways.

The inventive, poetic character of literary language is likewise a provocation to complex patterns of thought and action. A characteristic definition of the literary in the modern age is that it not only says new things but uses language in new ways to do so. The literary or poetic, in this sense, always implies pushing language into unfamiliar forms and paths, producing perceptual shifts and shocks by putting words together in surprising ways. This process produces a kind of variety that readers must initially encounter as uncoded: it exceeds their initial interpretive grasp by being outside the forms and usages they have encountered. But because it can be assumed or intuited that much of this noisy, uncoded variety can in fact be decoded, and will turn out to be part of a poetic mode of signification specific to the text in question, the difficulty of understanding becomes a stimulus to constructing more complex understanding. The encounter with the literary text thus becomes a cultural apprenticeship of complexity, of negotiating situations where the recognizable is mixed with the unfamiliar, information bound up with noise.[12] To have virtual experience—by means of reading—in coping with such situations is to be better prepared to participate appropriately and nonreductively to analogous interactions in other spheres of life. Complex verbal narrative constitutes a technology for encountering and knowing the real, for preparing oneself to negotiate the twists and surprises of life in the world.

ALTHOUGH the metaphors of steering and feedback evoke the circulation of information, as distinct from matter or energy, they do so in a context of devices and physical systems. Of course they are also human metaphors—the original *kubernetes*, the steersman, was a human being using his senses, wits, and muscles to realize the control circuit governing the ship's course on the sea. It may seem, however, especially in an age of ubiquitous automatic control systems, that the helmsman is a human being acting the part of a machine, like a lonely

---

[12] I develop this account of literature, its reading, and its cultural uses in *The Noise of Culture: Literary Texts in a World of Information* (Ithaca: Cornell University Press, 1988).

worker on an automated assembly line performing some irregular or flexible task for which no robot has yet been devised. The model of steering and control, in other words, while in many ways applicable to human behavior, derives more from the nonhuman, technical pole of collective life than from the human, cultural one.

We thus need a second figure for the use of culture in living in the world, one modeled on interaction with other human subjects in communities rather than with things in the material world. This figure, I propose, is that of dialogue, or—more accurately and generally—*networks of discourse.* The metaphor of dialogue is a traditional one to describe the scholarly or humanistic encounter between two minds, that of the reader or scholar and that of the often long-dead author. Despite—or perhaps because of—its attractive qualities of vitality and reciprocity, however, dialogue is a somewhat misleading figure for this situation, in that only one mind is "live" and the other is represented by written texts—texts that were not, in general, written so as to become part of "dialogues" in which readers try to cast them. Such written texts could be called, in Latour's terms, nonhuman delegates of humans, neither reducible to nor separable from their function as stand-ins for human speakers. More troublingly for the dialogue metaphor, readers and scholars don't primarily engage in one-on-one exchanges with singular authors: instead they read, quote, think with, borrow from, ventriloquize, rewrite, etc., a whole range of works in different genres and media. Dialogue, too, is by itself an overly Socratic, academic figure, implying the slow, reasoned conversation of a few individuals, whereas the symbolic transactions that matter in the humanities include the more urgent and disorderly speech of public square or parliament, the mimetic speech of the theater, the ritual speech of ceremony and worship. "Networks of discourse" should thus be taken as a generalization of dialogue, extended in space and time, to multiple, asymmetrical interactions in various forms and embodiments of language, including such object-like delegates of humans as manuscripts, books, films, and recordings.

To read, and then to think and sometimes speak or write on the basis of one's readings, to bring together readings in the mind or citations on the page, to conceive of the world via the language of poets and novelists and philosophers—to do all of these things, and others like them, is to engage in the making of networks in the field or medium of language. It is to extend the activities of human speech—conversing, listening, disputing, retelling, and the like—to the quasi-human, quasi-

objective category of texts. We could say that texts stand in, as delegates, for their absent creators from the past or from distant places, but
texts are always more than mere stand-ins: they are discursive entities in their own right, parts of the material, informational world in
which we live.

To participate in literary culture is to set up and use networks of language and ideas across time and space. This figure complements that
of steering on the basis of feedback: in making use of literary culture,
we intervene in networks of discourse on the basis of what we have
encountered in them. How does one go about changing and preserving the collectives that make up the life of the world? One major way
is to add to and modify their discourse networks, or, in other words,
to join in the ongoing conversations—oral, written, electronic, and so
forth—of their members—living and dead, known and anonymous. Of
course, one may also participate in discourse networks without making any attempt to steer the world: in this sense this model is more
general than that of feedback loops, since it includes within itself the
oppositional and tactical options as well as the strategic, purely disruptive negativity as well as efforts to change course. In a comple-
mentary sense, the model of feedback is more general than that of networks of discourse, since it includes the many processes of control and
interaction that proceed by nonlinguistic means and that often involve
nonhuman entities.

A principle of requisite diversity applies to the making and using of
discourse networks or generalized dialogue as a social activity: it is a
version of the principle that representative government requires genuinely representative, and thus—in a pluralistic society—diverse, representation. Networks of discourse are a form of extended representative democracy, a part of what Latour calls "the parliament of things,"
though perhaps somewhat closer to a "parliament of histories and cultures." To take in and react to works from the past, from other cultures and societies, and from the realm of the creative imagination is
to extend a kind of participatory citizenship to the dead, to members
of other polities, to invented beings. Of course this too is a metaphorical way of speaking because none of these beings participate directly
as subjects: it is their manifestation in quasi-human works that participates—whence the kinship between this notion of a parliament of
texts or works and the Latourian notion of a parliament of things. This
quasi-humanity underlies my recourse to *network of discourse* rather
than dialogue (or parliament) as a descriptive figure for these activi-

ties. To evoke a principle of requisite diversity or representativity in this case is to assert that in a culturally and historically complex world, structured in no small measure by residues of the past and crossovers from foreign societies and cultures and acts of inventive imagination, forms of discourse from these zones should be included in the conversations and networks in which the world, in both its human and nonhuman dimensions, is modeled and acted upon. In making writings from the past, for example, part of today's cultural and intellectual life, we enlarge the democratic conversation beyond the temporally, culturally, and imaginatively narrow scope of real people alive at the present day; we also expand the notion of conversation itself to include interaction with those nonhuman delegates known as texts.

In speaking almost indiscriminately of dialogue and discourse network in this context, I am deliberately turning my back on quarrels over humanism. It really does not matter much whether one uses the traditional humanistic figure of dialogue or a posthumanist, textual/ electronic figure such as "discourse network," as long as one understands that in either case one is working in a hybrid space, subject and object, social and technical. It has sometimes been assumed that the metaphor of dialogue, of the voice of the author, really implies the reader's passivity and submission to tradition, whereas analysis of the *text*, or critical scrutiny of the way texts go about making meaning, implies activity and contestation of the power received words have to shape us. By acquiring the critical faculty to become skeptical of all texts, according to this view, one becomes inoculated against the ruses of discursive representation. But both fear of the authorial voice and confidence in the liberating powers of textuality have been exaggerated. Texts written by humans are not mere expressions of human intentions and yet they are not just devices from which human intentionality can safely be removed. Embracing one extreme or another of dualistic alternatives will serve no cause but that of reductive stupidity. If we assume either that texts from the past are outmoded and therefore irrelevant or that they have an untouchable authority, external to our communities, we can learn nothing from them. If we suppose that culturally unfamiliar texts must be either dismissed as outside our traditions or admired as so authentically different that they are beyond our right to criticize, we will again learn nothing.

As Isabelle Stengers suggested, people who interpret cultural works should be able to address their makers with forthrightness and respect, though certainly not with deference or submission. Or, as Doris Sommer put it in a book about the resistance of minority writing to majority readings, "we should hesitate before dismissing the ghost" of the writer in a text: our awareness of a ghostly human presence may pull us away from the superficial supposition that the text is mere pretext for our work of interpretation, field for our free play.[13] Once we acknowledge that participation in the networks of discourse is at once dialogical and written, real-time and deferred, communicative and resistant, it becomes possible to see continuities, rather than oppositions, between the kind of intellectual exchange with texts of the past that Tzvetan Todorov called "dialogical criticism" and the ostensibly anti-humanist rhizomatics of Gilles Deleuze, who wrote of the response to reading: "It will never be asked what a book means . . . it will be asked with what it functions, in connection with what it does or doesn't transmit intensities, in what multiplicities it inserts and transforms its own. . . ."[14]

To sum up: since human reality is no single version of reality but an accretion of versions ranging from empirical realism to the most fantastic of fictions, culture needs fictions and poems past and present as part of its representation of its own latent possibilities. As Wallace Stevens wrote in a 1941 lecture, "it is not only that imagination adheres to reality, but, also, that reality adheres to the imagination and that the interdependence is essential."[15] The real-time life of the world needs the contributions of imagination, of past, of elsewhere, of fiction, and of literary language as part of the feedback signals it uses for purposes of control and invention, as part of the discourse networks it uses for cultural and political communication. In his essay on "Literature as Equipment for Living," Kenneth Burke wrote that "a work like *Madame Bovary* (or its homely American translation, *Babbitt*) is the strategic naming of a situation. It singles out a pattern of experience

---

[13] Doris Sommer, *Proceed with Caution, When Engaged by Minority Writing in the Americas* (Cambridge: Harvard University Press, 1999), 29.

[14] Tzvetan Todorov, *Literature and Its Theorists*, trans. Catherine Porter (Ithaca: Cornell University Press, 1987), and Gilles Deleuze, *Negotiations, 1972–1990*, trans. Martin Joughlin (New York: Columbia University Press, 1995), 10.

[15] Wallace Stevens, "The Noble Rider and the Sound of Words," in *Collected Poetry and Prose*, ed. Frank Kermode and Joan Richardson (New York: Library of America, 1997), 663.

that is sufficiently representative of our social structure, that recurs sufficiently often *mutatis mutandis,* for people to 'need a word for it' and to adopt an attitude towards it. Each work of art is the addition of a word to an informal dictionary. . . ."[16] To cope successfully with a world as complex as that of today, we need to maintain and strengthen our ability to use that dictionary's words.

History, culture, and politics are messier than virtually any theory of them would suggest, and a crucial reason to keep alive multifarious forms of knowledge, perception, and language is to acknowledge and grapple with that messiness and its attendant uncertainties. If history or even single epochs were all of a piece; if we could be confident of where history is headed, of how our present condition and modes of perception, thought, and discourse stood in relation to that heading; if, indeed, history could be safely described as progressive, so that the present state of affairs could be held to be an advance over previous states,then perhaps we could safely throw out the utterances of fiction and poetry, and texts left over from the past, for they would offer nothing but retreat, escapism, or satisfaction of idle curiosity. If, however, we are not sure where we are going, or whether where we are amounts to an advance over where we've been—if, therefore, it seems a bad idea to place our trust fully in the cultural here and now, and in constructions of what passes officially for being real—then it behooves us to listen to and network with textual voices from far outside our own society, from the past, from the inventions of story, poetry, and art.

[16] Kenneth Burke, *The Philosophy of Literary Form,* 3d ed. (Berkeley: University of California Press, 1973), 300.

5   Keeping Up with the Past

"THE TRADITION of all the dead generations weighs like a nightmare on the brain of the living." Marx's dictum sums up the fear many have of giving too much weight, in the making of cultural feedback and discourse networks, to inputs from the past. Isn't the continuity of books and literary culture one of the principal means by which this abusive influence of the past retains its force? If we are to escape from erroneous or oppressive ways of thinking that once flourished, shouldn't we give less heed to what was written down long ago, bidding good riddance to works that lend charm and prestige to ideas and assumptions we may well find useless, annoying, or unacceptable? Such characteristically modern questions may contribute to a sense that a major format shift in media and human attention, driven by technology, is coming none too soon to deliver present generations from the rigidity of print, the thralldom of old books, and the dead hand of dated ideas.

In this chapter, I will offer the decidedly nonmodern argument that it is unwise to give up on literary culture, to encourage teachers and students to turn away from it on the grounds of its technological or social obsolescence. If the "format changes" now taking place lead to a reduction in contact with the works that, in Kenneth Burke's formulation, make up part of our equipment for living, then the human ability to use language and thought to chart courses in the world will have been diminished. A loss of interaction with the textual traces of the past would impoverish education and culture, because—contrary to common opinion—the study of the past is less an escape from the world of the present than a means of encountering the conditions for making the world of the future. This is not, however, an argument for preserving the status quo. Literary culture and especially literary education will have to change considerably, perhaps radically, if they are to adapt to new conditions and to remain—or once again become—an attractive and dynamic force, something that will quicken the pulse of those who care about understanding their life in the world.

Considerations like these do not pertain to a purely intellectual or aesthetic realm of ideas or works; they belong to a material world of embodied thought, mediated communication, and situated knowledges. Any thinking done about these matters has to include the media—in the broadest sense, that of all possible networks of mediation—through which any connections between literary culture writ small and the life of the world writ large must pass. The processing of cultural feedback and the making and navigating of discourse networks require mediated communication.

We could say that the situation and future of literary culture depends on the interplay of technology and ideas—all the more so if we accept the lesson of science studies that ideas and technologies couldn't exist independently of each other in the first place. If there were no dissatisfaction with bookish ways or with the educational role of literature, then the possibility that new media could supplant print would be neither as attractive nor as threatening as it seems to be. Conversely, of course, if there were no new technologies, no new ways of storing and transmitting language and images, then disaffection with the existing cultural order would be far less capable of expressing itself as a critique of print or literary culture in general.[1]

As I noted in chapter 1, there may be something strange and even troubling about the comparatively direct access to texts of the past that the printed codex has provided over the last few centuries. Is it

---

[1] Nietzsche's essay, "On the Utility and Liability of History for Life," is in many respects a critique of print culture, though not explicitly formulated as such. See *Unfashionable Observations*, trans. Richard T. Gray (Stanford: Stanford University Press, 1995), 83–167. To an ancient Greek, Nietzsche writes, the "historically cultivated moderns" would be "walking encyclopedias" (110–111): " 'Are these still human beings,' we then ask ourselves, 'or are they perhaps merely machines that think, write, and speak?' " (119). He describes scholars as hens who lay ever smaller eggs "although the books have only gotten bigger" (136). The cultivated moderns have become blasé spectators incapable of being aroused for more than a moment by even great wars or revolutions, for "before the war is even over, it has already been transformed into a hundred thousand pages of printed paper" (116).

really a good thing to be able to go on receiving, with so little effort, so little sense of strangeness or unfamiliarity, messages sent one hundred, two hundred, four hundred years ago? To us it may seem normal that books from centuries past are still readable, and are actually read, but this persistence of the book format is no more natural than the gradual modification of an oral or manuscript tradition, or the obsolescence of last year's computer, or the incompatibility of a previous decade's diskettes; it's a product of technology and social organization like any other, perhaps a very odd one.

Oral cultures don't preserve their stories and traditions forever, though they may hold part of them fairly steady as they pass them from speaker to speaker over time. They certainly have nothing like the long-term access to fixed statements and accounts that writing, and especially printed books, have offered modern society. A digital culture in which massive format changes consign a large part of the cultural record of the past to near-oblivion every decade or so won't be the same as either print culture or oral culture, but it may be just as good as either, and of the three cases print may strike many people as the real aberration.

It has thus become possible and perhaps necessary to ask the question, "Are technological and social changes making literature a thing of the past?" The safest answers, of course, are "maybe" and "who knows?" Mountains of novels are still being published; there are about as many literature professors as ever; and it seems that Jane Austen and Henry James, through the delegate objects known as their novels, have found full-time work in the movie industry. On the other side of the coin, the proportion of college students majoring in English or foreign language and literature has been dropping steadily for a generation, and literary reading appears to play a diminishing role in the socialization of children and adolescents. Books, the vehicle for most of what we call literature, now compete for interest and attention with a greater quantity and variety of communications media than at any time since Gutenberg invented movable type.

Literary culture could thus lose, because of changing practices in communications and education, a significant part of the attention still paid to it today. Would this be a problem? Should anyone care about this possibility for reasons other than nostalgia or the protection of professional turf? One thing should be clear: what would change most is the relation of present-day culture to its past states. The present can keep up with its own cultural creations: whatever their format, it belongs to their era. But if society goes through a major "format shift" in cultural communication, its contact with the culture of previous eras— a printed, literary culture no longer easily readable—will probably be much reduced. A substantial loss of attention paid to books and literature would mean diminished cultural revisitation and recycling of the past as embodied in books—less contact with the works, problems, idioms, achievements, and embarrassments of times gone by.

A shift away from the habit of reading books would gradually make printed works obsolescent, rendering them stranger and stranger to the minds and habits of those who might read them. I use the term obsolescent rather than obsolete, because there would be no complete incompatibility, nothing like being unable to stick a vinyl LP into a compact disc player. It might be compared to what years of disuse have done to one's ability to speak or read a foreign language studied long ago. A still better analogy might be that of reading a manuscript from the Middle Ages, linguistic difficulties aside: even if we understand the words, follow the argument or the story, we may at the same time realize that we don't know how to be the readers of this manuscript in the way some people doubtless once did. If the languages of print and literature become less familiar, it will be just that much harder to pay attention to writings from the past; writings of the print era could become as estranged from the present as those of the manuscript era are today. Works written for print, or of the type written for print, can be transferred to computer media, but will generations raised in an electronic and audiovisual mediasphere care about them or know how to attend to them?

This potential loss of familiarity matters because interaction with works and materials from the past is crucial to the humanities. In the sciences, research from the past is gradually synthesized or superseded, its enduring parts summarized in textbooks rather than read in their original form. But in the humanities, the oldest surviving works can be just as seriously and attentively read as the most recent ones. Saying new things about, and by means of, words from long ago and far away has long been a central activity of literary culture, and this is one of its most distinctive features within the larger cultural formations of which it is a part.

As I noted in the introduction, the belief that new communications technologies can produce salutary changes in the human self implies that the world will benefit if the reading of books—sometimes stigmatized by hypertext theorists as "linear" reading—becomes a less dominant cultural practice. The literary past is also suspect, in the eyes of many students and scholars, because it often seems lacking, according to current criteria, in cultural diversity and because the teaching of works from past centuries was long associated with the compulsory organization of literary study along the lines of national histories. As a result, while explicit arguments against studying the past are rare, there is an undercurrent of resistance to granting it too much educational importance, to making temporal or chronological depth an organizing principle of literary curricula. (Whence the "dead" in "Dead White European Males.") There is less support than there once was for the view that directing attention away from the present to the past should be one of the central features of education in the humanities.

I suspect that the qualms about the past in contemporary literary culture have a parallel in the aversion felt by many in the humanities to strong claims on behalf of scientific truth, to the idea that science tells us about things out there whose forms, behavior, and existence are beyond our control. When physicists claim to define—or to be on the verge of defining—ultimate reality, when evolutionary psychologists announce that certain features of behavior long believed to be cultural are hard-wired in our brains by the ruses of our genes, they seem to be an unelected few who are interpreting forces and promulgating laws said to transcend the processes of politics and culture. Similarly, in Marx's nightmare and its many more recent avatars, the past appears to be that which summons and confines the culture and politics of the living with a voice of authority that comes from the undeparted dead.

The rush to leave behind the multiple epochs of history to concentrate on the contemporary, understood as the time over which living cultural communities have control, thus resembles the flight from the complexities of human and nonhuman collectives to the supposed autonomy of culture and of specific cultural formations. Focusing on our own time offers the humanities an extension of autonomy that entails major risks of increased isolation: the same delectable bargain that is offered by setting aside the material, biological, technological, and economic spheres of the world. The proper antidote to this temptation lies no more in submission to the authority of the past than in acceptance of transcendent natural laws. Just as it is important to understand that science and its discoveries are part of culture and politics, even while involving actors and entities outside humanity, so we should recognize that the past as we know it is something constructed in the present and yet constructed with the participation of things and people of another time. Material and mental traces of the past are not authoritative but untimely, differences that we articulate rather than traditions to which we must submit. To engage in serious commerce with the past is not to transcend political or cultural communities but to extend them in time. The literary past, I will argue, is a source of variety that is crucial to attempts to know and act in a complex world—complex not only in space and culture and materiality but in time, in its multiple relations to its own histories and prior imaginings.

A COMMON and often implicit argument for reforming education through placing more emphasis on images and electronic communications environments, and less on print and literature, goes something like this: the world is increasingly a place where what really matters in communication, what really reaches and affects masses of people, is the audiovisual and the electronic. This is where culture is going to take place, where much of politics will take place; it is a social space of growing importance. Not only in human communication, but in economic transactions, the world is electronically linked in real time. The Internet and related networks are the essential media of the economically linked, globalized world, and thus, at least potentially, they form the crucial space of the kind of global citizenship needed to address the transnational, hybrid problems of this interdependent world. Literary culture, by contrast, has often been nationalistic and elitist, especially as it has been used in schools and colleges; moreover, it may be inherently incapable of responding to, or helping people to understand, the new dynamics of worldwide exchanges, trade, communication, and citizenship. The age of the computer, the transmitted image, global networks, and virtual reality is upon us; schools had better get with it and stop trying to impose print literacy by fiat. In sum, the world has changed, and culture and education need to keep up to date, adapt themselves to the new form of the present.

This argument contains a crucial grain of truth. Culture and education ought to provide people with the means to understand the world as it is and to situate themselves, their lives, and their communities within it. These objectives should loom large for everyone concerned with knowing, interpreting, and teaching. To the extent that new media are a significant part of the world and of our means of knowing it, they must be a significant part of education. As for the teaching of literacy and the practice of literary culture, not all of their habits, traditions, and biases can or should survive in the new and coming era. Some of their most strongly print-based features—for example, the sharp separation between authors and readers, between elite and mass markets—will almost surely have to go. Yet to assume that the present must be closely identified with new technologies and communications media, and then to insist that cultural life and education should follow suit, is to oversimplify matters in a potentially dangerous way.

There is a powerful tendency in modern Western culture, perhaps best exemplified in the writing of universal histories and philosophies of history in the nineteenth century, to confuse a dominant cultural formation or a single place with an entire era. Universal histories conflate space and time: the "story of civilization" moves forward through chronology from the Near East to Greece to Rome, and after a somewhat less sharply defined though clearly European passage through the Middle Ages, arrives in Italy with the Renaissance, advances to France for the age of Louis XIV and the early Enlightenment, only to embark for England and Scotland to catch the beginnings of the Industrial Revolution, stop back in revolutionary France, and then cross the Rhine into German romanticism, and so forth. Of course at any given moment, people were living and making history in all these places and in many others, but the narrative assumes that each age should be represented primarily through its most innovative, powerful, or otherwise characteristic country.

This kind of structure often holds sway as well in thinking and writing about the history of technology: the ages of moveable type, of the steam engine, of the automobile—and more recently the jet age and now the computer age—all seem clear in our minds, and give shape to our sense of how people in each of those eras lived and worked. Likewise in the history of ideas: it is fairly customary to think that in the Age of Enlightenment people were animated by a critical spirit, that during the romantic era they turned both inward to their imaginations and outward to nature, that in our own century they have undergone the shock of the new in their encounters with art and the city, become preoccupied with their unconscious in accordance with the teaching of Freud, and felt their selves fragmented, dissolved, and reconstituted as ironic performances in the epoch of poststructuralism and postmodernism.

All of these developments in geopolitical dominance, technology, and ideas have their importance and do indeed mark their eras. But they are never the whole story. Life and history go on in the places and times passed over in the spatio-temporal trajectory of universal history. More to the point, technologies and ideas accumulate and coexist; accretion, not substitution, is the principle of their development. Take an everyday object of our own time, a car. It's often said that cars, like everything else, have gone digital: they have at least one on-board computer to control their engine, and in many cases more computers or at least digital information-processing devices to control other functions. But cars also have roofs and doors, early and fundamental technologies of human shelter; wheels, a famous neolithic invention and a basic part of land vehicles ever since; suspensions, not wholly unlike those first worked out for horse-drawn carriages around two hundred years ago. They contain much steel, a mass-produced material ever since the Industrial Revolution; internal combustion engines, whose basic principles were worked out at the end of the last century; rubber tires that would be recognizable to our grandparents, and so on. (Of course, there are losses as well, things that have dropped out: the wood of wheels and carriage bodies, the crank to start the motor, the polished or painted metal of unpadded dashboards.) In other words, for all its microchips, a car carries technologies and performs functions that indicate areas of continuity between the present and many different moments of the past.

This accretion of properties and technologies from different eras can be found not only in objects but in institutions. Consider the social and economic arrangements involved in the production and use of the car described above. Private property goes back millennia, corporations and stocks some four hundred years, assembly-line manufacturing over a hundred. Although superhighways are a creation of the last fifty years, the rest of the road network was built up slowly over centuries, and the institution of central governments building roads over large territories goes back at least to the Roman Empire. The unions representing the workers who assemble the car are the creations of nineteenth- and early twentieth-century social struggles, while the practice of "outsourcing" many of its components, often to shift work away from unionized workers or to countries with low wages, is much more recent. The car is usually priced for sale, at least in the United States, via a haggling process handed down from horse trading. Governmental authority to regulate its exhaust and safety features goes back some thirty years in the United States, but the Constitution under which such authority can be legislated is a product of eighteenth-century politics and thought that would surely not be adopted today if it were not in place as a holdover. (Once again, of course, many institutional features of the past have faded away as well: in labor-management relations in the U.S. auto industry, for example, both the violence of the twenties and the complacency of the sixties seem as out of time as can be.)

I offer this admittedly simple example to point out that whether we look at technology, institutions, language, or people, the present includes many things that have not changed much in a long time. The human being as creature was shaped by evolution over at least a million years, and has probably not changed much during the era of recorded history, even if today the body is sometimes repaired and supplemented by impressive surgery and high-tech add-ons. Languages change faster than the human organism, but to speak or write one today is to use words, expressions, and figures of speech that go back hundreds and in some cases thousands of years. Political, religious, and social institutions come down from a wide range of epochs. In doing something as simple as driving to the store and buying groceries, a person acts in continuity with an enormous range of practices begun long ago, such as gathering food, exchanging money for goods, and using a wheeled vehicle, combining these long-standing ways with others characteristic only of the very recent present, such as paying with a debit card and worrying about the cholesterol content listed on food labels.

It is thus absurd to suppose that we will soon leave our familiar world behind and enter an electronic or digital age. Claims that any new technology can usher in a new kind of world, utterly altering previous patterns of relationship, are vastly overstated. There is much talk of how modern medical and communications technologies are transforming the body and extending the sensorium, but despite the magnitude of current and impending changes the continuities with millennial pasts still outweigh the innovations. Many people, for example, wear eyeglasses, use hearing aids, or walk with ceramic hip joints, some using blood pumped to their legs by a heart with a plastic mitral valve. Changes in diet and the availability of antibiotics have modified the function of the human organism on a broader scale. Nonetheless, most of any person's body works the same way human bodies have worked for at least thirty thousand years, the way hominid bodies have worked for a million. Behind the glasses or contact lenses, such crucial features as binocular vision and peripheral motion detection continue in the form they evolved under prehistoric conditions; the hearing aid user follows conversations in a language whose grammar and lexicon, while always changing, have been recognizable for centuries.

In the sphere of communications media, the most sensible commentators on change always recognize that new techniques tend to be added to old ones rather than to replace them: television did not replace radio and neither of them replaced newspapers—which did not replace letters and gossip. Computer media may partially displace print and diminish the attention given to it, but are unlikely to replace it outright. Nor do the techniques, energies, and structures of "postindustrial" society replace those of its industrial predecessor: big companies with hierarchical organizations keep mining the earth and employing factory workers to produce substantial widgets, even if most consumer durables have at least six microprocessors, industrial companies have Web sites, and white-collar employees network over e-mail.

Much skepticism and a little resistance are thus in order when we are told that the world is entering the digital age and should accordingly hasten to educate its young people and organize its cultural life through digital media. The digital age may be as good a tag as any for what is conspicuously new and transformative about the current era, but if a label like this leads people to think that all experience or reality is now structured by digital media, then it is having a misleading and distorting effect. Terms like "digital age" or "postindustrial society" often function as textbook examples of James's "vicious intellectualism," which presumes the representativity of inadequately representative concepts, names, or abstractions. "Postindustrial society" powerfully suggests not only that a certain mode of industrial social organization has lost its dominance in the most economically "advanced" nations, but that the whole industrial age has been superseded, as if service, knowledge, and information sectors had replaced manufacturing—as if the hot, heavy, dirty, energy-consuming world of factories and industrial products had been replaced by a cool, light, clean world of offices and showrooms where small quantities of energy power ever faster and more capable computers. But of course energy use for industry and transportation is still enormous, and grows as more countries industrialize. Heavy industry has not disappeared, but rather has lost much of its hold on the collective imagination—in part because it is no longer a new and salient phenomenon, in part because it has been largely relocated to provinces or countries where its conflicts and problems are less visible. This material and economic situation, in which what we often take to be past and present still co-exist, corresponds to Latour's insight about the nonmodernity of the allegedly modern and postmodern worlds.

It is thus crucial to remember, when thinking about the role of literature, print culture, or any cultural product or formation from the past, that many institutions, practices, and assumptions associated with the print era are likely to persist for a long time, just as books are still being printed and read today. Liberal democracy, freedom of religion, and freedom of the press are arguably print culture institutions, and no amount of speculation about "electronic democracy" has even begun to suggest how they could be replaced. And as long as these and many other print-era institutions persist, works of imagination and reflection from the era of their formation and flourishing will continue to be a useful resource for understanding society and culture, not only of the past but of the present.

The past, in other words, is never really left behind: its residues are most of what makes up the present, sometimes with a large dose of reworking and reinterpreting, sometimes as relatively unchanging carryover. Furthermore, the decision to leave aspects of the past behind should be just that—a decision, made as democratically as possible, and not simply the consequence of acquiescing in a so-called march of progress. Thus if culture is to be used in education to help form an understanding of (and engagement with) the world, it is foolish, counterproductive, and fatalistic to rely on present-day or very recent culture alone. But, the reader may wonder, if the present contains so much that emerged in the past, can't the same be said for present-day culture, namely, that it too contains the past, so that we don't need the books of the last century any more than we need a time machine that could take us back to the era of the Civil War? To a degree, that's true. The most recent of cultural productions are not *sui generis* and they trail with them, directly or not, elements of the past. However, literary works, works of art, and *all* utterances that implicitly or explicitly represent or evoke a part of their world must necessarily reduce what they represent to something simpler than itself. One major tendency governing that reduction, at least in societies where historical change is considerable, is for works to focus on what is dominant or what stands out by being new, rather than on the full range of residues from many past times that actually make up the world they're talking about. They often emphasize, reflect on, and/or criticize the newest or most recently dominant features of their time and place.

The novels of Stendhal and Balzac, for example, which are often credited with inaugurating a new type of fictional realism that dramatizes recent history and current social and ideological conflict, foregrounded what was newest in French society around 1830: the interplay of money, press, and parliament; the conflict between the restored aristocracy and the increasingly prosperous upper bourgeoisie of finance and industry; the choices facing individuals in a society with little consensus on basic questions of political legitimacy. To the extent that these aspects of institutions, this kind of class conflict, still persist in today's society, the nineteenth-century novel, aesthetically dated though many may find it, remains one of the most powerful and freshest means of representing and conceptualizing them. A novel from 2001, in representing society, will often concentrate on what is most characteristic or distinctive of recent times, just as did a novel from 1830. So if we want to be reminded of what survives from 1830 in our own ideas and our own society, then we are probably best off reading the novel from 1830, and in so doing to engage in a dialogue between the novel and what we know about the world of 2001—part of which we learn from recent novels. As I noted above, industrial society persists, but it has become old news, at least in the most developed nations of the West, not the strange new phenomenon to which Dickens reacted in *Hard Times*.

Moreover, the continued reading of novels and other literary works from the past provides a dimension of understanding, and of verbal and conceptual enrichment, that is not provided by the study of history. For one thing, literature brings together the general and the particular, the abstract and the concrete, in ways that virtually no other discursive forms do. Fictional narrative swoops down from the heights of national events and social trends to details of interior decoration, gesture, and personal feeling; its perspective zooms out from the concrete minutiae of private life and material existence to the generalizations of philosophy and morality. Literary works thus articulate types of relations characteristic of their moment that leave scant traces in other genres. Even more important, perhaps, is that when we read, say, Flaubert's *L'Education sentimentale* instead of (or in addition to) a history of the French July Monarchy and Second Republic, we are reading words not simply *about* the past but *from* the past. We are complicating our knowledge of and ability to use a language—in this case, French—through an encounter with a text from that language's past;

we are, despite the inevitable changes in meaning and usage that come with the passage of time, experiencing something of the very word patterns, rhythms, and constellations of ideas and thought processes with which Flaubert and his contemporaries represented, imagined, and articulated their world. It is, of course, possible to read nonliterary historical documents, since these also provide something of this experience, but in general they have less ongoing appeal, less ability to bridge the gap of time. They often seem merely old, of "purely historical interest," as the saying goes, whereas the imaginative and indeterminate qualities of fictional and poetic works give them a continued freshness that enables them to bring something of the past into the present in a more lively and engaging form.

A society whose culture and educational system neglects (or forgets how) to read earlier literary works, such as nineteenth-century novels, will thus become not only a more present- and future-oriented culture but also a thinner, flatter, less verbally proficient culture. It will have become less capable of comprehending its own situation and development by virtue of having neglected a major residual mode of communicating within itself. In other words, although we are unlikely to transcend the conditions we associate with print culture, we may, if we emphasize temporally restricted, present-centered modes of communication over all others, become less and less well equipped to understand and engage those aspects of culture and society about which works from the past have the sharpest insights.

Although literary works often stress what is new and distinctive about the era when they are written, they can also harbor complex relations with the past and with residual aspects of their culture. Ever since romanticism, literature has often identified itself with interests that preceded and resisted the many perceived ruptures of modernity, from Newtonian science to the Industrial Revolution and on down to the uneasiness many writers and critics feel today at the prospect of technological obsolescence that haunts the printed book. As Lionel Gossman put it in an essay on literature and education, "the rediscovery and rehabilitation of the primitive world of origins—of the feminine, the maternal, the popular, the infantile—and the creation of a unified and total culture without ruptures or exclusions was a major enterprise of Romantic poetry, historiography, and philology."[2] In more

---

[2] Lionel Gossman, *Between History and Literature* (Cambridge: Harvard University Press, 1990), 36.

general terms, literature has long had an affinity for exploring what Virgil Nemoianu has called "the secondary," i.e., the cultural eddies and backwaters behind the dominant flow of development—the residual ideas, feelings, and ways of thinking and seeing that at any moment have been left behind along the major route society is taking toward its future.[3] This has been especially the case under the assumptions and interests of modern literary institutions—roughly speaking, those that have been in place ever since the market replaced patronage as the dominant mode of economic life in letters, and since literature came to be identified essentially with written works in the imaginative genres of poetry, theater, and the novel. Literature's tendency to tarry over the archaic, the dominated, the neglected byways of cultural development, may be more than ever one of its distinctive features now that print is under suspicion of obsolescence. Literature is beginning to seem "secondary" not only in its content but in its very form, and is thus both menaced with a new level of irrelevance and gifted with new possibilities of differentiation from the most prominent interests of the present day.

In addition, cultural artifacts such as literary works are shaped by, and respond to, the histories of their forms or genres, the works that have gone before them. Different forms of cultural production bear the mark of their respective paths of development; they carry within them something of the conditions inherent in the moments when their genres were arising and flourishing. Literary works refer implicitly and explicitly to their predecessors, sometimes simply through the way they respond to conventions and expectations, sometimes through specific allusions. Novelists work in a genre largely shaped in the eighteenth and nineteenth centuries, though continuously updated; lyric poets work in a form whose basic properties go back to the Troubadours. Joyce's *Ulysses* borrows its structure from *The Odyssey*; Borges and Kathy Acker play with *Don Quijote*.

This relation of cultural production to its own antecedents is by no means unique to literature or writing. As anyone who takes film seriously knows, the visual language of cinema and the audience's ability to read it depend on its development in prior works. Films allude to earlier films, both in content or theme and in such matters as camera work, the nature and rhythm of editing, the types of shots used, and

---

[3] Virgil Nemoianu, *A Theory of the Secondary* (Baltimore: Johns Hopkins University Press, 1989), xi–xv, 3–25, 173–203.

so forth. In the case of film, this kind of engagement with the past can go back to the end of the nineteenth century when the Lumière brothers filmed a group of workers coming out of a factory in Lyons. For television, the earliest allusions are likely to be to programs of the fifties, when the medium was freeing itself from the influence of radio and when viewing became widespread enough to leave behind a significant collective memory.

In literature, of course, the possibilities for "looking back," for reinjecting something of the past into present-day creation, extend much further back in time—back to Homer and the Bible, to invoke only the major Western reference points. Thus literary works, even the most recent, are apt to draw on a longer-term range of historical moments than do newer media with shorter histories. Pynchon can make use of eighteenth-century language and novelistic convention to produce the stylistic pastiche so essential to his *Mason and Dixon,* but a movie about Bougainville's voyage around the world can't draw on the look or conventions of eighteenth-century cinematography. Essayists work in a genre shaped by Montaigne's temperament, his publishing practices, and his use of quotation, digression, and addition, but the director of a television essay on PBS cannot conceive of how a sixteenth-century camera crew or editor would have framed or cut Montaigne. These examples are overly simplistic, to be sure. The shaping of the literary present by the pathways and traces of the past is usually a subtle process, one that is not consciously identified as such but that gives the written word multiple resonances over a long span of time.

There are two major reasons to care about our access to a broad temporal spectrum of culture. The first, as already suggested, is that the world of the present is no smooth well-integrated whole that can be understood solely in the context of currently dominant modes of organization, but is instead a conglomeration or accretion of entities and activities formed at many different times and in a wide variety of contexts. Cultural texts from the past can thus help their readers and students to understand the complexity of the present. Moreover, the cultural past is important because it provides perspectives outside the reach of the present, outside the dominant influences now shaping thought and action. Even those many features of past works that seem to be of no relevance to understanding today's world can be extremely important in showing that the range of human possibilities is larger than what a given society or even the entire world offers at any given time. This is not to say that culture lies outside of history, or that people or works can transcend their era, or that anyone should aspire to a timeless, objective contemplation of human history and culture and the possibilities they offer. You do not *transcend* your culture by turning to cultures of other peoples and other times; you simply add features to it, extending and multiplying your perspective without ever making it universal. The past need not and should not be used as a source of external authority over the present, but acknowledged as the major source of the present's own temporal complexity. With some help from the works of cultures distant in time and/or space, you can manage to equip yourself with other concepts, forms of perception, ways of speaking and thinking. You can manage to cast sidelong glances at your more immediate world, never becoming a universal observer, but with luck a somewhat less parochial one.

Nietzsche tried to describe and advocate the use of the past to enlarge and open the present in his great essay, "On the Utility and Liability of History for Life," perhaps better known in an earlier translation of its title, "On the Uses and Disadvantages of History for Life." Referring to his own field of classics, which was then the major discipline devoted to the study of temporally distant cultures, Nietzsche wrote, "I have no idea what the significance of classical philology would be in our age, if not to have an untimely [unfashionable] effect—that is, to work against the time and thereby have an effect upon it, hopefully for the benefit of a future time."[4] His essay is, among other things, a scathing critique of a superficial historical culture, of the tendency in scholarship, education, and middle-class cultural life to use the works and records of the past as an entertaining, consoling, or prestigious diversion from the challenges of living in the present and building the future. It is a call not to bury the past so that it will cease to intrude on the present but to engage the past seriously so that it will trouble the present in quickening, vivifying ways.

Nietzsche has harsh words for the idea that a general acquaintance with a broad range of cultural achievements from the past can suffice to form a liberal, cultivated outlook. "Its result, when viewed in a vulgar empirical manner, is the historically and aesthetically cultivated philistine, the quickly dated up-to-date babbler about the state, the church, and art, the *sensorium* for a thousand secondhand sensations,

---

[4] Nietzsche, *Unfashionable Observations*, 87 (translation modified). Subsequent references given in parentheses.

an insatiable stomach that does not even known the meaning of genuine hunger and thirst" (160). In some respects the recent shift of emphasis in the humanities—away from historically comprehensive literary curricula and toward contemporary concerns, recent culture, and issue-oriented, politically engaged teaching and research—responds to Nietzsche's call to cast aside accumulative erudition and connoisseurship and instead bring knowledge of the past into projects for acting on and in one's own time. The advantage that much activist and Cultural Studies scholarship has over literary historical or formalist work lies in its vigor and sense of moment: because it embodies a project for the future, it has stronger motives for existing than scholarship or teaching that aim only to satisfy curiosity or provide cultivation.

Unfortunately, however, attempts to reform literary curricula so as to make them less out of step with the diversity of present-day society, or to keep them from reinforcing and lending aesthetic prestige to inegalitarian institutions and values, often wind up reducing the attention paid to works of the more distant past, even as they enlarge the geographic and cultural diversity of what is looked at from recent years. Activist scholarship and teaching also run the risk of relating to the past in judgmental and thus ahistorical ways, condemning or approving elements of it, in a characteristically modern gesture, according to today's presumably clarified standards. This sort of judgment borders on making the past safe for the present, on organizing and arranging it in a fashionable or timely way so that it does not intrude or disturb too much. (And yet there are dominant and emergent aspects of the present as deserving of resistance as any scandalously outmoded residues of the past.) In addition, the recent activism characteristic of academic literary culture tends to frame its project for the future primarily in terms of issues in which the cultural and subjective poles of collectives predominate—problems of power, fairness, access, and identity, for example—and not their natural and material dimensions. Nonetheless, for all their limitations, attempts to make the humanities an active force in constructing a just future have a strength and a conviction that are all too often lacking when literary and humanistic studies are pursued as exercises in appreciation, edification, or pure curiosity.

In arguing that the humanities should continue to pay close attention to the literary past, therefore, I am not suggesting a return to formalistic or literary historical concerns, nor do I wish to imply that knowledge and appreciation of cultural works from the past can constitute an educational ideal or program. And in suggesting that politically and socially oriented criticism has focused on an overly narrow set of questions, I mean to advocate not a return to supposedly timeless questions of esthetics or "enduring values" but instead—as I argued in chapters 3 and 4—an enlargement of what is understood by the political and social so as to include, rather than sidestep, some of the most important features of today's transformed world: its long networks and large-scale systems, notably those of economics, ecology, technology, and science.

The view that the influence of the past should be reduced—if necessary simply by cutting back the attention paid to it, the place accorded it in educational and cultural practice—goes hand in hand with a view that present-day, living generations should have as full control as possible over their destiny, that the possibilities of the current historical moment should be developed as much as possible and with as little inertial resistance from what has been left behind by those who have gone before. This may sound like a reasonable position, especially if the alternative seems to be submission to a starchy construction of the past brandished by those in power as a transcendent source of authority. In fact, however, the impulse to flee or condemn the past entails two great problems, which come from opposite directions. The first is that if we think not of a few ideas, doctrines, or texts but of the totality of human affairs, the idea that present generations can determine their destiny is so far from reality as to be absurd. The second is that, given this situation, attempts to remake the world according to the dictates and desires of the present alone are necessarily reductive and abusive, and potentially totalitarian. According to the imperative to bring the world up to date, the "is" (or "is becoming") of history implies an "ought" of morality or politics—the better to reinforce and ensure the triumph of the "is" or "is becoming" as understood by whoever is interpreting it. When pushed to its limits, this kind of argument implies both an impulse to homogenize the world in the present (by eliminating residues of the past) and a perversion of morality via historical relativism ("whatever is, is right"). And who would want to live in a world completely ordered according to the ideas, imaginings, and wishes of one's contemporaries?

History is no smooth succession of homogenous eras, each one complete and coherent in itself; rather, change and inertia are always mixed together, with different aspects of the human lifeworld enduring and changing at varying rhythms. If this is the case, then it is vain to hope that at any given time this world can be radically remade, though of course crucial aspects of it can and will change much more rapidly at certain times than at others. And, to return to the questions of literary culture that are the real issue here, if culture is to be used in education to help form an understanding of the world, it is foolish to rely on contemporary culture alone.

It's worth remembering, as Michel Serres likes to point out, that the present moment isn't necessarily the most important or the wisest one in history just because we're living in it.[5] (Of course, living in it gives the present a special kind of importance for us, but that importance doesn't include a monopoly on truth or knowledge or even pertinent thinking.) The present is made up of far too many pasts to be reduced to something as temporally thin as the present, but if in some sector of culture access to the past is curtailed, that sector risks becoming temporally solipsistic, overconfident of its own rightness. If fiction from the past, for example, were no longer read, the result would be that fiction would suddenly have become a much more solipsistic and reductive source for learning about the world, even the world of the present itself.

Of no less importance, the decision to go on networking with the literary past provides a concrete opportunity to resist the modernist temporality of inevitable, unidirectional development, of progress always experienced and understood as the globalization of communications and markets, the expansion of technoscience, the extension of rationality and economism to ever more areas. Do we want to live among books or in the World Wide Web? Doubtless in both, in various degrees depending on who is answering. But the most striking features of the question are, first, that for much of humanity neither books nor Web are within reach, and, second, that for those who believe in a certain march of progress, it is an absurd thing to ask. Of course we will get the Web, they say, and books will rapidly become residual. Yet an enlarged vision of democracy, along the lines suggested by Latour's nonmodern constitution or his expanded conception of political ecology, would provide for more explicit choices about what kinds of technologies and communications to have, what sort of networks to build, what manner of technosocial environments to live in. Decisions about what to do with the written past, the culture of codex

---

[5] See Michel Serres, with Bruno Latour, *Conversations on Science, Culture, and Time*, trans. Roxanne Lapidus (Ann Arbor: University of Michigan Press, 1995), 48–52.

and print, can be seen as a modest opportunity to convene a "parliament of things" and have a say about the kinds of networks among which humanity will go on making its history.

I WANT to close this chapter with a brief plea for the compatibility of my emphasis on the past with the goal of cultural diversity in the present. The two are no more than superficially at cross-purposes. It is far from certain that a turn away from literature to the creations of high-technology media will foster genuine diversity in cultural attention. Because of rapid changes in cultural markets and the technological and economic resources needed to compete in them, the electronic and audiovisual present runs the risk of being less diverse in its cultural creations than virtually any past, including the residual literary culture that is still producing new works today. In other words, there is every reason to fear that electronic and audiovisual media under global capitalism are promoting sameness, or more precisely a superficial, market-niche-driven diversity, rather than fostering expression by the plethora of local cultures the world has produced over the long term. Highly technologized media impose much of their own form on those who work with them, demanding adherence both to their own complex technical constraints and to the current (and transitory) consensus on how information needs to be presented so as to maximize its reception. Print may be obsolescent in many ways, but its very familiarity, one might even say its banality and its increasingly residual character, means that the formal constraints it imposes on would-be cultural producers are relatively low and familiar, and this enables its appropriation in many contexts and to many purposes. Web sites, as dazzlingly varied an array as they may seem, resemble one another more than do poems, because poems derive from longer, looser, and above all more multiple traditions, ultimately connected to the diversity of local and regional cultures and languages as they have developed and changed over the long term.[6] Thus attention to the cultural creations

6 The late Octavio Paz contrasted poetry's temporal depth with the presentism of those who aim to set politics right: "... the uniqueness of modern poetry lies in its having been the expression of realities and dreams rooted more deeply in the past than in the intellectual geometries of the revolutionaries and the conceptual prisons of the utopians. [...] ... poetry is the *other* voice. Its voice is *other*, because it is the voice of passions and visions. It is otherworldldy and this-worldly, of days long gone and of this very day, an antiquity without dates." *The Other Voice*, trans. Helen Lane (New York: Harcourt Brace Jovanovich, 1991), 150–51.

of the past, and to lower-technology, historically rooted creations of the present such as literary works, may well prove to be an important strategy for preserving and involving cultural and geographic diversity—no matter how demographically small and narrow the community of poets and their readers may seem in comparison to the community of Web surfers.

The history of media change, which is one of nonmodern accretion as well as modern replacement, strongly implies that print, and the literature now associated with it, will survive, and that even if they are more and more perceived as residues of the past, they will have a place in the new mediasphere in which they are no longer dominant. What kind of place this will be will depend in large measure on the implicit and explicit choices before us concerning the forms and practices of literary culture. It is up to today's communities of literary culture—including readers, teachers, students, scholars, and writers—to invent and preserve ways of using literature that lead away from the here and now, that expand minds by giving them something of the multiple languages, stories, and concepts that have taken form in words at other times and in other places.

6 Reinventing "Language and Literature"

A New Media Environment

IN THE LAST three chapters, I have tried to propose new ways in which the literary humanities could conceptualize, practice, and/or enlarge their intellectual missions. Such proposals, however, are unlikely to do more than add to an already dispiriting cacophony of ideas unless they are accompanied by changes in the internal practices, legitimation strategies, and institutional situation of the literary disciplines. If literary culture is worth continuing, if it is to have a dynamic role in the future, then its institutions need to be adapted to the media environment of today's transformed world, a world radically different from the one in which modern literary culture took shape.

Scholars and teachers need to bring forth practices and institutions that will help make literary culture pertinent to articulating experience, knowledge, and desire in the world as it is today, not as it was in the nineteenth century when the contours of literary culture were becoming familiar, or in the late 1960s when literary education received the impetus for its last major reconfiguration. Communications media are changing rapidly and will continue to change; there is virtually no possibility of restoring the dominance of print. At the same time, everything in the prior history of media suggests that changes will continue to be additive or accumulative: print and books will not disappear because of electronic media any more than speech disap-

peared because of writing.[1] Whether printed books, and the texts written to go into books, will persist on a scale comparable to that of
speech, or handwriting, or radio, however, remains to be seen. There
is uncertainty and room for maneuver concerning the future role of
print and, more important, of the literary culture so strongly identified with it. There are, in other words, opportunities to shape and define the role of the written word and of literary culture in a largely
electronic and audiovisual mediasphere.

Now that print has lost much of its dominance among media, it is
also losing—and needs to lose—its pretensions to universality, the illusion that it was the natural and obvious way to communicate about
almost anything. The emerging media environment thus provides an
opportunity to confront the specificity of print and the literary within
culture, to map their niches in the ecology of communication. What
is print most useful for in comparison to other media? When and why
are reading and writing preferred forms of communication? What can
students get by reading and working with literature that they can't
get as successfully from other cultural forms? How does the experience of reading, especially of literary reading, fit in with other cultural practices? Print and literature, exiled (but also liberated) from
the dubious privileges of dominance, from being confused with communication and culture in general, will increasingly find themselves
confronted by these unsettling and exhilarating questions. I can only
begin to address them in this final chapter, with the hope that my observations and proposals will encourage further thought and invention from others.

Language and Literature

IF NEW MEDIA do not replace the old but are instead added alongside
them, if the culture of the past and the inventions of fictional and poetic language are as relevant to living in the world as any of today's
cultural spectacles, and if—above all—the kind of technological and

---

[1] A recent book on technology and the humanities that is very lucid on this point
is James O'Donnell, *Avatars of the Word: From Papyrus to Cyberspace* (Cambridge:
Harvard University Press, 1998).

social institutions we have in the future is a matter of human choice and not of techno-economic fatality, then there is no general reason to turn away from literature. As I've suggested, there are many particular reasons to maintain and reinvigorate its cultural role in the face of the admittedly powerful forces working to consign it to a bygone past. We scholars should be prepared, then, to give up or transform some of the features of literary culture, especially in its academic incarnation, in order to preserve and extend the networking between past and present, far and near, that takes place when people read and respond to literature. To harrow the soil of autonomous literary institutions so as to foster the profusion of literary hybrids, to cultivate rampant networks linking literature to the world and its people rather than to tighten and refine the networks of the literati—this is the non-modern alternative agenda I wish to place before literary culture. Its first order of business should be a revitalization of the connections between language and literature.

Literature is of course made of language. Although written, printed discourse is in some ways distanced from readers, and lacks the reciprocity of oral communication, works made of written language retain a direct connection, in their very stuff, with the words we use to think and talk to ourselves and to talk to one another. And this connection is stronger in literature than in many other forms of writing. The language of poems, novels, and plays, though it is by no means identical to spoken language, usually has a stronger connection to oral culture—to storytelling, gossip, dialogue, proverbs, and word play, for example—than do administrative reports, laws and rulings, user's manuals, or many other forms of written discourse.

That literature uses language, as does almost every person past infancy, should be regarded as a most important feature of literary culture. This was acknowledged negatively by Stéphane Mallarmé, who complained that the ubiquity of literature's linguistic medium hampered attempts to purify poetry into a sphere of abstract, formal beauty and invention. Mallarmé tried as hard as anyone to turn poetry into a pure and autonomous art, its works and practices accessible only to initiates. And yet, in an early article, he complained with undisguised peevishness that language is seriously compromised as the medium for such a project *because too many people use it*. The same printed characters so carefully placed by the poet on the page are spread all over the newspaper, every day! If only poetry could have something

like musical notation, he groused, so as to keep out those who don't
know anything about it.[2]

Literature's reliance on everyday language, which Mallarmé saw as
a scandal and a liability for the autonomy of poetic art, I see as a
tremendous asset—one so obvious, in a way, that it has been insufficiently noticed or utilized. Teachers and students of literature should
remember that its specificity (along with that of other forms of serious writing) as a cultural practice lies in its use of language and thus
in its potential connection to the writing and speech of its readers. The
sharing of language helps assure that literature will always have a
fuzzy, permeable border with other kinds of discourse—with history,
autobiography, memoir, diaries, letters, anecdotes, everyday conversation, journalism, even memos and reports. More important, there
can be interpenetration and influence between the ways of language
in literature and those of everyday speech. To read and study the literary written word is potentially to add to one's own repertoire of language, to be exposed to ways of augmenting and transforming one's
capacity to speak, write, and think. When the reader temporarily appropriates the language of a writer, she is adding something to her brain
that she can use in kind: you can think with and against new words,
new relations between words. There is an overlap between the language with which you express yourself to others in speech and writing and the textual languages from which you have learned. They are
never, of course, identical, but they belong to a continuum, not to separate domains. It is much more possible to respond in this way to texts
than to images, or even to mixed forms such as television shows, films,
and virtual reality games, which use language, to be sure, but which
are also powerfully structured by using images and sound in a technologized way that most people cannot begin to answer in kind—
whether in their heads or their hangouts or their homes.

The French philosopher Maurice Merleau-Ponty developed this idea
in *La Prose du monde*, an extended meditation on literature and language written around 1952 and posthumously published in 1969.
Painting (and presumably the art of images in general), he wrote, "is
recorded only in works and cannot manage to underlie people's daily
relations," while "man feels *at home* in language as he never will be

---

[2] Stéphane Mallarmé, "Hérésies Artistiques. L'Art pour tous," in *Oeuvres com-
plètes*, ed. Henri Mondor and G. Jean-Aubry (Paris: Bibliothèque de la Pléiade, 1945),
257–60.

in painting."[3] The reader, in reading, takes on the author's language, undergoing a kind of identification with the specific possibilities of thought and perception that this language brings. The process can begin, of course, because language is socially shared and thus can serve as an instrument of communication, but reading only becomes significant, and transformative, when the reader begins to adapt to what is particular, unique, and *not* entirely shared or predictable in the writer's language. Words undergo "a secret twisting" in the hands of the writer, leading readers in thought and perception to places they have never been (12). Reading Stendhal, he writes, is an operation that winds up "establishing in the mind of the reader, as a now available instrument, the language of Stendhal" (13). When a book works in this way, it becomes a kind of perceptual and mental prosthesis, for the reader "lets [the book] transform him and grant him new organs" (22). This effect of literature, according to Merleau-Ponty, is akin to what happens in a genuine dialogue with another person, in which one goes beyond conventional or ready-made forms of expression so as to understand and be moved by the other's singularity: in both cases, the operation is one of active reception and influenced response.

The American novelist, philosopher, and art critic William H. Gass has likewise suggested that works in language offer possibilities of appropriation and response not found in nonverbal forms of expression. Imagining the conversation at a dinner party, Gass writes that

> all these words are but humble echoes of the words the poet uses when she speaks of passion, or the historian when he drives his nails through time. . . . Even if the world becomes so visual that words must grow faces to save themselves . . . we shall never talk in doodles over dinner, or call up our spirit to its struggle with a little private sit-com or a dreary soap. Could we quarrel very well in ink blots, or reach a legal understanding in the video arcade?[4]

The language of poets and historians matters, Gass argues, because it enlarges upon, and thus enriches, the language human beings use in

---

[3] Maurice Merleau-Ponty, *The Prose of the World*, trans. John O'Neill (Evanston: Northwestern University Press, 1973), 110, translation modified. Subsequent references given in parentheses in the text.

[4] William H. Gass, *Habitations of the Word* (New York: Simon and Schuster, 1985), 208.

social conversation, in carrying on and resolving disputes, and—most important, perhaps—in talking to ourselves, that is, in using language as an internal instrument of thinking, feeling, and desiring. Language, he tells us, could not be replaced in these contexts by visual or audio-visual forms of communication, because we do not make use of such forms either to talk to ourselves or in most of our encounters with others.

It's true that Gass was writing over a decade ago, and that if you turn to media theorists today, there's a good bit of brave new thinking on behalf of making images and hypermedia into a space of discourse where everyone can, as it were, "talk" back electronically in doodles or video. In *Imagologies*, Taylor and Saarinen write, "Since image has displaced print as the primary medium for discourse, the public use of reason can no longer be limited to print culture. To be effective, writing must become imagoscription that is available to everyone."[5] Now we may or may not see such universal imagoscription and we can imagine that for at least a very long time it would be far less democratically shared than Taylor and Saarinen dream of its becoming. The populist promise of computing ("in a few years, these things will be so cheap that everyone will be able to afford them") seems to be forever deferred because of the spiraling commercialization of technological advances in microchips and the increasing complexity of software: your old computer is worth only a fraction of what it cost five years ago, but to keep up with the ever increasing bandwidth of the internet, you need a new, more powerful one that costs almost as much as ever. Since this dynamic keeps significant computer access from extending very far downward on the worldwide ladder of wealth, imagoscription for the masses always remains a long way off.

In the meantime, it seems worth remembering that there still is—and probably always will be—something fundamental about language as a vehicle of human communication and sense-making; because of this, *verbal* texts remain, in comparison to other forms of cultural production, peculiarly central to the formation of human minds and thus to the educational and cultural tasks of fostering thought and its expression. People lead their mental lives and live with one another by means of words, in the milieu of language. And if the need for well-used words as means to thought and knowledge is taken seriously, if

---

[5] Mark Taylor and Esa Saarinen, *Imagologies* (London: Routledge, 1994), "Communicative Practices," 4.

people are to think about their lives and their place in the world in ways that matter, then they can use the kind of quickening to life and its singularities that literary texts sometimes offer, the refreshing of perception that comes from unfamiliar and inventive language, the interface that fiction and poetry provide between language, society, sensation, and emotion. These features may be difficult to equal in media less oriented toward language, more dependent on long chains of technical mediation, such as film, television, and the creations of hypermedia and the Web.

As Merleau-Ponty implied, people can respond in kind to literature simply by virtue of being language users. Their own use of language in thought and speech can be affected whether or not they "write back" or "talk back" in some explicit form. They do not need to be painters, sculptors, Web-site designers, or expert users of digital audiovisual systems to do so. They do not need to use language in the same medium of transmission in order to remain within the continuum of language. This is not to say, however, that different technologies of the word do not shape people's disposition and ability to respond to them. New and highly technologized media increase human exposure to forms of communication to which we cannot respond in kind, at least not directly, and this may inhibit the larger possibility of response to language through language. Print itself, as the high tech medium of its day, was already subject to this problem: though its readers can respond implicitly and indirectly via their use of language, along the lines suggested by Merleau-Ponty, most of them do not write for print, and so do not respond in kind as directly as is the norm in oral (or even manuscript) culture. Nietzsche's "cultivated philistines" and his scholars "read to ruin" by age thirty were typical avatars of the reader as bulimic devourer of printed material. They could, of course, still respond in language, and their reading could augment and shape the language they used to think and communicate, but the input/output ratios could get so far out of balance as to be stifling or inhibiting—to make it difficult, for example, to shift to the kind of balance needed in conversation. (This is the well-known problem of pedantry.) In a classic essay, "The Storyteller," Walter Benjamin describes the reader of novels as a consumer of information, a being far more passive than the storyteller's listener, who could shift to an active role by retelling the story to others.

The preponderance of images and highly technologized audiovisual effects in new media brings a different danger of passivity, not that of talking like a book or feeling disempowered into silence by the distant and superior tone and status of authors, but that of being the spectator of a slew of images and words that require little imagination or activity to understand and imagine. This is why the television viewer risks greater passivity than the reader. The Web surfer, though capable of interacting and intervening in certain ways and thus more active than the television viewer, is still largely a browsing spectator, a consumer of words and images even when not an outright consumer of the products they advertise.[6] In this new media environment, in which print is no longer high-tech—as it was in Nietzsche's day—but low-tech, the works in language embodied in print can and should take on a new role in formation of active participants in culture.

The tendency toward passive cultural consumption can perhaps best be countered through new kinds of cultural and pedagogic practices that aim to use the experience of reading so as to enlarge people's capacity to think, speak, and write in ways that clarify and intensify knowledge of self and the world. The connections between literature, other cultural works in words, and everyday language are today more central than ever to the survival and cultural value of literature. Conversely, as we see the written word and the cultural reservoirs that reside in it displaced from their former position of dominance, it becomes pointless and counter-productive to maintain hierarchical, social, and aesthetic distinctions between genres of written works, between the guild of authors and the public of readers, or between the naive credulity of unschooled readers and the skeptical sophistication of critics. Now that literature embodied in books has thus lost much of its aura of cultural inevitability, literature ought to be valued and

---

[6] Much of the commentary praising computers for offering their users creative empowerment and interactivity now sounds somewhat dated, a holdover from the era of "personal computing," when it seemed plausible that universal access to computers would a bring a great measure of equality and reciprocity to the communications environment. Aside from the fact that universality of access is continually being deferred into the future, the development of the Web as an entertainment and commercial medium has made reciprocity and empowerment recede even further toward the horizon: individuals may, to be sure, have their own Web sites, but they hardly compete for attention on an equal basis with the sites of organizations that can invest heavily in dazzling graphics and in the acquisition of proprietary information. As a result, computer networks continue to provide the conceptual promise of interactivity—and some genuine spaces and possibilities for it—while encouraging minimally active, grazing spectatorship on a large scale.

read not so much for its absolute distinction from the words and speech of everyday as for its integral connection to the ordinary language that it both echoes and expands.

In colleges and universities, literature is mostly taught in "language and literature" departments: English Language and Literature, Romance Languages and Literatures, Germanic Languages and Literatures, and so forth. They bear these names in part because their faculty often includes linguists as well as literary scholars, in part because students begin—in the case of foreign languages and literatures, at least—by studying the language and then turn to literature once they have achieved some ability to read, speak, listen, and write. (Similarly, in English departments, a course in written language, usually called composition, generally precedes introductory courses in literature.) The curricular relation between language and literature, in other words, is largely sequential: first you master the foreign language (or the conventions and techniques of formal writing in your own) and then you advance to the study of literature. When this type of curriculum was put in place in the late nineteenth-century American university, literature printed in books was unchallenged as the serious and exemplary cultural material from which to learn once one knows enough of a language to make reading possible. Today, however, there are far more options, because language has been materialized in far more forms than print. In the study of foreign languages and literatures, in particular, recent generations have seen increased tensions between the traditional assumption that language should be followed by literature and the more eclectic and "multimedia" contacts with cultural productions that students routinely enjoy and expect. Many professors, meanwhile, have come to see the ethos and nationalistic ancestry of literary studies as overly conservative, its emphasis on canonical literary works as a distraction from the more important task of teaching students to think critically about the popular culture in which they are immersed. "Language and literature" is thus often denounced as a rather tired curricular model, too instrumental in its view of language and too exclusive in its emphasis on literature as the cultural payoff for achieving linguistic mastery.

Gandhi is said to have remarked, à propos of "Western Civilization," that "it would be a very good idea." I would say the same thing about "language and literature": old-fashioned and criticized as it may be, it's a pairing that was not taken seriously during much of the twentieth century, and I think it would be a very good idea to give it a try in the twenty-first. The sequential coupling of language and literature—master language *and then* study literature—does not really exploit or explore their intimate connection. Often stigmatized as an unholy alliance of the instrumental and the elitist, "language and literature" has not really existed, at least not as a central principle of literary education, since the decline of the rhetorical teaching of literature toward the end of the nineteenth century.

Pedagogies

CULTIVATING the connection between language and literature implies transforming the literary pedagogy developed under print culture in this century—and such a transformation, fortunately, is already under way. It implies the use of technologies both old and new—and both are available. It calls for putting new technologies in their place—and many people are already reacting against the exaggerated millennial potential so often ascribed to them. There are, in other words, good reasons to believe that a renewal of the educational and cultural potential of literature is possible.

As the printed word, and thus the written and literary word, faces increasing competition from media and forms far more dependent on the image, literary pedagogy has to let go of habits it picked up when print ruled the roost unchallenged, habits that often made the study of literary works into a bitter pill or a test to separate the strong from the weak. Gerald Graff has shown that late-nineteenth-century professors of literature faced the task of "making English as difficult as Greek" so that it could become a respectable university subject.[7] The project of producing difficulty typified the teaching of literature in the twentieth century: given that the reading of printed texts was the obvious, self-evidently dominant mode of acquiring information, literary study could define its special niche by demanding that reading be subtle and problematic. Its mission became that of questioning and corroding everyday, instrumental, and pleasurable modes of reading books while sorting students out according to their ability to interpret difficult texts under severe intellectual constraints. But now that the

[7] Gerald Graff, *Professing Literature* (Chicago: University of Chicago Press, 1989), 38, 74.

printed word has lost its communicative hegemony, we literature professors cannot afford this kind of monopolistic stance. We have to teach literature in ways that make it attractive and engaging vis-à-vis other cultural forms and practices.

It seems likely that reading and writing, if they are to survive and hold interest, will have to make more and stronger connections with their roots in orality—in storytelling, play, and performance. This is, of course, a major rationale for the widely offered prescription of having parents and other caregivers read aloud to children: children will be more comfortable reading if they have been able to make a gradual transition from oral to written language, and their desire to read will be greater if it has been nurtured by association with the human closeness of listening to familiar voices.[8] (Reading aloud is certainly not the only activity that fosters children's entry into reading: active cultivation of other aspects of speech, such as conversation and word play, are also important in raising children who will be at ease in all dimensions of language.)[9]

To read aloud is to draw on the power of the spoken word in service of the written, to fuse literacy and orality. As a technique to build interest in reading, it has been used not only by parents but by classroom teachers, and not only in the earliest grades. In a best-selling essay on the pleasures of reading, *Comme un roman*, the French high school teacher and novelist Daniel Pennac tells how he reads aloud to get "difficult" students interested in literature. Pennac, the author of many children's stories and the popular series of Malaussène novels, realized that as a teacher he could not just assume that his students were already readers—from whom he could demand the analyses, commentaries, and interpretations dear to twentieth-century literary pedagogy.[10] So he would often begin a literature class by getting out a big fat novel and starting to read it aloud to his class. Many of the students

[8] See Jim Trelease, *The Read-Aloud Handbook*, 4th ed. (New York: Penguin, 1995), 1–223.

[9] For an extensive and intelligent discussion of the interdependency of orality and writing in education, see Kieran Egan, *The Educated Mind: How Cognitive Tools Shape Our Understanding* (Chicago: University of Chicago Press, 1997), 33–103, 181–84, 210–37.

[10] Daniel Pennac's essay, *Comme un roman* (Paris: Gallimard, 1992), has been translated into English in both North American and British versions: *Better Than Life*, trans. David Homel (Toronto: Coach House Press, 1994) and *Reads Like a Novel*, trans. Daniel Gunn (London: Quartet Books, 1994).

responded by continuing to read the novel, and then others, on their own. Pennac's point is not that reading aloud is a panacea, or that literary education can't go beyond it, but that reading will only be embraced by young people today if they are in touch with what makes it pleasurable. And the possible pleasures and unpleasures of reading exist in the context of what Debray calls the contemporary mediasphere. When students feel the reading of novels to be in continuity with storytelling, they find it attractive; when they feel it to be in competition with movies and television in the presentation of visual material, as when they struggle with the long descriptive passages of nineteenth-century fiction, they find it deadly.

Written language, in other words, no longer a hegemonic medium, must be allowed to do what it does best. The function of textual works within the new mediasphere is both to provide the kinds of awareness and knowledge best conveyed via writing and to enrich the speech, thought, and writing of their readers. If the teaching of literature is to adapt itself to these tasks, it needs to change accordingly—as, unofficially, it is surely already doing. Long oriented to reinforcing print's hegemony as a medium and literature's distinction as a genre, and more recently attuned to a theoretical and critical scrutiny of language, literary pedagogy needs to become more interactive and invention-oriented—borrowing a leaf, perhaps, from the discursive spaces of electronic computer media but without giving up on the print-era texts in which so much of culture and history reside. We need to rethink the teaching of literature at all levels so as to encourage reading that stimulates responses in kind, whether in thinking or speaking or writing.

The new electronic technologies, if they are not taken as The End of the Book, can help print and literature overcome some of their own most dubious features. The future media environment in which books and literature will thrive (or fail to do so) will be strongly shaped by the electronic and the audiovisual. Electronic communications are changing the social and institutional conditions of reading and writing, the meaning of "publication," and the roles of authors and readers. As it becomes easier for anyone to reproduce either printed or electronically displayed writing, the distinctive position of the writer as provider of copy to the printing press becomes diluted. New technologies, even if their practical consequences in the book publishing industry have so far been limited, thus foster the idea that readers are also potentially writers, that speech and writing circulate and recombine with more fluidity and reciprocity than was the case under the social regime of print culture. In the emerging media environment, writing and literature can become less and less a medium in which authors are distinguished from readers, producers from consumers, and more and more one in which these roles are provisional and subject to exchange. We should therefore be able to stop treating the author as either intrinsically dead (and thus negligible) or as a larger-than-life presence (whom we need to declare dead in order to save ourselves from suffocation). Increased reciprocity and respect between writers and readers should encourage the realization that the language of each person's thought and expression can be altered and enlivened by contact with that of others.

One way to do this is to give more explicit attention to the connection between reading literature and writing—to exploit the fact that English departments contain both literature and creative writing programs, that foreign language departments teach conversation and composition as well as literature and culture. Henry Miller affirms in *The Books in My Life* that it is through writing that one can become a better reader, and through "reading one's favorite authors that one becomes supremely aware of the value of practicing the art of writing." He points to the strange one-sidedness of most reading and to the cost of this practice in unrealized potential stimulation and development of the reader's mind:

> If it is a book which excites and stimulates us to thought, we race through it. We cannot wait to know what it is leading to; we want to grasp, to possess, the hidden message. Time and again, in such books, we stumble on a phrase, a passage, sometimes a whole chapter, so stimulating and provocative that we scarcely understand what we are reading, so charged is our mind with thoughts and associations of our own. How seldom do we interrupt the reading in order to surrender ourselves to the luxury of our own thoughts! No, we stifle and suppress *our* thoughts, pretending that we will return to them when we have finished the book. We never do, of course. How much better and wiser it would be, how much more instructive and enriching, if we proceeded at a snail's pace! What matter if it took a year, instead of a few days, to finish the book?[11]

In effect, Miller is saying, the reader slides comfortably into the position of literary consumer or spectator or student, hooked on enter-

[11] Henry Miller, *The Books in My Life* (New York: New Directions, 1969), 36, 131.

tainment, novelty, and information, reading on so as to find out what happens or to be able to write the term paper. Miller's view of the typical reader's acquisitive haste parallels Walter Benjamin's portrait of the reader of novels in "The Storyteller": driven by a burning desire to find out what happens, the reader "destroys, he swallows up the material as the fire devours logs in the fireplace"[12] This easy path, at once greedy and passive, is all too typical of print-culture reading. It blocks an alternative potentiality of literary culture, namely, that of stopping to think about what you learn from reading, of talking back (at least in your own mind) to what you read so as to develop your thoughts and your language for expressing them. In the oral culture of storytelling with which Benjamin contrasts the reading of novels, the hearer of the tale learns to become its teller.

There are clear indications that pedagogy has begun to move—both with and without inspiration or practical help from new technologies—in a direction Miller and Benjamin would have applauded: away from the split between writing and reading. One sign of this incipient transformation is the increasingly common practice of requiring students to keep reading journals, a form of student assignment that encourages students to record and explore the ideas they pick up from the texts they read, ideas about human psychology and society, insights into history, examples of words memorably used. Perhaps an even more striking harbinger of pedagogical change is the related but distinct practice of assigning creative writing projects, often pastiches or other forms of imitation. On the basis of anecdotal evidence gleaned in many conversations, I believe that pastiches and other forms of creative writing assignments related to literary readings have become much more common over the past decade, often without much official or institutional notice that this is what is happening. It would only be a slight exaggeration to say that every literature professor believes that he or she and a few like-minded colleagues are striking the first blows for this silent revolution.

This type of assignment reduces rather than reinforces the distance between famous literary writers and the potential or incipient writers—and, in any case, users of language—who are our students. Jacques Bourgeacq points out that imitating the style, turn of phrase, vocabulary usage, and music of literary authors "constitutes a particularly

[12] Walter Benjamin, "The Storyteller," in *Illuminations*, trans. Harry Zohn (New York: Schocken, 1969), 100.

productive school of composition" and also leads to "precise reading" and to the experiential realization that "no text is ever completely transparent or gratuitous."[13] This kind of writing also encourages students to *respond to* their readings in an open-ended, emergent, and constructivist vein, rather than being expected to *account for* texts within explanatory paradigms (whether old or new, traditionally edifying or radically critical). Pastiches and other creative assignments are often used as small additions to courses in which traditional themes or critical essays remain the main focus. In my own experience (and that of Bourgeacq) they work best when they are made one of the principal activities of a course and become the object of active discussion and preparation by groups of students.

The pastiche (or imitation, or continuation) can, of course, be presented as primarily a stylistic exercise, and it is a very good one, often enabling students to get a close feel for what makes a text tick. But it can also be presented as a process of inquiry and knowledge-production, as an exercise in thinking and imagining through specific forms of literary language. If one writes, for example, an episode of one's own childhood in the manner of Rousseau's *Confessions* or Camara Laye's *L'Enfant noir*, one must experience something of the self-knowledge that their specific kinds of writing make possible, and encounter their blind spots as well. This technique allows the author to be conceived not as authority but as process and procedure; the students' task becomes that of enlarging their own knowledge and repertoire of expression by letting themselves be temporarily borne along by the otherness of a style and a certain narrative logic. The making of pastiches can be understood as a written version of vocal imitation, just as responding to literature through journals or creative pieces can be conceived as a form of dialogue. Students can also be encouraged to use pastiches and other forms of imitative writing as occasions to experience and think concretely about the interplay of individual invention and conventional scripting in the making of culture.

---

[13] Jacques Bourgeacq, "Le Pastiche: pédagogie de la langue et de la littérature," *French Review* 71 (1997): 20. This article is the first published discussion of this phenomenon of which I am aware in my own field of French studies; the situation in English is far more complex, with much commentary published in composition circles on nontraditional forms of student writing, but less focus on the role of literature, probably because of the sharp professional division between composition and literary studies.

A sense of writing as procedure, influenced by forces of chance and constraint, can also be conveyed through formal and combinatorial exercises in literary writing (or transformation of previous writing) of the type cultivated and publicized by the (largely French) group *OuLiPo*. A contraction of *Ouvroir de Littérature Potentielle* (Potential Literature Workshop), OuLiPo was founded in 1960 by the mathematician François Le Lionnais, and the polymathic writer Raymond Queneau. The basic idea of the group was to use combinatorial and algorithmic methods, often involving the adoption of difficult constraints and/or the injection of arbitrary doses of randomness, to produce new literary texts that presumably would not have been thought of using more conventional techniques of invention and composition. One key example is the *lipogram*, whose writer adopts the constraint of not using one or more letters of the alphabet so as to be forced to use the remaining subset of language in unfamiliar ways. The best known example of this technique is arguably George Perec's novel *La Disparition* (in its astonishing English translation, *A Void*), which eschews the letter e; Perec followed it up with another example, *Les Revenentes*, which, like the phrase "eschews the letter e," avoids the four other vowels.[14]

The pedagogic point of such a seemingly strange exercise is to reconceive the composition of a text as a process or game rather than as an act of inspiration or genius. Students today see obvious affinities between OuLiPo's techniques and the information-manipulating capabilities of computers: the techniques of OuLiPo could clearly be converted into algorithms for generating computer-authored or assisted texts.[15] Italo Calvino, who along with Perec and Queneau was the best known of OuLiPo's members, wrote that modeling the writing process as a material act of combining and permuting words, a task that might be assigned to a machine, corresponded better to his own sense of verbal artisanry than did traditional, idealistic, subject-centered notions of what writers do. "Writers, as they have always been up to now, are

[14] Georges Perec, *La Disparition* (Paris: Denoël, 1969); *A Void*, trans. Gilbert Adair (London: Harvill, 1994); *Les Revenentes* (Paris: Julliard, 1972); *The Exeter Text: Jewels, Sex, Secrets*, in *Three by Perec*, trans. Ian Monk (London: Harvill, 1996).

[15] A software package for creative writing based on Oulipian principles has recently been published in France: Antoine Denize, *Machines à écrire* (CD-ROM) (Paris: Gallimard, 1999).

already writing machines; or at least they are when things are going well."[16] He also saw affinities between such combinatorial composition and the methods of oral storytellers, who would recombine a familiar repertoire of figures, situations, and actions so as sometimes to come upon something new that would resonate with mythic significance among their listeners.

However bizarre the activities of OuLiPo may seem, however up to date and technological our metaphors for its games and for the related practice of pastiche may be, there is nothing postmodern or even very new about a pedagogical prescription for continuity and mutual influence between reading, writing, and speech. It is more like a non-normative return to *rhetoric,* that traditional practice of the ancient and medieval worlds. Rhetoric was already pushed away from the center of education and toward the domain of expressive ornamentation in the sixteenth and seventeenth centuries, and finally all but eliminated or driven underground, at least as a *literary* pedagogy, by the print-culture modernism of the twentieth century. A rhetorical teaching of literature implied the use of literary texts in the teaching of eloquence, of techniques for ordering ideas, of commonplaces and figures with which to illustrate them, of styles appropriate to different forms of subject matter and situation. The emulation of models and constrained composition were among its fundamental techniques. The young Denis Diderot's first assignment at boarding school in the early eighteenth century was to write the speech the serpent used to seduce Eve; a century and a half later, Arthur Rimbaud and his classmates were composing Latin verses with the aid of a handbook of rhymes, figures of speech, and topics.

This rhetorical approach to the teaching of literature—or, no less accurately, this literary approach to the teaching of rhetoric—was largely purged in the teaching practices associated with literary history and with modern critical formalisms and historicisms, all of which placed critical, scholarly, and student writing in discontinuity, rather than continuity, with the literary writing that is their nominal object. Twentieth-century pedagogy, in other words, largely made the writing associated with reading literature into an apprenticeship in (and thus an imitation of) critical or professorial commentary, rather than an

---

[16] Italo Calvino, *The Uses of Literature,* trans. Patrick Creagh (New York: Harcourt Brace Jovanovich, 1986), 15.

imitation of literary works or more generally a composition in the pertinent literary genre.[17]

The non-rhetorical literary pedagogy begun in the nineteenth century (whether historical, biographical, or formal, edifying or demystifying) treats literature as something distant to be analyzed and interpreted, spoken and written *about*, rather than as a set of discursive practices to be joined into. All this, we now can realize, was the pedagogy of the high print age, the epoch of literary autonomy and of the radical split between the guild of artist-writers and the public of consumer-readers. It was also the pedagogy of the age of C. P. Snow's two cultures, literary and scientific, the latter having a de facto monopoly on knowing the real and the former a self-appointed role as guardian of traditions, beauty, higher values, and the social distinction that accompanies disinterestedness. If literary works are gratuitous, self-referring artifacts, radically distinguished from other forms of discourse, then it is a travesty to imitate them or to learn from their contents, but it can be a respectable exercise in scholarship to explain them, or an act of quasi-literary invention in its own right to speculate on their formal inexplicability. If, on the other hand, literary works are understood to be strong instances of rhetoric and narrative—parts of the discourse networks by which human beings both register and invent their realities—then it is possible to learn from and interact with both their form and their content in multiple and unpredictable ways (with the proviso that *form* and *content* designate hypothetical extremes that never really exist without each other).

Two things must be made clear about this proposal for renewing rhetorical pedagogy. First, I am not saying that pastiches, constrained compositions, and the writing of personal reactions in journals should become the sole writing activities connected with the study of literature, or even that this study should be entirely rhetorical in nature. There is every reason to preserve the best features of current practices and also to try other forms of innovation. Second, the renewal of rhetoric should not (and, indeed, could not) imply using literature as a model for inculcating a single, distinguished way of writing—for assuring, in other words, the inheritance of upper middle-class cultural capital.

---

[17] See Judith Schlanger, *La Mémoire des oeuvres* (Paris: Nathan, 1992). On the late nineteenth- and early twentieth-century transition away from the rhetorical teaching of literature in American colleges and universities, see Graff, *Professing Literature,* 41–118.

That kind of model is too far gone to be restored, even if people were foolish enough to want to do so. As John Guillory pointed out in his magisterial study of literary canons, being familiar with literature or having a literary writing style carry far less social prestige than they used to.[18] Moreover, literary writing has become, over the last two centuries, far too varied and at times outrageous to function as a normative model for discourse. When the literary was defined by way of distinctions in diction and tone, it could serve as a model of gentility or refinement, but its entire history since romanticism has been to make it less directly suitable for that usage. Imitate Baudelaire? Joyce? Georges Perec? Kathy Acker? Hardly the stuff of either normativity or social refinement. Indeed it may well be that the pedagogic shift from imitating literary writing to imitating scholarly or critical discourse was a tactic for preserving a residual, normative role for literary studies in the teaching of writing when literature itself—at least in its most prestigious, challenging manifestations—had become too strange and unpredictable to serve as a model. A turn to rhetorical pedagogies of literature, then, should imply not a return to an outmoded model of linguistic distinction but rather the destabilization and diversification of styles, ultimately the production of creative, individual styles with shared elements.

The conditions of possibility for new forms of literary pedagogy are, moreover, marked by dynamic change rather than stasis or return to a lost past. With the rise of new writing technologies and print's loss of hegemony among materializations of language, literary culture's old hierarchical distinctions between the literary and the nonliterary, between geniuses who write Great Books and students who write criti-

---

[18] John Guillory, *Cultural Capital: The Problem of Literary Canon Formation* (Chicago: University of Chicago Press, 1993), 45–46, 63–82. Guillory notes that the literary canon, and particularly the linguistic norms it underlies, have long been a form of cultural capital distinguishing the dominant class, i.e., the upper bourgeoisie. However, he argues, recent reorganization of class structure and the corresponding modes of social discourse have given rise to a new kind of managerial-technical class for which literary culture and language no longer function as cultural capital to any significant degree: "The professional-managerial class has made the correct assessment that, so far as its future profit is concerned, the reading of great works is not worth the investment of very much time or money" (*Cultural Capital*, 46; see 45–46, 63–82). The social process described here by Guillory, I would argue, prepares and accompanies the technological shift that is diminishing the role of print, and thus of the literature associated with it, in education and socialization. As always, technological and social changes occur in tandem (see chapter 3, above).

cal essays, become ever more out of step with the material forms and practices of culture today. As Richard Lanham and others have pointed out, the cultural models, practices, and concepts that arise from electronic writing and networks help create the conditions for a renewal of rhetoric and thus for new forms of connection between language and literature. To be sure, I am far less optimistic than Lanham that the educational use of computer hypermedia will lead *directly* to a revival of rhetoric, since I suspect that what we gain from the new technology in flexibility and interactivity may well be more than offset by what we risk losing in diminished contact with a wide variety of works in written language, especially if we herald the shift to new media as the means of resolving old problems. I nonetheless agree with him that new media create a new environment for cultural practices and that those of us devoted to literary education must work with rather than against the new media environment. Remembering Latour's call for a nonmodern dispensation in which neither novelty nor tradition should be embraced for itself or even regarded as constituting a coherent option, we should try to identify and construct the most promising hybrids possible of old texts and new models for responding to them. Some of these models will involve the active use of new technologies, such as "writing back" to a classic print text in hypermedia; others may be as quaint as making entries in a leather-bound journal with a fountain pen, but all will have to offer something that can be experienced as pleasurable and rewarding in a dynamic world of cultural and communicative practices shaped by rapidly changing electronic technologies.

The Two Poles

MANY READERS may, by now, be shaking their heads in surprise or dismay over the course taken thus far by the present chapter. I have been calling for a literary pedagogy of pleasure rather than seriousness, of creative and personalized response to texts rather than an accurate or collectively shared accounting for them. Does this prescription belong in the same book as the brief for literary and scientific interdisciplinarity of chapter 3, the call to include literature in the practice of cultural feedback and the making of discourse networks in chapter 4, the praise of extensive cultural contact with the past in chapter 5? Moreover, mine is by no means the first voice raised in favor of rhetorically and creatively oriented teaching of literature and writing, and such a shift in the aim and focus of what we do with literature has already been stringently criticized.

David Simpson, for example, in an intelligent and well-argued book entitled *The Academic Postmodern and the Rule of Literature: A Report on Half-Knowledge,* indicts the tendency to substitute the telling of stories for the search for truth as a characteristic failing of both research and teaching in much of the humanities.[19] Concentrating on such figures as Richard Rorty and Clifford Geertz, Simpson describes what he calls the mainstream academic embrace of postmodernism in both the humanities and the social sciences as a retreat from more serious knowledge claims about either the real world (the domain of the empirical social sciences) or the structure of discourses and texts (the domain of an intellectually rigorous literary criticism and theory). This postmodernism, understood as a preference for what Lyotard called small narratives (*petits récits*) over collectively shared explanatory frameworks, amounts to the "rule of literature," he argues, because in preferring the making of stories, fictions, and new languages to the quest for truth, it generalizes the option chosen by literary culture since the beginning of the nineteenth century: the self-validating, autonomous, sometimes gratuitous invention of languages and forms as an oppositional alternative to scientific culture's pursuit of truth within consensual frameworks and to the bourgeois economy's insistence on practical efficacy. In a larger sense, the postmodernism of storytelling and self-fashioning is an avatar of rhetoric in its old quarrel with philosophy, its academic triumph a new victory for the Sophists in their 2,500-year posthumous war with Socrates and Plato. Simpson sees self-expressive and playful techniques for the teaching of literature—perhaps most prominently advocated by Jane Tompkins, in a series of articles and interviews and in an autobiographical memoir—as an extreme instance of this rhetorical and romantic turn that he considers widespread in the academy.[20]

My advocacy of an interactive pedagogy bringing together reading and writing notwithstanding, I agree with Simpson that the making of stories and the expression of subjectivities alone do not suffice as an

---

[19] David Simpson, *The Academic Postmodern and the Rule of Literature* (Chicago: University of Chicago Press, 1995).

[20] See Jane Tompkins, *A Life in School: What the Teacher Learned* (New York: Addison Wesley, 1996).

intellectual mission for literary studies or the humanities. And, like
Richard Lanham, I see the competition between rhetoric and philosophy as a necessary and constitutive tension in education (at least
within the Western cultural traditions that go back to ancient Greece).
My advocacy of a reinvented form of rhetorical pedagogy is much more
than a call to fiction and subjectivity. In the first place, it represents
an attempt to preserve contact with a diverse cultural past in a mode
compatible with the interactivity of the cultural present—and in a
manner other than that of prescribing cod liver oil. Moreover, imitating the style of an unfamiliar writer or the form of an archaic literary
genre is an exercise neither in expressing subjectivity nor in affirming
interpretive mastery over the text. Quite to the contrary: it is an experience of renouncing the privileges of interpretation and of bending
one's subjectivity to the constraints of otherness. It is a matter of enacting, via writing, something of the enlargement of self through contact with another voice or style of which Merleau-Ponty wrote when
discussing the reading of Stendhal. Of course it contains a strong element of individual creativity; of course the expression of subjectivity
will be part of the picture. But it is at the same time a testing and an
expansion of the shape of one's own subjectivity through the temporary adoption of unfamiliar languages and forms. Writing pastiches or
writing under constraints is thus the opposite of the despised but ubiquitous pedagogic practice known as paraphrase, in which literary contents are summarized in dull, up-to-date prose, usually under the cover
of claims to critical analysis.

   This being said, there remains a contrast between the intellectual
ambitions of the last three chapters and the pedagogic prescriptions of
the first half of the present one. The former are predominantly philosophical (in the broad sense of aiming for reliable knowledge of the
way things are) and the latter primarily rhetorical (in the no less broad
sense of cultivating forms of discursive expression and human interaction). The tension between the two is great enough that at one point
I considered having the section on rhetorical and creative pedagogy
serve, vis-à-vis the rest of the book, as a *palinode:* a coda that is also a
retraction. Perhaps, I thought, I have tried to take literature much too
seriously in suggesting that it can be thought about together with
knowledge of the natural world, that it can be a means to complicating and improving our engagement with a temporally complex present by providing access to the inventions and imaginings of the past,
that it can enter into processes of cultural feedback whereby we try to

steer a course for ourselves and for the world, or can connect to networks of discourse through which we relate to others and their textual delegates. Maybe literature is much more frivolous and gratuitous than I wanted it to be, valuable because it provides pleasure and possibly a bit of guidance for the parts of life that have as little as possible to do with the world on a grand scale—those matters of individual desire, pain, pleasure, and serenity that touch society only in the everyday ways in which people living their lives come into relation to one another.

What if literature and its culture were less like a great network of historical and cultural articulation stretched over space and time and something more like one of life's little pleasures, an embroidery, a discreet musical accompaniment, a modest supplement to the real that turns out to be just part of a richer-than-otherwise real? or a mode of human relations that resists the making of knowledge, the desire for mastery or control? A palinode to this effect, with only modest suggestions for keeping literature in local circulation after all those ringing declarations about its global import, would lead some readers to judge me inconsistent, but might well keep even more of them from writing me off as fanatical or totally un-cool. Reader, I would have said, it's your choice: accept the book's main argument or, if it strikes you as too serious or overblown, go with the palinode.

Friends can sometimes help us find things when we've lost them right in front of our eyes. I showed my colleague Santiago Colás an outline of my book-in-progress that ended with the palinode described above. "Does this palinode really have to be a palinode?" he asked me when we sat down to talk about it. I don't remember his exact words, of course, but the challenge he posed to me went something like this: "show us the connection between what you want to say in the main body of the work about literature and education for life in the political, economic, and ecological sphere, and what you say in the palinode about an education that contributes to having languages with which to live one's own life."

Indeed, I realized. Santiago had seen the central stakes of my arguments better than I had. Literature is something both very large and very small, serious and frivolous, solid and tenuous. A novel like *Heart of Darkness* can be a source of many insights into the era and society in which it was written and into the forms and language of fiction as such; it may be a crucial reference point for understanding the national literature to which it has always been assumed to belong and the alternate tradition of colonialist writing in which recent criticism has placed it; at the same time, it may be a magical or loathsome book to you or to me for very private reasons. *Madame Bovary* may be the prototype of modern novels, a fictional lesson in the delusions of fiction, but it is also that surprising book you read in French as a freshman, and your memory of how Flaubert's prose insinuated itself into your mind, teaching you that certain sound and shape of a French sentence. Every work has both public and personal significance for each of its readers.

To take part in literary culture is to shuttle between these two poles of literary experience: the vast domain of time and space over which texts stretch their networks of form, meaning, and reference; the intimate complications with which a single mind encounters and internalizes its readings. It is also to move between what we can call referential and semiotic poles: between looking as much as possible *through* texts toward what they point to in the world, and trying to look entirely *at* them to understand how their language is structured and works on us. And it is, as well, to maneuver between philosophical and rhetorical poles of intellectual life: between the use of literature in a project of knowing the world, with its history and cultures, and its use to produce new moves in the language games in which people compete with and try to persuade their fellows, or resist their persuasions.

For each of these polarities, what really matters are not the ideally theorized ends but the hybrid traffic in the middle. Readers, students, and scholars all find themselves at the apparent center of a relatively localized network of communications and social transactions: what they read, watch, and hear; what they say and write to others. They occupy, in other words, specific social positions as subjects, and the forms in which they communicate and interact with other people, media, and works (such as texts) are obviously of crucial importance to them. They also belong to an enormous, object-like world, a real, functioning entity that is not necessarily anything like an enlarged version of the situations that locate and define the individual's access to knowledge and experience. We cannot neglect either pole. What matters most is their conjoining. Literary culture should contribute to the educational task of enabling people to link their experience of their own small-scale interactions to their knowledge of the larger world in which they live. We need to teach literature on more than one level, as part of multiple but ultimately interconnected projects: on the one hand, using it to enlarge students' possibilities for writing, speaking, and thinking; on the other hand, connecting it to nonliterary ways of knowing the world.

Another way of putting this would be to say that those of us who teach language and literature should try to instill connections between reading and writing as paths toward knowing (and acting in) the world, and reading and writing as matters of no less serious but individually-oriented liberation or awakening. This should happen not just because both kinds of education can involve the same readings of the same texts, but ultimately because humanistic education should help provide tools for understanding the linkages between private lives and collective life. People should be encouraged and assisted in thinking about the relations between their lives and the social, historical, and economic contexts in which they live them, and about which, as citizens, they're called to make decisions. Too many of these decisions, at present, are either made completely undemocratically or else by way of shallow and narrow systems of representation that almost certainly lack the requisite diversity for constructing and regulating complex and nonreductive futures. Not only do we need to enlarge, improve, and provide greater access to such systems of democratic representation, we need a culture that encourages people to see steering one's own course and participating in the steering of one's society and the world as interconnected.

The languages, texts, and ideas of literary culture, I submit, can foster thinking and further speech or writing about the large-scale and small-scale poles of life: living collectively and historically, living out individual paths of becoming. The highest and most central task of teaching in the humanities may thus be to help students encounter words, narratives, and concepts that make it possible for them to think and communicate broadly and deeply about their life in the world in all its dimensions. A verbal culture worth having would be one that enables people to navigate the networks of meaning, energy, and substance that tie their desires, thoughts, and actions to the natural and social worlds in which they find themselves, worlds not of their making but that they are called upon collectively to remake and sustain. To learn and enrich the languages with which we can speak, write, and think about the connections between our lives and the world, and to challenge routine habits of thought and speech by means of new conceptual and rhetorical tools—such should be the goals of both education and research in the literary humanities.

The need for balance and mediation is no less crucial when we turn to the polarity of the semiotic and the referential. Richard Lanham, who sees great things ahead for the humanities if they can shift the locus of their activity away from print and into electronic media, has written extensively about this polarity under the terms of "looking *at* and looking *through*." He argues that the choice of looking *at* or *through* any medium, and in particular language, is a very basic two-way mental option, an either/or, digital distinction—one or zero, on or off—that he likens to the throwing of a toggle switch. Either we look *at* or we look *through*. Although he describes the opposition as symmetrical, Lanham, like many of his literary colleagues, also makes clear that since he regards the dominant Western ideology to be that of looking *through*, he will devote his critical and pedagogical energies primarily to the importance of looking *at*. He argues that opaque styles, which tend to throw their readers' switches to the *at* position, are as basic to humanity as transparent ones because they satisfy the impulses to competition and play, which are no less fundamental than the impulse satisfied by transparent style, that of effective action based on knowledge.

Lanham's development of the *at/through* distinction's cultural implications is impressive and far reaching.[21] Yet it rests, I would argue, on a fundamental dualistic reification: the belief that this must be a bedrock, digital distinction, a mental toggle switch hard-wired in the human brain. I suspect instead that it is an artifact of history and culture and not a foundation, and that its either/or character is, like the Latourian polarity of pure nature and pure society, a product of socio-technical work and stabilization. We come to believe that we can look *through* language when we come to have stable objects and a separate nature to look through *to*. The same process enables us to separate out a cultural and linguistic pole and to practice looking *at* it. Meanwhile, of course, our language was working both ornamentally and referentially all along. Lanham's image of *oscillation* between the poles of *at* and *through*, something he advocates as an educational and cultural practice, thus strikes me as sensible in its thrust but overly dualistic in its concept. I would suggest that *balance, blending,* or *simultaneity* of the two modes are what we should strive to model and instill in

[21] Richard Lanham, "*At* and *Through:* The Opaque Style and Its Uses," in *Literacy and the Survival of Humanism* (New Haven: Yale University Press, 1983), 58–86.

education. Such balance or coexistence, in fact, is something that most people manage successfully enough in the perception and speech of everyday life. It only becomes a problematic antithesis when thrust on the stage of confrontation between idealistic humanism and the demystification offered by critical theory.[22]

Just as today's science studies scholars understand science as thoroughly constructed and yet all the more capable of providing knowledge by virtue of its constructed character, we specialists in language and literature should allow works to be simultaneously textual constructions and meaningful exercises in communication and transmission. We should teach the contrast between these two perspectives not as a fundamental conflict or as an occasion for virtuoso oscillation or heroic dialectic, but as an idealization of the extrema in a continuum that we negotiate and balance all the time, for example, when we study chemistry, or watch baseball on television, and not just when we study texts. There is no reason why literature should have to bear the burden, or more accurately undergo the deformation, of being the chief object for object lessons in the reflexivity, self-referentiality, or opacity of language. To make it serve this function is but one possible mode of putting it to educational use, one that closes off certain forms of knowledge based on literature even as it opens up others. Literature surely bears within itself the requisite balance between—and simultaneity of—the semiotic and the referential.

The same can be said when we turn to the related polarity of the rhetorical and the philosophical. What is at issue here is the kind of project in which we place our acts of reading, our use of literature. The rhetorical project is one of inventing, proposing, and evaluating new ways of speaking in the marketplace; it is one of competition, cooperation, and negotiation with our fellows in real time. The philosophic project is that of obtaining stabilized knowledge about the way things are, knowledge that may be produced in isolation but to which all reasonable people, like Socrates' straw-man opponents conceding points to him in Plato's dialogues, are supposed to assent. To read or speak

---

[22] On nonheroic, nonagonistic versions of this kind of balanced reflexivity, see Bruno Latour, "The Politics of Explanation: An Alternative," in *Knowledge and Reflexivity: New Frontiers in the Sociology of Knowledge*, ed. Steve Woolgar (London: Sage Publications, 1988), 155–76, and Morris Berman, *Coming to Our Senses: Body and Spirit in the Hidden History of the West* (New York: Simon and Schuster, 1989), 297–344.

rhetorically, in other words, is to presume that the ultimate context of one's knowledge and action is a social world of malleable subjectivities; to read or act philosophically is to assume as one's context an objectified world that it is our task to know.

The rhetorical and philosophical are, in other words, the modes associated with what Richard Rorty, following C. P. Snow, labeled the literary and scientific cultures of the modern world, with what Isaiah Berlin called the conflicted heritage of romanticism and the Enlightenment. It is no surprise, therefore, that the literary disciplines, despite their neglect of rhetorical pedagogy, have operated of late primarily in the mode of rhetoric as opposed to philosophy. Not only does it seem to be the mode of successive forms of literary language and discourse, seductive and mortal; it also seems to be that of democratic politics, of multiple voices raised to seek recognition for themselves and those around them, as opposed to the authorized monologue of the expert or philosopher-king. It is the mode of speaking out, of taking the floor, rather than that of *ex cathedra* teachings: the mode of May 68's anti-technocratic protest. The serious, strategic business of knowing and mastering the real—or of claiming to know so as to abusively master it—already weighs heavily enough in education and intellectual life, through the natural and empirical social sciences, that the humanities (and some interpretive social sciences) have largely chosen to declare themselves in opposition and pursue an alternative project, one centered in the give and take of sociability and the modification of subjectivities.

Yet as I have tried to suggest throughout this book, this stance, however progressive it may seem, now leaves the humanities in an impasse. Neither in practical nor in theoretical terms can we separate an instrumental, economic, and technical sphere from one of intersubjective relations, justice, and recognition so as to devote ourselves to the claims of the latter against the former. The human world—to say nothing of those parts and aspects of the world from which humans are all but absent—is made of much more than what is generally known as sociability, including power, desire, competition, culture, and language. It is made, too, of its relations to the physical and biospheric environment, of the many objects around which social relations are formed and mediated, of large and complex institutions and structures of exchange, too large to be understood solely with reference to the projects and relations of the human beings associated with them. And the world of today is also made of its histories, of the still present traces of its many pasts; without reference to this temporal dimension it would be impossible even to begin to grasp the many tangled and uneven paths of development that collectively make up its movement toward the future.

The world, in other words, is so large and complex, our cultures, societies, and politics so deeply implicated in that size and complexity, that a full education for life in the world must join together the philosophic project of knowing this "place . . . not our own and, much more, not ourselves" (Stevens) with the rhetorical project of inventing, using, rejecting, and refining languages and other forms of cultural expression with which to relate to one another. Literary education, of course, cannot alone make up a complete education, but it need not and should not restrict itself to one end of the polarity. To so limit it would be both to forgo much of what works of literature can tell us about the many places and moments of the human world and to reinforce the division between the rhetorical and philosophical poles rather than to stitch threads of connection between them.

What Is to Be Done?

NO PALINODE, then, for this book; no reassurance that we can take it less seriously, that it's only literature, after all, or that perhaps we scholars can content ourselves with looking at things from the standpoint of our special semiotic or rhetorical expertise—instead, a resolute argument, right to the end, for occupying and cultivating the middles of all these polarities. But how? What is to be done?

The renewal of close ties between language and literature, and the cultivation of a sense of pleasure and participation in literary reading and writing, are no more than first steps, foundations, a fertile irrigated soil. They may well be necessary, but they are surely not sufficient. We should open up possibilities of talking back to books, as Henry Miller suggested, without shutting down the still necessary task of reading them. Finishing books, after all, has its advantages as well: without it, where will be the informed stimulus for thoughts and reactions to reading worth pursuing? That is precisely why we have literary and philosophical education, why it is important to read much, to study the contexts of what one reads, and to become familiar with theories and methods that enrich and complicate the process of learning from what one reads. To be sure, as traditional assumptions that have underwritten literary education give way, and as readers are less inclined to see themselves as radically distanced from authors, it seems important to provide teaching that advances students' own powers, that calls them to develop, sharpen, and expand their impulses to use their languages for serious thought and creation. But this goal should never be isolated from the acquisition of a broad and diverse familiarity with what others have written and with techniques of reading.

Beyond knowledge of texts, contexts, and methods of reading, however, the humanities need to be complemented by much more cross-traffic between disciplines, by a working together of humanities disciplines with fields outside them. Little ultimate purpose is served by pure knowledge of literary or artistic works if this knowledge is not in some way put into larger circulation. We do not study Shakespeare in the hope of solving the "Shakespeare problem" and then, building perhaps on our solution, move on to something else. The plays of Shakespeare may, of course, be viewed as objects of knowledge in themselves, topics on which societies and thus universities must have specialized researchers. But when we consider how little use or appetite there is for the definitive outcome of such a quest for knowledge, we realize that this stance must really be a method for making the works of Shakespeare as productively and subtly stimulating as possible, for learning more original things from his plays than we could if we did not treat them so seriously as objects of knowledge. In the end, however, such treatment and the objective knowledge it might produce are not really the goals of the humanities. Shakespeare is ultimately read and studied so that the language and ideas of his works, and probably also our knowledge of how those works related to their social and historical contexts in Elizabethan and Jacobean England, can become part of the cultural tool kits with which we experience and think about the world. And that project will go largely unfulfilled if there are no mechanisms for bringing the knowledge gained in the study of Shakespeare into contact and circulation with other forms of knowledge.

The academy these days is nothing if not self-consciously interdisciplinary. Yet much of what goes under that rubric turns out to depend on recourse to cultural theories common to the humanities and the less empirical social sciences: in other words, on what David Simpson called "the rule of literature" in a sizable sector of the contemporary university. This kind of crossover, congenially based on shared theoretical assumptions about the centrality of culture, doesn't really address the more serious interdisciplinary problem, the relation of the more human, social, and cultural aspects of the world to its more nonhuman, natural, and technical features. So it would be good to make the interdisciplinarity often claimed by literary studies into something more real by paying deeper attention to what other disciplines, and not just the neighboring ones, are actually up to. Sometimes what they are doing will not look congenial or even legitimate to those whose outlook has been forged primarily by literary rather than scientific culture. But disagreement and discomfort are often the price to be paid for engaging with others in ways that are democratic, respectful, and productive of reliable knowledge, as Isabelle Stengers suggested in her comments on the "science wars." Genuine interdisciplinarity should accept and even welcome the alterity of the other field, the possibility that its views and ways won't be easily compatible with our own or, even worse, will force us to rethink what we thought we could safely assume. A little modesty wouldn't hurt.

Modesty should also be a watchword when professors writing books are tempted to propose remaking the university. Universities are large and deliberately conservative institutions; their professional and disciplinary subcultures are particularly hard to change. No one can or will persuade (or, worse yet, order) everyone in the humanities to start working with fields foreign to them. Fortunately, no one needs to. The path to change lies not in getting professors to do things they don't want to or don't know how to do, but in curricular and structural realignment—something that is not exactly easy but that universities are more capable of than they are of changing the cultures and mentalities of their disciplines.

My proposals for change concern the structures of education, both undergraduate and graduate, and the mode of recruitment and initiation into the professoriate, up to and including the criteria for academic tenure. Their potential for realization depends on two key assumptions. First, and more generally, that change in the disciplines should come through the education of the next generations of scholars, who, on the basis of different formative experiences and initiatory requirements, will remake their fields as they grow into them. Second, and more specifically, that interdisciplinary education does not have to—indeed, should not—take place in every course, or even in many courses: its locus can be the minds of students, trained seriously in different disciplines by the practitioners of each.

This second point is crucial. Most of today's faculty are not trained or inclined to offer the kind of interdisciplinary teaching called for by the general argument of this book. Team teaching is a useful option, but on a large scale it is costly and hard to organize. If, however, we turn over to students the task of putting ideas, outlooks, and problems together in their minds—that is, if we structure educational programs so as to be sure that they are exposed to other things, and try to teach so as to provoke the desire and curiosity to make the connections— then we are using the university's resources in a plausible and efficient way, while helping students to develop and mature by giving them more active and creative responsibility for their own education.

My first proposal for undergraduate education is thus extremely simple: *require every humanities major to be a double major*—the "second" field being an empirical one, outside the humanities. Of course the exact modalities of such a plan will have to be worked out by the faculty on every campus that adopts it: people will reasonably come up with a variety of solutions concerning the boundary of the humanities, the size and nature of double majors or concentrations, and so forth.[23] One feature that strikes me as crucial, however, is the provision of some form of major integrative experience for every student, whether in the form of seminars, tutorials, or independent projects. (This is where the relatively scarce resources of team teaching and innovative course development would have to go.) It is important that students work actively to develop a sense of relatedness, at a minimum, between their education inside and outside the humanities. After all, many humanities majors are already double majors today— a fact that indicates the feasibility of my proposal—but all too often they keep their fields in two separate mental compartments: for example, economics so as to qualify for a job in business, French for cultural enrichment and prestige. The requirement for a synthetic project or seminar would aim to counter this kind of two-track thinking. Of course, the integrative intellectual experience I would like to see

---

[23] I've referred here to the humanities and not just to the "language and literature" fields. In doing so, I realize that I am enlarging my proposal somewhat beyond the sphere of my overall arguments. Obviously any reader who wishes to do so may consider the idea only in the context of the languages and literatures; certainly a college or university could decide to adopt it just for those departments and not for all of the humanities. However, I suspect that many of the reasons for adopting such a plan in the literary humanities would also apply to such fields as philosophy and the history of art.

will not work out wonderfully in every case, and many of these "new" double majors will be no more intellectually inclined than were the "old" ones—but I am talking about a workable structural reform and not a great awakening of the undergraduate population.[24]

Readers may well ask, why require everyone who wants to specialize in the humanities to be a double major? Shouldn't your proposal really be to strengthen general education requirements? Give freshmen and sophomores a better grounding in the humanities, the social sciences, and the natural sciences, and then let them specialize as they see fit!

To this objection I have two replies. First, to complement a humanities specialization and counteract its often isolating tendencies, I believe it necessary to require more in-depth work in other fields than could be called for by general education requirements alone, whether of the "distribution" or "core curriculum" variety. (If an institution were to adopt *much* more substantial general education requirements, along the lines of "at least a minor in a humanities field *and* in a social science *and* in a natural science," I would consider that a version of my proposal for double majors.) Second, I propose a new approach to general education requirements, one that would complement and reinforce the plan for double majors inside and outside of the humanities.

The great weakness of college general education requirements is that they are not general enough; the courses in them are almost all taught from a disciplinary perspective. "This is how we do things in sociology, this is how you go about becoming a chemist, here are the Great Books as taught by a humanities professor." This kind of course, however successful, often has something of the unhappy compromise about it: too discipline-specific to help students acquire general cognitive maps of their world, often too watered-down to draw on the passion and scholarly expertise of the faculty. Such courses do a better job of helping students to become consumers of course offerings and ma-

---

[24] Perhaps if humanities departments, or at least the languages and literatures, went on record as saying that what they have to offer educationally is a very important part, but only a part, of a liberal education for life in today's world, a similar spirit of modesty might encourage other fields to require their own majors to spend more time on the humanities. Such an outcome cannot, of course, be guaranteed, and in my judgment should not be made a condition for adopting the "no humanities major without another field" plan, which strikes me as beneficial in and of itself.

jors than of preparing them to be citizens of the world or original thinkers.

So my proposal would be to distinguish between two kinds of general education courses and have students take a certain number of each. The categories would be called something like *knowing the world* and *pursuing curious interests.* (I first called them *relevant* and *irrelevant*—until someone pointed out to me how vulnerable to every budget cut the second category would be.) The first group would consist of integrative courses, not necessarily disciplinary at all, aimed at providing students with a very general picture of what is known about the physical universe, organisms and the environment, forms of human society and culture, and the state of the present-day world. No question about it: these courses would be expensive to develop, controversial, and hard to teach. If they succeeded, however, they would give students maps and linkages for relating their education, both in those courses and beyond, to the world they encounter around them. The second group of courses would be seminars in which professors would present examples of the most fascinating work in their fields, however irrelevant to anything they might be—the only condition being that they teach it in ways that students not yet initiated into work in the disciplines could understand.

As with the proposal for double majors, a key element of this plan would be to encourage students to take an active role in making connections, both across fields and between the specialized activities of education and the general project of understanding one's place in the universe. A liberal education would be thus defined: an overview or set of maps to help you situate your life in the natural and social world, together with the often surprising and unexpected stimuli and connections that come from pursuing what may seem like gratuitous interests—things you would never have thought about if professor so-and-so hadn't pushed you to do so. Notice that there is no mention of a judicious balance among disciplines—though an institution could certainly require some such balance among the "curious interests" courses if it so desired. I readily admit that this proposal reaches beyond any conceivable definition of my own expertise, and also that it is by no means a necessary condition for adopting the more temperate proposal for double majors. I believe, however, that the two plans would complement each other well, would provide some stimulating but not insurmountable new teaching tasks for faculty, and could improve both the liveliness and relevance of undergraduate education in the arts and sciences.

Changes such as these would also, after a few years, modify the background and outlook of students entering graduate programs in languages and literatures. My hope is that they would arrive less disposed to accept the notion that graduate study in the humanities is an initiation into a guild or counter-society of enlightened cultural critics. It's wonderful that thinkers and scholars in the humanities contest commonsense ways of looking at language and the world, that they offer critical perspectives, that they question stereotypes, ideologies, and received ideas. Humanities teachers rightly want to give these gifts of perspective, criticism, and new languages to their students so that they may enrich and complicate their minds and their relation to the world by adding new tools, new tricks, new ways of seeing, speaking, and writing. But something troubling occurs when the gift of new perspectives and forms of expression becomes a matter of community identity, or more precisely an entry criterion for community membership. "Be one of us, think as we do, come over to our side, leave your benighted commonsense modes of thought behind, join the group in the know": such are the seduction lines of critical theory in the humanities, such is the link between the sense of autonomy and oppositionality borrowed from the literary field and the reproduction through co-optation characteristic of academic disciplines.

A major curse of graduate education in the humanities in the age of theory is its over-identification with the posture of critique, of being critical. Since intellectual respectability requires a self-conscious, constructivist position on the relation of language to reality, it is all too tempting for teachers, students, and scholars to judge one another according to how rigorously they pursue such a stance. It becomes easy to produce readings and interpretations (or anti-interpretations) that are all valid, at least on their own terms, but collectively redundant, repeating the same kind of intellectual operations on a wide variety of texts with relatively little sense of learning anything from those texts' diversity and specificity. It also becomes efficient to produce new critiques by criticizing previous critics for lapses in self-reflexive awareness or in other forms of critical vigilance.

To a degree this is simply the conflictual norm of academic rhetoric as it applies to the humanities. One may question the overall dependence of academic culture on ritual confrontation, but such questioning would not be specific to literary or humanistic fields.[25] The rush to be critical, however, carries a particularly high cost in disciplines devoted to the study of texts and other culturally created works: it can short-circuit the process of learning from the works under study. Here is how the intellectual historian Michael Roth put it: ". . . as the goal of education has become the creation of a class of professional unmaskers, we have seriously limited our ability to make sense of the world. In overdeveloping the capacity to show how texts fail to accomplish what they set out to do, we may be depriving students of the capacity to learn as much as possible from what they read . . . our students may become too good at showing how things *don't* make sense."[26] Why this is so, and what is lost in reading as a result of premature negativity, was brilliantly set out by Nietzsche in *Human, All Too Human:*

> *Love as a device.* Whoever wants really to get to *know* something new (be it a person, an event, or a book) does well to take up this new thing with all possible love, to avert his eye quickly from, even to forget, everything about it that he finds inimical, objectionable, or false. So, for example, we give the author of a book the greatest possible head start, and, as if at a race, virtually yearn with pounding heart for him to reach his goal. By doing this, we penetrate into the heart of the new thing, into its motive center: and this is what it means to get to know it. Once we have got that far, reason then sets its limits; that overestimation, that occasional unhinging of the critical pendulum, was just a device to entice the soul of a matter out into the open.[27]

Nietzsche is no advocate of edifying or submissive reading; criticism and distancing, he recognizes, are a necessary moment of any process of knowledge, but are best postponed until after one has learned as much as possible by means of generous identification. This moment of love, complicit in the project of using language to signify something beyond itself (and thus suspect from the standpoint of those who wish

[25] Deborah Tannen comments on the adversarial practices of academic culture and specifically of graduate school, and their relation to larger trends in American society, in *The Argument Culture* (New York: Random House, 1998), 256–76.

[26] Michael Roth, "On the Limits of Critical Thinking," *Tikkun* 11, no. 1 (January–February 1996), 85–86.

[27] Friedrich Nietzsche, *Human, All Too Human,* trans. Marion Faber, with Stephen Lehmann (Lincoln: University of Nebraska Press, 1984), 257; aphorism 621.

to look primarily *at* the language of texts so as to make plain its workings) occurs all too rarely in the graduate education and intellectual life of today's supposedly philological disciplines.

Bringing more broadly educated humanities majors to graduate school may help create the conditions for overcoming a disciplinary fixation on critique, but it is only a first step. It may or may not help to alleviate a related problem: the overemphasis graduate programs place on reproducing the professoriate. Universities seem addicted— via an economic reliance on large numbers of teaching assistants, and a professorial fondness for graduate teaching—to turning out far more potential professors than they are actually willing or able to hire. If this situation is to change, either we have to produce fewer Ph.D.s (unpleasant for those of us who enjoy graduate teaching), hire more professors (how?),[28] or decide that the goal of advanced education in the humanities should not be limited to producing replacement professors, i.e., researchers who will produce specialized knowledge of the disciplinary objects of the humanities. There is no call for such researchers outside the academy and thus no reason to train more humanities scholars of this kind than are needed to teach the next generation of humanities students. Yet might there be other kinds of graduate education, less single-mindedly devoted to reproducing pro-

---

[28] It is often said that the main culprit in the poor job market of the humanities (and some other academic fields) is the crassness of universities, which, instead of hiring new Ph.D.s as tenure-track professors, have hired them at lower salary and poorer working conditions under the guise of various adjunct positions, from the decent if modest position of regularly employed non-tenure-track lecturer down to the abject status of part-time section instructor. It is surely true that universities have, to a degree, done this, and professional organizations and unions do well to pressure them to improve employment conditions, especially those that are blatantly exploitative. But it is difficult to see why or how the universities would or could pay for all their elementary-level teaching, especially in labor-intensive subjects such as foreign language and composition courses, at professional rates. Professors' comparatively good salaries and low teaching loads are justified by production of research and its value in attracting students, primarily graduate students. Since there is more than enough research being done in the literary humanities and since there are more than enough professors available to teach the next generation of graduate students, it is hard for universities to find reasons to hire more of us. The best way to improve the economic lot of increasingly numerous adjunct faculty would be to produce a smaller pool of them and/or to help many of them find attractive employment options outside higher education, so that the potential adjuncts would be in shorter supply and could command higher salaries. At that point the economic incentives to use adjunct instead of "regular" faculty would be reduced, and a somewhat less inegalitarian system might begin to emerge.

fessors, for which there might be nonacademic demand? We hear often enough that the intellectual or cultural level of a B.A. in English isn't what it used to be—might there not be many positions for which people with additional education in literary studies, though not necessarily training designed to make them professors, would be highly suitable?

Most universities, unfortunately, have not even begun to ask this kind of question. The few existing initiatives to help Ph.D.s find nonacademic employment presuppose, for the most part, that the configuration of the Ph.D. itself (and even of humanities graduate study in general) will not change. But why not? Is the narrow focus of Ph.D. preparation really all that useful *inside* the academy, either? Do present-day patterns of disciplinary initiation produce people well suited to using literature to educate their students for life in the world?

I leave the answer to these prickly questions to my readers. For my part, I believe that some of the problems evoked here—the overemphasis on critique, the mentality of a guild that fancies itself a counterculture, the lack of true interdisciplinarity, and the excessive focus on reproducing the professoriate—might usefully be attacked by a change in the structure of academic careers from graduate school through tenure review. As in the case of my proposals for undergraduate education, this idea applies most properly to the "language and literature" fields, though I think it deserves consideration in the humanities as a whole and perhaps beyond them.

Academic tenure is granted on the basis of achievement in research and teaching, with high research output the *sine qua non* at research universities and prestigious colleges. In the humanities, research is virtually synonymous with published writing addressed to other members of the academy, in one's own and allied fields. This form of publication is substantially subsidized by universities, and is evaluated by members of the academic community. Subsidy and peer review provide the kind of autonomy that literary cultural producers hold dear, and that scholars rightfully regard as guaranteeing a degree of independence from external pressures. But it should come as no surprise that the people produced under this system have a hard time communicating outside of it, or that its symbolic products find little echo in a larger economy of communications that is radically different. Many outside the academy find the works and ideas produced under these conditions irrelevant or impertinent, not simply because they are inherently anti-intellectual or hostile to professors, but because they can find little in the preoccupations and modes of discourse of the academic profession that engages their concerns or that corresponds to their ways of seeing.

The form of the academy itself as mediating institution, now that its nineteenth-century structure and print-culture habits make it ever more out of step with dominant communications practices in society, risks posing an ever greater obstacle to the circulation or reception of the ideas and languages that people who work in the humanities might contribute to present-day society and culture. As Columbia University English professor David Damrosch notes, "in our contemporary 'postindustrial' economy, we need a strengthened *economy of circulation* . . . If we are not to retreat within the sheltering confines of the nearest disciplinary or ideological coterie, we need to coordinate and share knowledge better. . ."[29] Unfortunately, if you wanted to invent a method for writing a lot while not reaching or influencing an audience outside a restricted circle, you couldn't do much better than to reinvent the rules and practices of academic discourse.

To counter this problem, colleges and universities ought to consider a dual requirement for publication (or other creative work) in at least the humanities. Candidates for tenure and further promotion should be expected to produce two kinds of work: one for academic audiences and one for a broader public. (Schools of music and art might serve as models in this regard.) Just how broad, just what form of work, would have to be left open to individual institutions and their evaluation committees to decide. The fundamental criterion could well be negative: a portion of one's publications would have to be *outside* the subsidized academic circuit.

It is important to emphasize that I am not talking about eliminating the specialized and necessarily subsidized preserve of academic publication so as to force scholarship to sink or swim in the free market. It would be foolish to want to abolish the freedoms and special circumstances of the academy, for they provide a niche in which cultural activity is not directly subjected to the full force of the market, the present, today's dominant media, and the imperative to provide either immediate utility or amusement. The problem, then, is that of ensuring *both* the separate, protected space of the academy *and* the existence of strong and creative communications across a permeable boundary between academia and the larger culture. The academic cul-

[29] David Damrosch, *We Scholars* (Cambridge: Harvard University Press, 1995), 212.

tural preserve is now so heavily weighted toward autonomy that it is in danger of collapse under the tedious productivity by which it affirms its internal values and regulates its internal relations. A two-track publication requirement, which asks that humanities scholars express themselves *both* for their peers and for a more general public, would attempt to redress the balance and increase the social circulation of work in the humanities without eliminating the virtues of scholarly autonomy.

Obviously such a plan would have to be phased in and the expectations would need to be modest at first. In order for it to work, it would have to start with graduate education. Students earning the Ph.D. in the humanities would have to be given encouragement and instruction—almost certainly not seminar-based—in writing for nonacademic audiences. In practical terms, this will not be easy, because it adds to the already heavy demands of graduate education at a time when universities are under pressure to reduce the time it takes to earn a Ph.D. But in intellectual terms, it is far less difficult than it sounds, because of a great advantage graduate students have over their professors: they are not yet fully socialized academics. They are still in the process of being co-opted by the academy and their disciplines, of learning a specialized discourse and perspective. They have to make efforts of mediation and translation to become academics, to fit into the disciplinary practices they are encountering. As of now, they usually try to overcome as efficiently as possible their resistance to the academic way of thinking and speaking about society, culture, and literary works. Everything encourages them to repress their pre-disciplinary ways of looking at things. (Some graduate students, of course, do not embrace this repression, resisting academic socialization so effectively that they drop out.) However, if graduate students were encouraged or required not to exchange one language and outlook for another, but to become fully bilingual, able to express themselves in the language of the their new discipline but also to articulate their new thinking in the language they would need in order to talk about it with their mothers or their college roommates, they would become interpreters and mediators of their scholarly fields, just as bilingual children of immigrants routinely become mediators and interpreters between their parents and their new societies.

My own department at Michigan recently took a modest first step in this direction by adding to its Ph.D. requirements the preparation of a portfolio of work related to one's studies and field but outside of scholarship *per se*. As of now, this requirement can be—and probably will be, for most students headed for academic careers—satisfied by a teaching portfolio, which by itself is not unconventional; in fact, it is increasingly something that graduate students need to prepare when looking for an academic position. But we deliberately defined the requirement broadly, not limiting it to teaching, because we saw it as an opening for students who want to think about the relation between their graduate work and other types of careers. Given the ingenuity and breadth of interests of our graduate students, I expect to see unexpected and unconventional work start to turn up in fulfillment of this requirement.

An expectation of work addressed to a nonacademic audience might do a good deal to break down barriers to cultural circulation and exchange between academia and society. It would start by nudging the pattern of recruitment into academia away from that of initiation into a counter-society. It might even help the academy withdraw from its addiction to self-reproduction through teaching and the co-optation of its most successful students. To ask students to write about their new learning for a nonspecialist audience would be to encourage them to reflect on, rather than simply undergo or overcome, the transition from a "commonsensical" to a disciplinary or theoretical perspective. It would better prepare them for dual citizenship in the academy and in the larger society, with the latter considered not simply as the place where one lives the unintellectual part of one's life but as a world where culture, languages, and ideas matter.

Envoi

I HOPE that this chapter will not leave the impression that literary culture's role in the life of the world can be renewed solely by a few pedagogical innovations here, a curricular or tenure reform there. The problems and possibilities are larger in scope than any such adjustments alone. A book like this one is written in the hope of provoking thought, discussion, moments of recognition and realization—and, with luck and grace, some changes in outlook, redirection of energies, and above all further work and conversation along related lines. If the arguments and ideas I've offered should fail to stimulate any renewal of thinking about why and how literature is read and taught, about how old works should (or shouldn't) be carried forward into changing times, about how different aspects of the natural and social world might be understood in continuity rather than in opposition, then the suggestions for educational change will fall by the wayside as well. But if the ideas I've tried to set forth here find echoes with enough readers to make some kind of difference, then one of the responses ought to take the form of further thinking about how the academic institutions of literary culture might better conceive of and carry out their tasks. Such further thinking might or might not, of course, follow the lines I have tried to trace in the last pages. What matters is a recognition that the issues concerning literary culture's role in the world are, by their nature, not abstract but embodied, situated in practices and institutions. A book that stressed the media environment and institutional situation in which ideas and works find themselves could hardly end without proposing practical and institutional measures—however modest or improbable—to complement its intellectual arguments. Real change must involve both individual minds and the external structures through which people communicate and carry out human activity.

There is no lack of opportunities for change in the way literary culture is structured and used. The often isolating effects of literary and disciplinary autonomy are rightly perceived as a problem by the many scholars who characterize their work as interdisciplinary or as part of Cultural Studies. Whatever reservations I may have expressed about the often anti-literary stance of Cultural Studies, or about its maintenance of the culturalist and immaterial focus of literary culture, I see the energy and commitment of its practitioners as a hopeful sign and a resource for the renewal of the humanities. No less important, there is already much work in science studies that can provide models for a literary and cultural study no longer intimidated by the prospect of referring to the things of the world that lie outside of language or that cannot be reduced to human constructions and meanings. And even the pace of media change, with all its risks of faddishness and of diminished contact with earlier forms and texts, has the merit of forcing a rethinking of educational practices and thus of shaking literary studies out of any temptations of complacency.

The beginning of the millennium, then, should be an exciting and inventive time for literary culture in all its senses—its communities, its works, its beliefs and activities. The stakes are not small. The texts known as literature are a crucial locus of cultural memory and diversity, a web of words through which we access and activate an enormous range of attempts to know, imagine, and reinvent the world. The institutions, outlooks, and communicative practices of literary culture still form a major part of the cultural space for learning, exchange, and invention. The changes now being faced by both literature and the world at large, I've tried to argue, should encourage readers, writers, and teachers to consider how best to make literary culture a vital part of an enlarged humanism (or post-humanism, if you will), one that locates our creative and constructive tasks as human beings not just in an aesthetic, intellectual, or even cultural sphere but in the entire project of making and remaking the social, cultural, and material collectives to which we belong.

Individually and collectively, we need to steer our courses in this world. To face the complexity of that task in a nonreductive manner, we need to continue to draw on the manifold variety of what has been invented and recorded in human languages. Poetry (in the largest sense) does not and should not take us away from the alterity of the material world, but keep us in contact with it. "From this the poem springs," wrote Stevens, "that we live in a place/That is not our own and, much more, not ourselves." It should be possible for the practice of literary culture to contribute to maintaining that place, the ever-transformed world in which we live. Life must rule over knowledge, Nietzsche wrote, but to say this is also to say that knowledge follows its highest calling when contributing to life. Sustaining and enhancing the life of the world should be the ultimate vocation of literary culture, of that branch of knowledge named philology, the love of language and its works.

Bibliographic Essay

Rather than a list of works cited, which are already documented in the notes, this is a chapter-by-chapter guide to works that I have found helpful and that interested readers may wish to look into. I have tried to emphasize sources that may not be familiar to readers from the literary disciplines.

Introduction

There are by now many books on the implications of digital media for literary culture, most of them quite favorable to the prospects for change. Among those that I have found most useful are Richard Lanham, *The Electronic Word: Democracy, Technology, and the Arts* (Chicago: University of Chicago Press, 1993), James O'Donnell, *Avatars of the Word: From Papyrus to Cyberspace* (Cambridge: Harvard University Press, 1998), and Mark Taylor and Esa Saarinen, *Imagologies: Media Philosophy* (London: Routledge, 1994).

One of the best contributions from the techno-skeptical side is Mark Slouka's *War of the Worlds: Cyberspace and the High-Tech Assault on Reality* (New York: Basic Books, 1995). An unusual and iconoclastic look at the problems faced by humanities with the dominance of audiovisual media is provided by David Marc, *Bonfire of the Humanities: Television, Subliteracy, and Long-Term Memory Loss* (Syracuse: Syracuse University Press, 1995).

A very good introduction to the broader intellectual and cultural implications of computer networks is Pierre Lévy, *Collective Intelligence: Mankind's Emerging World in Cyberspace,* trans. Robert Bononno (New York: Plenum Trade, 1997). For an even broader historical and philosophical perspective, see the recent works of Régis Debray on what he calls "mediology," notably his *Cours de médiologie générale* (Paris: Gallimard, 1991). In English, see Debray's *Transmitting Culture,* trans. Eric Rauth (New York: Columbia University Press, 2000).

Chapter 1

On the beginnings of modern literary culture, see Walter J. Ong, S.J., "Romantic Difference and the Poetics of Technology," in *Rhetoric, Romance, and Technology* (Ithaca: Cornell University Press, 1971), 259–82; Alvin Kernan, *Samuel Johnson and the Impact of Print* (Princeton: Princeton University Press, 1989); Clifford Siskin, *The Work of Writing: Literature and Social Change in Britain, 1700–1830* (Baltimore: Johns Hopkins University Press, 1998); Isaiah Berlin, *Vico and Herder: Two Studies in the History of Ideas* (London: Hogarth, 1976) and *The Roots of Romanticism* (Princeton: Princeton University Press, 1999); Raymond Williams, *Culture and Society, 1780–1850* (London: Chatto and Windus, 1958).

For sociological analyses of the autonomy of the literary field, see Pierre Bourdieu, "The Market of Symbolic Goods," in *The Field of Cultural Production*, ed. Randal Johnson (New York: Columbia University Press, 1993), 112–41, and *The Rules of Art: Genesis and Structure of the Literary Field*, trans. Susan Emanuel (Stanford: Stanford University Press, 1996). Sections of Peter Bürger's *Theory of the Avant-Garde*, trans. Michael Shaw, foreword by Jochen Schulte-Sasse (Minneapolis: University of Minnesota Press, 1984) are also very useful on this topic. A wide-ranging history of the literary field in the nineteenth and twentieth centuries that emphasizes the centrality of "art for art's sake" autonomy is that of Gene Bell-Villada, *Art for Art's Sake and Literary Life: How Politics and Markets Helped Shape the Ideology and Culture of Aestheticism, 1790–1990* (Lincoln: University of Nebraska Press, 1996). In his final chapter, Bell-Villada argues that autonomy and aestheticism are important characteristics of contemporary academic literary studies. On the delayed and distinctive turn to literary modernism in Latin America, see Julio Ramos, *Desencuentros de la modernidad en América Latina: Literatura y política en el siglo XIX* (Mexico City: Fondo de Cultura Económica, 1989).

Chapter 2

As I suggested in the text, one of the best works on May 1968 in Paris remains Michel de Certeau's *La Prise de parole*, first published in the fall of that year and reissued in 1994 by Editions du Seuil, Paris. It contains a remarkable annotated bibliography of contemporary materials on the May events. The English translation is *The Capture of Speech and Other Political Writings,* ed. Luce Giard, trans. Tom Conley (Minneapolis: University of Minnesota Press, 1998). The most serious study of the connections between May '68 and poststructuralist theory is Peter Starr, *Logics of Failed Revolt* (Stanford: Stanford University Press, 1996). Also of interest is Thomas Pavel's often scathing history of structuralism, *The Feud of Language: A History of Structuralist Thought,* trans. Linda Jordan and Thomas Pavel (Oxford: Basil Blackwell, 1989), which discusses the relationship between rising economic prosperity, exuberant theoretical production, and student rebellion in France of the 1960s under the category of "discretionary intellectual behavior."

A major recent theorist of the social implications of environmental crisis and related problems is Ulrich Beck, whose works include *Risk Society: Towards a New Modernity,* trans. Mark Ritter (London: Sage Publications, 1992) and *World Risk Society* (Cambridge: Polity Press, 1999). On the need for reinventing political ecology in a way that brings its social and environmental aspects together, see Bruno Latour, *Politiques de la nature: comment faire entrer les sciences en démocratie* (Paris: Editions La Découverte, 1999). An unusual and original approach to the relations between language, scientific knowledge, and ecology is proposed by Will Wright in *Wild Knowledge: Science, Language, and Social Life in a Fragile Environment* (Minneapolis: University of Minnesota Press, 1992). For connections between feminism, ecology, biodiversity, and cultural diversity, see the works of Vandana Shiva, notably *Staying Alive: Women, Ecology, and Development* (London: Zed Books, 1989). For an educational program attentive to the needs of the environment, see David Orr, *Ecological Literacy: Education and the Transition to a Postmodern World* (Albany: State University of New York Press, 1992). A major recent synthesis of ecocriticism is Lawrence Buell's *Writing for an Endangered World: Literature, Culture, and Environment in the U.S. and Beyond* (Cambridge: Harvard University Press, 2001).

On technology as a form of materiality not reducible to culture, and thus on the limits of much cultural analysis of technology, see Mark Hansen's important and insightful *Embodying Technesis: Technology Beyond Writing* (Ann Arbor: University of Michigan Press, 2000).

Chapter 3

Fundamental works in the Sociology of Scientific Knowledge include David Bloor, *Knowledge and Social Imagery* (London: Routledge and Kegan Paul, 1976), Barry Barnes, *Scientific Knowledge and Sociological Theory* (London: Routledge and Kegan Paul, 1974), and Barnes, *Interests and the Growth of Knowledge* (London: Routledge and Kegan Paul, 1977). Among the most important feminist works on science are Evelyn Fox Keller, *Reflections on Gender and Science* (New Haven: Yale University Press, 1985), and Sandra Harding, *The Science Question in Feminism* (Ithaca: Cornell University Press, 1986).

The major works of Bruno Latour (in their English versions) include *Science in Action: How to Follow Scientists and Engineers Through Society* (Cambridge: Harvard University Press, 1987), *The Pasteurization of France*, trans. Alan Sheridan and John Law (Cambridge: Harvard University Press, 1988), *We Have Never Been Modern*, trans. Catherine Porter (Cambridge: Harvard University Press, 1993), and *Pandora's Hope: Essays on the Reality of Science Studies* (Cambridge: Harvard University Press, 1999). A key article is "The Politics of Explanation: An Alternative," in *Knowledge and Reflexivity: New Frontiers in the Sociology of Knowledge*, ed. Steve Woolgar (London: Sage Publications, 1988), 155–76. An important paper on the "generalized principle of symmetry" by Latour's colleague Michel Callon is "Some Elements of a Sociology of Translation: Domestication of the Scallops and the Fisherman of St. Brieuc Bay," in John Law, ed., *Power, Action, and Belief: A New Sociology of Knowledge?* (London: Routledge and Kegan Paul, 1986), 196–233.

Latour is no stranger to controversy. A major published debate between Latour and representatives of the Sociology of Scientific Knowledge can be found in *Science as Practice and Culture*, ed. Andrew Pickering (Chicago: University of Chicago Press, 1992): H. M. Collins and Steven Yearley, "Epistemological Chicken," 301–26; Michel Callon and Bruno Latour, "Don't Throw the Baby Out with the Bath School! A Reply to Collins and Yearley," 343–68; Collins and Yearley, "Journey into Space," 369–89. A more recent and in some ways more important exchange appeared in the journal *Studies in the History and Philosophy of Science*, 30, 1 (1999): David Bloor, "Anti-Latour," 81–112; Bruno Latour, "For David Bloor... and Beyond: A Reply to David Bloor's 'Anti-Latour'," 113–29; Bloor, "Reply to Bruno Latour," 131–36.

Susan Squier rewrites Latour's rules of method from *Science in Action* for use in the study of "literature and science" in "From Omega to Mr. Adam: The Importance of Literature for Feminist Science Studies," *Science, Technology, and Human Values* 24, 1 (1999): 132–58. On

Latour's relation to Foucault, see T. Hugh Crawford, "Give me Fragile Networks and I will Shake the World," *Critical Texts* 7, 2 (1990): 29–39. I develop the implications of Latour's and Stengers's work for literary studies in "For a Cosmopolitical Philology: Lessons from Science Studies," *SubStance*, no. 96 (2001): 102–120. Mike Michael draws on the work of Latour, Donna Haraway, and Michel Serres to propose a social theory of such contemporary hybrids as road rage and couch potatoes in *Reconnecting Culture, Technology, and Nature* (London: Routledge, 2000). In a recent and popular work, and without making reference to science studies, Michael Pollan gives a striking example of how the roles of subject and object can be redistributed among humans and nonhumans: *The Botany of Desire: A Plant's-Eye View of the World* (New York: Random House, 2001).

Works by Donna Haraway of interest in the humanities include *Simians, Cyborgs, and Women: The Reinvention of Nature* (New York: Routledge, 1991), *Modest_Witness@Second_Millennium .FemaleMan©_Meets_OncoMouse™* (New York: Routledge, 1997), and a major article, "The Promises of Monsters: A Regenerative Politics for Inappropriate/d Others" in *Cultural Studies*, ed. Lawrence Grossberg, Cary Nelson, and Paula Treichler (New York: Routledge, 1992), 295–337. For an engaging retrospective interview, see *How Like a Leaf: An Interview with Thyrza Nichols Goodeve* (New York: Routledge, 2000).

Recent works by Isabelle Stengers available in English include *The Invention of Modern Science*, trans. Daniel W. Smith (Minneapolis: University of Minnesota Press, 2000), and *Power and Invention: Situating Science*, trans. Paul Bains, forward by Bruno Latour (Minneapolis: University of Minnesota Press, 1997). The final volume of her *Cosmopolitiques* series, which has yet to be translated into English, should be of particular interest to readers in the social sciences and humanities: *Pour en finir avec la tolérance* (Paris: La Découverte, 1997).

Another science studies scholar, not discussed here but whose work is of great potential interest for literary and cultural study, is the American sociologist Andrew Pickering. His main programmatic book is *The Mangle of Practice: Time, Agency, and Science* (Chicago: University of Chicago Press, 1995). A debate consisting of four brief critiques of this book and a response from its author can be found in *Studies in the History and Philosophy of Science* 30, 1 (1999): 139–71.

Chapter 4

On tactics versus strategy, see Michel de Certeau, *The Practice of Everyday Life*, trans. Steven Rendall (Berkeley: University of California Press, 1984), and Anthony Wilden, *The Rules Are No Game* (London: Routledge and Kegan Paul, 1987).

Concerning the model of feedback, my thinking has relied first and foremost on the work of Gregory Bateson, especially the papers in *Steps to an Ecology of Mind* (New York: Ballantine, 1972). Bateson's first use of what would only later be called feedback and cybernetics to analyze culture can be found in his *Naven*, originally published in 1936; 2d edition (Stanford: Stanford University Press, 1958). I also picked up much of this style of thinking from two books by Anthony Wilden: *System and Structure* (London: Tavistock, 1972), and his somewhat more reader-friendly *The Rules Are No Game* (see above). Related arguments on the liberatory and/or ethical import of cybernetics can be found in the work of Humberto Maturana and Francisco Varela; see, in particular, Maturana and Varela, *The Tree of Knowledge* (Boston: Shambhala, 1987), and Varela, Evan Thompson, and Elanor Rosch, *The Embodied Mind: Cognitive Science and Human Experience* (Cambridge: MIT Press, 1991).

Readers interested in pursuing this approach further should also consider the synthetic works of two major European sociologists, Edgar Morin and Niklas Luhmann. Luhmann's major work is available in English: *Social Systems*, trans. John Bednarz Jr. with Dirk Baecker (Stanford: Stanford University Press, 1995). Morin's multivolume series, *La Méthode*, remains untranslated into English: Vol. 1, *La Nature de la nature* (Paris: Seuil, 1977); Vol. 2, *La Vie de la vie* (1980); Vol. 3, *La Connaissance de la connaissance* (1986). A briefer and more accessible synthesis of Morin's approach, with an emphasis on ecological crisis and other global issues, recently translated, is *Homeland Earth: A Manifesto for the New Millennium*, with Anne Brigitte Kern, trans. Sean M. Kelly and Roger LaPointe (Creskill, N.J.: Hampton Press, 1999).

Another major work that uses the concepts of adaptive feedback in cultural study is the magnum opus of my late Michigan colleague, Roy Rappaport, *Ritual and Religion in the Making of Humanity* (Cambridge: Cambridge University Press, 1999). On the history, vicissitudes, and cultural avatars of cybernetics during the second half of the American twentieth century, see N. Katherine Hayles, *How We Became Posthuman: Virtual Bodies in Cybernetics, Literature, and Informatics* (Chicago: University of Chicago Press, 1999).

Chapter 5

The most powerful and stimulating writing on relations to the cultural products and trances of the past remains Nietzsche's essay, "On the Utility and Liability of History for Life," in *Unfashionable Observations*, trans. Richard T. Gray (Stanford: Stanford University Press, 1995), 83–167. Among recent and contemporary thinkers, Michel Serres is without peer in showing works from the past to be pertinent and enriching resources for approaching the most up-to-date of issues. For a general discussion of his thinking and—if one can really use the term with respect to Serres—method in this area, see the book of interviews he did with Bruno Latour, *Conversations on Science, Culture, and Time*, trans. Roxanne Lapidus (Ann Arbor: University of Michigan Press, 1995), especially the second conversation, "Method," pp. 43–76. See also chapter 2 of *The Natural Contract*, trans. Elizabeth MacArthur and William Paulson (Ann Arbor: University of Michigan Press, 1995), 27–50.

One of the richest and most wide-ranging studies of relations to the past is David Lowenthal, *The Past is a Foreign Country* (Cambridge: Cambridge University Press, 1985). On the practice of "reading medieval texts medievally" as a form of intellectual relation to the past, see Catherine Brown, "In the Middle," *Journal of Medieval and Early Modern Studies*, 30, 3 (2000): 547–573. On literature's kinship with the residual, see Virgil Nemoianu, *A Theory of the Secondary: Literature, Progress, and Reaction* (Baltimore: Johns Hopkins University Press, 1989).

There are many essays from a conservative perspective on the importance of continuing contact with literary traditions—most of them too reactive to be very thought-provoking. By far the best one that I have encountered is Danièle Sallenave, *Le Don des morts: sur la littérature* (Paris: Gallimard, 1991).

Chapter 6

My reflections on language and literature have much aided by Maurice Merleau-Ponty, *La Prose du monde* (Paris: Gallimard, 1969); in English *The Prose of the World*, trans. John O'Neill (Evanston: Northwestern University Press, 1973), Kieran Egan, *The Educated Mind: How Cognitive Tools Shape Our Understanding* (Chicago: University of Chicago Press, 1997), Daniel Pennac, *Better Than Life*, trans.

David Homel (Toronto: Coach House Press, 1994), Judith Schlanger, *La Mémoire des oeuvres* (Paris: Nathan, 1992). See also Richard Lanham, *Literacy and the Survival of Humanism* (New Haven: Yale University Press, 1983).

Among the works of recent commentary on universities, and particularly on the place of the humanities, the following have been particularly useful to me (though they should by no means be regarded as taking positions similar to my own): David Damrosch, *We Scholars: Changing the Culture of the University* (Cambridge: Harvard University Press, 1995), Bill Readings, *The University in Ruins* (Cambridge: Harvard University Press, 1996), John Guillory, *Cultural Capital: The Problem of Literary Canon Formation* (Chicago: University of Chicago Press, 1993). See also Antoine Compagnon, "L'Exception française," *Textuel*, no. 37 (2000): 41–52.

A 1999 "Conference on the Future of Doctoral Education" held at the University of Wisconsin, Madison, generated an excellent set of papers on the status and problems of graduate study in the modern languages and literatures; the proceedings are published in *PMLA*, 13, 5 (October 2000): 1136–1276. Of particular interest are the contributions of John Guillory on "The System of Graduate Education" (1154–63), Walter Cohen on "The Economics of Doctoral Education in Literature" (1164–87), and Robert Weisbuch on "The Humanities at Work" (1202–4).

Index